Cowboy Song

Cowboy Song

The Authorised Biography of
Philip Lynott

Graeme Thomson

Constable • London

*For all those who put fifty pence in the jukebox of the
Richmond Springs, Bristol, between 1988 and 1992.*

CONSTABLE

First published in Great Britain in 2016 by Constable

13 5 7 9 10 8 6 4 2

Copyright © Graeme Thomson, 2016

All lyrics written by Philip Lynott reproduced with the permission of the Lynott estate.

A CIP catalogue record for this book
is available from the British Library.

ISBN: 978-1-47212-104-2 (hardback)
ISBN: 978-1-47212-105-9 (trade paperback)

Typeset in Great Britain by SX Composing DTP, Rayleigh, Essex
Printed and bound in Great Britain by Clays Ltd, St Ives plc

Papers used by Constable are from well-managed forests
and other responsible resources.

MIX
Paper from
responsible sources
FSC® C104740

Constable
An imprint of
Little, Brown Book Group
Carmelite House
50 Victoria Embankment
London EC4Y 0DZ

An Hachette UK Company
www.hachette.co.uk

www.littlebrown.co.uk

Contents

Introduction

'The Irish are the niggers of Europe, lads,' Jimmy Rabbitte tells his band of white would-be soul singers in Roddy Doyle's *The Commitments*. 'An' Dubliners are the niggers of Ireland . . . Say it loud, I'm black an' I'm proud.'[1]

If Dubliners were the blacks of Ireland, then being an *actual* black Dub was a veritable double whammy of otherness. In 1957 on his first day at the Christian Brothers' School in Crumlin, the eight-year-old Philip Lynott stood in the playground while his classmates lined up to touch his hair.

'Automatically, he was like a peacock,' says Paul Scully, a fellow Southside Dubliner. 'He was exotic. He stood out. I remember Philip coming to my mother's house and she whispered to me, "*Does he drink tea?*"'

The long, lean, coffee-skinned boy with no father and an absent mother became a celebrity simply by existing.

By the 1970s he would be Ireland's first ever bona fide rock star.

By 1986, he was gone.

For Philip Lynott, fame was a self-fulfilling prophecy. Its outline was always there; he simply needed to fill in the detail. It did not

1

take long. He was a local band leader at the age of fourteen, the singer in Ireland's best rock group at eighteen, and had formed Thin Lizzy by the time he was twenty. When the full force of his talent finally caught up with his looks, drive and charisma in his mid-twenties, Lynott seemed unstoppable.

Thin Lizzy's gold-standard records – *Jailbreak*, *Johnny the Fox*, *Bad Reputation*, *Live and Dangerous* – are both powerful and strangely beautiful. They are often described as a hard-rock band, even heavy metal, which undersells the soulful mix of machismo, melody, poetry, mischief, rhythm and attack Thin Lizzy conveyed at their peak. Amid the swagger, there was always a lightness of touch; beyond the smoke-bombs and sirens lay a determination for things to be better and smarter than they needed to be.

On stage, Thin Lizzy became masters of the live ritual. For five years in the second half of the 1970s, Lynott was the quintessential rock-and-roll frontman. He controlled and coaxed and electrified crowds to the extent that he became synonymous with the image on the front of their classic concert album, *Live and Dangerous*, a Dionysian study in leather trousers, studded wristband, clenched fist and gypsy earring.

He was so ridiculously good at being a rock star, he inhabited the role with such obvious relish, it's easy to overlook all the other attributes Lynott had going for him. 'He could speak freely in the language of music,' says drummer Mark Nauseef. 'Not many rock guys can do that. He had so much going on. People didn't see a lot of it.'

Had he never written a single song, his voice alone would have marked him out. It's not really a rock voice at all. The wood-smoke timbre, the high-wire sense of timing and off-beat phrasing position Lynott closer to folk and jazz. He was a crooner seduced by high voltage and heavy wattage, but the mournful grain was always an essential part of his appeal.

If his voice brought out the soul of Thin Lizzy, his words delivered the substance. Lynott's early lyrics have a poetic flourish. They are a young man's words, anxious to impress, but often very beautiful. The tenor of peak-period Thin Lizzy, on the other hand, was all cinematic street-smarts, every adjective and noun armed with a flick knife and a sharply turned-up collar. Few lyricists have proved so adept at placing the listener right in the centre of the action.

He wrote melodies that have endured. Although numerous hard rock and heavy metal bands – from Megadeth to Metallica, Foo Fighters to Def Leppard – cite Thin Lizzy as a key influence, perhaps more telling is the diversity of artists who have performed Lynott's songs, among them Pulp, Sade, the Hold Steady and the Corrs.

He was a fine bass player. He was a phenomenal band leader. He was a wired-up perfectionist who affected the lassitude of Johnny Cool. He knocked around with poets and snooker players, fishermen and gangsters, Johnny Thunders and Georgie Best. He read comics and Camus and had a deceptively sprawling hinterland.

This is a story about Lynott's life in Thin Lizzy, but it is also a story about all the other things he was and could have been, inside and outside of music.

It is a story with an unhappy ending. Lynott did not always behave well, nor did he always make the smartest choices. In later life his addictions and insecurities made him a difficult man to be around, and ultimately they overpowered him.

But there is also much to celebrate. As the first full-blooded rock star to break out of his homeland, Lynott signalled the possibility for a new kind of Ireland: confident, swaggering, unbowed. His image, aspects of which can seem faintly ridiculous in retrospect, was potency writ large. As the late Irish writer Bill Graham said of Lynott. 'He was the most masculinely sexual of any Irish star before or since, at a time when we were struggling to escape the prison of our repressions.' The 'jailbreak' Lynott sang about was real. The Boomtown Rats and U2 tunnelled out after him. In time it became an exodus.

That it took a black, illegitimate, English-born, Irish-Guyanese man to roll back the frontier is rather wonderful, even if Lynott regarded himself as an Irishman first, last and always. 'He entirely viewed himself as Irish,' says fellow Dubliner Bob Geldof, returning to Jimmy Rabbitte's theme. 'The old Black Irish thing – you're an outsider anyway. He was totally Irish, in every sense. He couldn't *be* more Irish.'

And yet no matter how Irish he *felt* or sounded, Lynott appeared to be the precise opposite. This distance between the seeming and the being is part of his story. It was an existence filled with tensions and contradictions, playing out over thirty-six years. They resulted in some wonderful times and music, and some soul-scouring lows. 'He lived many different lives,' says Noel Bridgeman, a friend since their days together in Skid Row. 'There were different levels. His personality was paradoxical.'

The Irish poet and publisher Peter Fallon told me: 'Philip rose and he fell, and somehow that rise and fall was simultaneous.' At times in this tale Lynott looks like someone who threw it all away. At other times he looks like a man who spun gold from a fistful of thin air. Of course, he was both, and more, all at once.

PART ONE
Dublin

1

There are several recurring archetypes in the songs of Philip Lynott, each one a form of self-portrait. The streetwise hustler (let's call him Johnny; Lynott usually did) of 'The Boys Are Back in Town' and 'Johnny the Fox Meets Jimmy the Weed'; the flinty Celtic warrior of 'Eire' and 'Róisín Dubh (Black Rose): A Rock Legend', chiselled from Irish mythos; the amped-up main man of 'The Rocker' and 'Black Boys on the Corner'; the sad-eyed lothario of 'Romeo and the Lonely Girl' and 'Randolph's Tango'.

And there is the orphan, a supporting character throughout much of his work. Lynott named his pre-Thin Lizzy band Orphanage, and his earliest songs in particular wrestle again and again with family and identity. 'Shades of a Blue Orphanage', 'Saga of the Ageing Orphan', 'Mama and Papa', 'Diddy Levine', 'Philomena' and many more are complex triangulations involving mothers, fathers and sons. They are sometimes characterized by a wild, questing romance; more often, by an aching awareness of absence.

Lynott was seven years old when he was sent from Moss Side in Manchester to live with his grandmother in Crumlin, in the Southside of Dublin. Those first years of his life are ill-defined, but absence is a recurring theme. The absence of his biological father and a number of potential surrogates; of two younger siblings given up for adoption; of a settled and stable home, until finally he is faced with the absence of his mother.

If there is any substance at all in the old Jesuit proverb – *Give me the child for the first seven years and I will give you the man* – then Philip Lynott makes a particularly fascinating case study.

Crumlin was built in the image of Holy Ireland. The names of its main streets – Leighlin, Clonmacnoise, Ferns, Kells, Bangor, Clogher, Lismore – are taken from the dioceses of the Irish Catholic Church, and were laid out to approximate the shape of the Celtic cross of the Eucharist.

Named from the Gaelic *Croimghlinn*, 'Crooked Glen', the area had been settled since Anglo-Norman times. In the 1930s, when the Irish government began clearing out the cramped, crumbling tenements in the centre of Dublin and relocating their inhabitants to landscaped sites further out of town, the ancient lines of Crumlin Village were redrawn to accommodate a vast new social housing development of 3,000 homes.

Lynott's grandparents, Frank and Sarah, were part of the exodus. By the time the Lynotts were moved there from the Liberties, in the heart of old Dublin, in 1936, Sarah had given birth to six of her nine children. After the noisy, head-to-toe confines of the tenements, Crumlin promised space, order and civic pride. For a modest sum the family secured the tenancy of a modern Corporation House at 85 Leighlin Road, with running water, a kitchen, two upstairs bedrooms and a plumbed-in toilet.

It offered a new kind of stability, but in a poor country shaped – literally, in the case of Crumlin – by the Catholic Church, and the drip-feed of religious, moral and social censure it meted out, ambition was strictly rationed. Growing up, Philomena Lynott felt keenly not only the lack of immediate opportunities, but the awareness that Ireland would not change quickly enough to alter the course of her own life.

Born on 22 October 1930, the sixth of Frank and Sarah's children, Philomena – known as Phyllis to those close to her – was in many respects a very different personality than her siblings. Irreverent, wilful and eccentric, her spirit would not be contained. As so many of her compatriots had before her, including two of her older sisters, she left Ireland. She could hardly wait.

On the first occasion, she ran away to England, and an older brother was despatched to find and return her. At the age of fifty-one, Sarah Lynott was expecting her final child, Peter, and Philomena was needed at the house to help with her two younger siblings, Timothy and Irene.

She came back, but she did not stay long. Philomena was seventeen when she arrived by boat in Liverpool. By eighteen she was pregnant.

In a photograph taken when he was in his twenties, Philip Lynott's father wears the same suavely minimalist pencil moustache later adopted by his son.

Cecil Joseph Parris was born on 21 April 1925 in the port city of Georgetown, the capital of what was then British Guiana. A colony on the northern coast of South America, wedged between Venezuela and Suriname, the country was renamed Guyana in 1966 after gaining independence.

He was Afro-Guyanese, a descendant of the millions of African slaves shipped to the east coast of South America during the eighteenth and nineteenth centuries. The Afro-Guyanese were regarded as socially superior to the Indo-Guyanese, the country's large population of indentured workers from the Indian subcontinent which was granted minimal opportunities for education and social mobility. Parris's father, Eustace, worked as a schoolteacher in Georgetown, part of the educated, urbanite middle-class who arrived in the city following the abolition of slavery. Eustace was married to Jeanetta, and Cecil was one of several children.

The flow of migration from British Guiana to the United Kingdom in the 1940s and 1950s was closer to a trickle than a flood, particularly in comparison to Jamaica, Trinidad and Barbados. It was a promising colony, and in those days Georgetown was a fine garden city, with canals, tree-lined streets and elegant buildings. British Guiana was a remote outpost, however, and the cost of travelling to Britain was prohibitive. Migration was available primarily to members of the educated elite who had the means and the connections.

Cecil Parris died in 2012. When he left Georgetown almost seventy years ago, it's impossible to know whether he was running from the past or sailing towards the future. Later in life, he told his wife Irene that in 1947 he made a decision to emigrate to New York. His family have always believed that he stowed away on a steamer. Once the ship was seaborne and sufficiently far from Georgetown port, Parris revealed himself to the crew and worked his passage in the ship's kitchen. The family were also told that he still mistakenly believed his boat was bound for America, and he arrived in Liverpool thinking it was New York.

There is a chance he came to Britain via an alternative route. A passenger list for a Pan American Airways flight from Georgetown to New York on 13 August 1947 names Cecil Parris among those on board. His British passport had been issued three months earlier, and his New York address is listed as 24 Halsey Street, Brooklyn – a long, lively thoroughfare in the Bedford-Stuyvesant district full of theatres, dance halls and boxing arenas. This may be an entirely different Cecil Parris. The surname is not uncommon in Guyana and the passenger's age is recorded as twenty-five rather than the twenty-two Cecil would have been at this time. The alternative conclusion is that Lynott's father succeeded in his original aim to emigrate to New York and lived there for a spell before travelling to Britain.

What is certain is that within a year of disembarking, Parris had met a fellow runaway. Irene Parris believes that her husband first knew Philomena Lynott in Liverpool, the great port city of north-west England where they had entered the country at almost exactly the same time. However, Philomena has recalled that their first encounter was in Birmingham, at one of the regular weekend dances held at a local displaced-persons hotel in the city. In post-war, post-*Windrush* England, such institutions were plentiful. They were often given a gloss of gentility they rarely merited by calling themselves hotels. Primarily, they were hostels providing accommodation for Eastern Europeans and newly arrived West Indian immigrants.

Parris and Philomena Lynott hit it off. He was already in possession of a nickname, 'The Duke', bestowed in honour of a rather ostentatious sense of style and his reputation for charming the opposite sex; the pencil moustache was not the only trait he shared with his son. Regular dances lead to regular dates, which lead to more, and early in 1949 Philomena Lynott discovered she was going to have a child.

Her son was born on 20 August 1949 at Hallam hospital in West Bromwich, weighing nine-and-a-half pounds. His first name was the male counterpart of his mother's name. His middle name was Parris, after the father who, according to both Philomena and Irene Lewis, proposed marriage before he was born, an offer that was not accepted.

Philip Parris Lynott's first home was Woodville House, 176 Raddlebarn Road in Selly Park, in south-west Birmingham. A large Victorian building formerly in use as a workhouse, since 1943 it had been a home for unmarried mothers run by the Birmingham Diocesan Rescue Society, now known as Father Hudson's Society. Woodville was overseen by the Sisters of Charity of St Paul the Apostle and could accommodate up to fifteen young women and their babies at one time. While his mother slept in a communal dormitory and worked for her bed and board, Lynott was put in the children's dorm elsewhere in the building. He was baptized – there was no choice in the matter – on 4 September 1949, at St Edward's, the Catholic church situated a short walk down the road, where the young women and their children attended Mass each Sunday.

Since 1944, the Birmingham Diocesan Rescue Society had been a registered adoption agency, free to arrange for the children in its care to be taken on by more 'suitable' families. After three months at Woodville, mothers could either agree to give up their babies or leave and make their own way in the world. The choice was harder than it should have been. It was a time of post-war austerity. The Family Allowances Act had been introduced in August 1946, but the payment of five shillings per week in welfare was only applied from the birth of the second child onwards; first-time mothers such as Philomena Lynott were excluded. Socially as well as financially, there was an enormous amount of pressure and coercion applied to force women and their infants apart.

In the event, she managed to keep her baby and find a place to live. It was the start of a transient and uncertain period lasting several years in which Philomena and her son were subject to close supervision and regular intervention from both the Catholic Church and local social services. When she moved, as she did often, she earned money as best she could. Philomena shuttled between a series of boarding houses, halfway hostels and attic rooms in the less salubrious parts of Birmingham, Liverpool,

Leeds and Manchester. Her child was minded by babysitters – some familiar, some strangers – and on occasion was left alone while his mother worked at night. It was a rootless, unsettled life, pockmarked by prejudice and the looming threat of the next moonlit flit. New rooms, new streets, new cover stories. Lynott spent at least some time – and possibly quite a lot – in the care of welfare services.

An already challenging start in life was complicated further when Philomena became pregnant again. Now living in Liverpool, she gave birth to a daughter, Jeanette, in Sefton Park hospital in Liverpool in April 1951. Cecil Parris is listed as the father on her birth certificate – the baby was named after his Guyanese mother and 'Parris' was once again conferred as a middle name. He and Philomena appear to have maintained an irregular relationship in the time since Philip had been born, but each lived unsettled and transitory lives. In reality, Jeanette's father was not Cecil Parris but a white US serviceman, who had already departed the scene.

Shortly afterwards, Parris moved on, too. He settled permanently in London, where one of his brothers, Alan Parris, was now living and working as a policeman. More family members would subsequently make the trip over from British Guiana. It would be another twenty-five years before he re-entered his son's life. 'Cecil was always very upset about [leaving] because he was a very strong family man,' says Irene Parris. 'It was taken out of his hands . . . He wasn't able to be a father to Philip.'

Shortly after Parris had left, Philomena was living in Manchester, where she met a black American G.I. she called Jimmy Angel. He paid the rent for her flat at 96 Everton Road, a run-down street in the district of Chorlton-on-Medlock, later demolished as part of the inner-city slum clearance. Once again, she became pregnant, giving birth to a third child, James Arthur Lynott, at North

Manchester General Hospital on 27 June 1952. The father provided basic support but soon he was heading back to the United States. Lynott, now three years old, 'took his absence very badly'.[1]

Having given birth to three children by three different fathers – none of whom assumed the role of parent or provider – before she had passed the age of twenty-one, Philomena was faced with impossible choices. In early 1953, when Jeanette was still not quite two, her mother gave the child up for adoption. The same pattern occurred with Lynott's half-brother, James, who was given up for adoption in 1954, at the age of two.

The trauma was both profound and heart-breaking; that Philomena didn't merely survive but flourish is testament to her remarkable fortitude. The impact on her son remains harder to discern.

By 1957, Lynott was attending Princess Road Junior School in Moss Side. On his report card, Conduct is graded D, Attendance C, Punctuality E. 'Philip must be helped to form a regular habit of punctuality,' writes the teacher, pointedly. 'Rather disappointing,' adds the principal, who attaches an accompanying note upbraiding the pupil for being 'deliberately careless' for losing the report in the street on his way home. It does not require much reading between the lines to identify the outline of an erratic home life; years later Lynott recalled that nobody was ever there to collect him from school.

It is not possible to know what he witnessed or felt during the first few years of his life. He simply didn't talk about it. 'I never remember a word from him about that [time],' says Jim Fitzpatrick, the Irish artist who became one of Lynott's closest friends. 'I think his life began in his head when he was seven or eight. Maybe that's a way of psychologically adjusting for a child. He never went into any negative stuff. I tried to talk to him about it a couple of times and it was like pulling teeth.'

14

There are mysteries and secrets at the heart of his childhood. The pieces don't quite fit. There are parts missing. Time slips and bends. The absolute truth remains elusive to outside observers and family members alike – much as it was to Lynott himself. He made no indication as an adult that he possessed any knowledge of having a younger brother and sister. He was very young when they were born, and perhaps they faded quickly from his memory and existed only as a hazy outline, a dream that never quite connected to his own reality. It is not inconceivable that circumstances dictated that he was elsewhere at the time they were born, that his care in England was provided by someone other than his mother. In time Lynott grew extremely close to Philomena, and came to understand her vibrant spirit and to love her unconditionally, but there were still things about her past that he didn't know, and perhaps didn't want to.

Shortly before he died, in the autumn of 1985 Lynott learned conclusively of the existence of his half-sister, Jeanette, who had recently traced her birth mother and had made contact with her. (Philomena Lynott's other son, James, now known as Leslie, did not make contact until 1996, ten years after Lynott's death.) Re-christened Philomena by her adoptive parents, Jeanette was now a teacher, living in Derby in the East Midlands of England. Lynott showed no indication that he was being given information which he already knew, although his reaction to the news was subdued. Troubled as he was at that time in his personal and professional life, confirmation that he had a sibling was a further complication he did not necessarily welcome. Within three months he would be dead, without ever meeting the 'other' Philomena.

His mother's resilience saved Lynott from the fate of numerous other children, including his siblings, born in similarly testing circumstances. He was not snatched away by the Catholic

Church, sold to the highest bidder or farmed out for adoption in the United States or Australia. The price of maintaining the blood ties of family, however, was an undoubtedly harrowing start in life. Full of 'fear and paranoia',[2] Philomena eventually ran out of options. In the summer of 1957, Lynott was sent to live with her parents at 85 Leighlin Road in Crumlin. He was almost eight. The solid anchor of Ireland awaited him.

2

Lynott wrote two songs called 'Sarah'. The second, and most famous, appeared on *Black Rose: A Rock Legend* and was released as a Thin Lizzy single in 1979. It was written for his daughter, born at the end of the previous year.

The first was for the woman who had saved him from an uncertain fate. Recorded in 1972 on Thin Lizzy's second album, *Shades of a Blue Orphanage*, 'Sarah' is a tender piano ballad, which pays poetic homage to the grandmother he adored. His characteristically romantic imagining of Sarah Finn as an impassioned young woman, snaring the heart of Frank Lynott, contains a pun on the family name: *'Schoolboy eyes would stare in innocent fun / Never told no lies'*. This was Lynott's traditional means of advising people how to correctly pronounce his name. 'It's Lie-not,' he would say, 'cos I tell no lies,'[1] a definition that deliberately tested the boundaries of credibility.

Born in north Dublin in 1898, Sarah Lynott was a typical Irish 'mammy', a tough, can-do, unsentimental rock of reliability for a child who had previously known only turbulent waters. Lynott would quote her no-nonsense aphorisms to friends and until the day he died afforded her the utmost respect. Frank Lynott was a more distant figure. He enjoyed a drink, could be taciturn and did not always see eye-to-eye with his own children, but he was idolized by Lynott as the first real father figure he had known who hadn't vanished. When he did leave, dead from a heart attack on 20 May 1964, his fourteen-year-old grandson was crushed.

Lynott arrived in Crumlin at the beginning of the summer holidays in 1957, accompanied by his mother and a long-forgotten school friend from Manchester. Within a few weeks he was at the centre of a conventional Irish Catholic family: hard-working, durable and absolutely steeped in the idea of their own Irishness.

Though the Lynotts weren't fully aware of all the facts – they knew nothing of Philomena's two adopted children – they exhibited a degree of disapproval over the manner in which she was managing her life. For the next few years she focused on building a more solid existence for herself in Manchester. There were letters to and fro – 'Dear Mammy, I hope that you are well, I think of you all the time' – but close contact between mother and son was minimal. Lynott made the transition from boy to man in a two-up two-down in Leighlin Road, under the supervision of his grandmother.

Give or take a splash of colour, the proliferation of satellite dishes and the number of cars lining the pavement, Leighlin Road – pronounced *Leg-lin* – was much the same in the late 1950s as it is now. It is a long, gently curving street of featureless pre-war constructions, clustered in groups of fours and fives. 'These little boxes,' as Lynott later described them. 'Every house looked the same.'[2] The area was certainly too pedestrian for the Republican poet, playwright and wild man Brendan Behan, whose family grew restive when moved to Crumlin in 1937 from Russell Street in central Dublin. Behan went further than Lynott in regarding the homes as 'dolls' houses'. In his autobiographical play *Moving Out*, he refers to Dublin's new housing developments as 'Siberia', likening life in Crumlin to enforced exile from the beating heart of the city.

No. 85 Leighlin Road was tiny. 'You couldn't swing a cat in the kitchen,' recalls Michael O'Flanagan, who befriended Lynott in the 1960s while filming and photographing many local bands. 'It was a *very* small house.' There was a small patch of greenery at the front set back from the road, while a larger garden at the rear was designed to encourage families to grow their own produce and become self-sufficient. The Lynotts were not persuaded.

The family lived on the section of Leighlin Road where the street grows increasingly narrow, giving the impression almost of a country lane that has been gripped and squeezed by the hand of modernity. 'That end of Leighlin Road was the rough end,' says Martin Duffy, a Crumlin native who went on to become a successful editor, film-maker and writer. 'I hated going down it as a kid because there were a lot of tough kids there.' Although Duffy was a couple of years younger than Lynott, and a self-confessed 'nerd', the pair became teenage friends.

In common with most families in the area, the house had been overrun with offspring, raised and then shooed out into the wider world. By the time Lynott arrived only three children remained – his aunt Irene and his two youngest uncles. He came to regard the older of the two, Timothy, as a cross between an adult big brother and a surrogate father; Peter, the last in line, and only 14 months his elder, was closer to a sibling. It was the kind of set-up not unfamiliar in large families. Brothers could seem more like fathers; uncles like brothers.

Relationships and roles were fluid, which suited Lynott. He arrived in Crumlin without an accompanying explanation. There was no identifying label attached. Timothy, Irene and Peter were not told that this was their nephew, Philomena's boy. 'My mother and father knew the full story,' said Timothy Lynott, 'But we didn't because we were young and it wasn't explained to us.'[3] As much as a decade later, there still existed members of the Lynott family who did not know that Philip was Philomena's son. The neighbours, meanwhile, assumed that he had been adopted, a story which the family had little appetite to correct. The taking-in of children born into extreme hardship or what was then regarded as 'disgrace' was not uncommon in Catholic Ireland. Within that cultural context, the arrival of a 'poor black baby' was unusual but not entirely implausible.

In the absence of absolutes, alternative narratives were constructed for the sake of convenience and propriety. Misunder-standings were allowed to stand. 'We had hidden it from a lot of people,' Philomena Lynott told me. 'I remember taking him to the shops and an old woman put her hand on his head and said, "Oh God bless him and protect him and take him back to Africa to them that own him." She was a real old Irish lady. That's how it was then. Nobody would have believed that I was his mother, no matter what.'

Eventually, those who needed to came to recognize the truth without ever asking – day-to-day life was so frantic, no one seemed to care much one way or the other. 'When I think about Crumlin now it's almost like a Monty Python sketch, all these kids falling out of these tiny little houses,' says Martin Duffy. 'My mother had fifteen children, and we weren't the biggest family. The Butlers had a family of twenty kids. There was a huge amount of kids. Too many kids, not enough work. Tough times and tough people. Everybody was accepted for what they were if they measured up. I didn't register Philip's family situation. I didn't even notice it. At that time, with so many kids around, we weren't analysing things like that.'

'Philip was accepted,' says Frank Murray, one of Lynott's closest friends and Thin Lizzy's road manager for much of the 1970s. Murray grew up next door to Crumlin, in Walkinstown. 'It was a working-class district, we accepted lots of things. We accepted poverty, fashion sense, families – it didn't matter. It was that kind of community. You just didn't go up to a guy and say, "Look, you're living with this all-white family, you're a black guy – what the fuck happened?" People would say, "Isn't that guy great?" but they didn't mention his colour.'

In Moss Side, by the late 1950s non-Caucasian children were a not unfamiliar sight. There was a vibrant Afro-Caribbean population and a sizeable Sikh community was forming. In Ireland, Lynott belonged to a world few people recognized or even understood. There were precisely four indigenous black children in a city of more than 600,000 souls. Dublin was home to a tiny and transient group of African students, enrolled at the College of Surgeons at Trinity College, but for the vast majority of those who encountered him in the first years following his arrival from England, Lynott was – symbolically, if not literally – the First Black Irishman.

It was in August 1957, during his first days as a pupil at the Scoil Colm Christian Brothers' School (CBS) on Armagh Road, that Lynott stood in the playground while his fellow pupils clamoured to touch his hair. 'We were envious, because one of our nightmares was our mothers untangling our hair with a comb, and we reckoned he wouldn't have had to comb his hair at all,' says his classmate Liam O'Connor. 'We were only babies. There wasn't any racism. We weren't sophisticated enough to be threatened.'

At Catholic schools across the country, including Lynott's own, each week pupils would collect money for the 'Black Babies'. The proceeds were spent on sending missionaries to Africa and elsewhere to deliver aid, establish charitable work and spread the gospels. 'If your parents paid 2/6 [two shillings and six pence] you could "buy" your own black baby for life,' says O'Connor. 'We just assumed someone had paid their 2/6 and they had sent Philip over from Africa. That was the logic of a child.'

Ireland had many problems at that time, but immigration was not one of them. Human traffic invariably travelled in the other direction, and the default reaction to Lynott was a kind of benign incomprehension rather than the kneejerk hostility of those who feel threatened or invaded. Only rarely did cultural confusion spill over into physical altercations. His uncle Peter, in the year above Lynott at CBS, was assigned the role of brother protector. He recalls taking Lynott to school and running the gauntlet of astonished children, some of whom registered their shock with mocking shouts of 'Blackie!' and 'Baluba!'

Future Thin Lizzy drummer Brian Downey, also a fellow pupil at CBS, recalls 'one occasion when some guy called him "Sambo", and Philip took exception to that. He called the guy into the schoolyard, and there was an arrangement for later that day to have a bit of a scrap outside the school gates. I was on Phil's side, there was a couple of guys on the other guy's side, but we all just stood off and let them have it – and Phil won hands down. Phil was pretty tough. It was only a five-minute skirmish, but Phil had him pinned to the ground and could have beat this guy to a pulp. Nobody was going to intervene, but he just let him up and said, "If you say that again I really will hurt you." That was a typical example of what Phil was like. He was a fair guy.'

Like many whose roots might be open to question before they even open their mouths, Lynott quickly seemed to become *more* Irish, *more* Dublin, *more* Southside than those who had been born and raised there. He quickly developed, says Duffy, 'a perfect

Dublin accent', which he deployed quietly but effectively, folding in the local idioms, rhythms and sly wordplay.

His colour was simply there, as he put it, like having 'big ears',[4] but he recognized that it afforded him a certain status. He rarely had to shout to get attention. The world came to him. Once he understood this, he used it.

He was already a budding hustler. For obvious – if dubious – reasons, the teachers at CBS often sent him out to collect for the Black Babies. 'He told me that he used to rob the box at night time because he *was* one of the black babies,' Philomena Lynott told me. 'He used to turn the box upside down and slip a knife up and let some of the pennies slip down.'

On the bus in Dublin, children would point and say, 'Mummy, Mummy, there's a black man!' 'He thought that was hilarious,' says Michael O'Flanagan. A budding *cineaste*, O'Flanagan wanted to make a short film of Lynott's first band, the Black Eagles. Lynott asked whether it would be shot in colour or black and white. 'Oh, colour,' said O'Flanagan proudly. 'I come out better in black and white,' came the reply.

He would make jokes about having a 'beauty spot all over', and about the size of his 'mickey'. During taxi journeys Lynott would often pretend that he was a Nigerian medical student at Trinity College, and converse with the driver in stilted pidgin English. During one trip in April 1968, when he arrived home the driver told him the fare would be ten shillings.

'Suddenly Philip reverted back to his broad Dublin accent and said it wasn't ten shillings but only seven-and-six, as it had been every other night,' recalls O'Flanagan, taking up the tale. 'The taxi driver still insisted that it was ten shillings. Philip said, "You'd better take me around to the cop shop, then, and we'll see what it is." The taxi driver relented and slid a half-crown across the seat to Philip, who took the money, pocketed it, got out of the taxi and walked away. The driver jumped out of the taxi and shouted after Philip, "I'm glad they shot Martin Luther King!" which indeed they had that very day. He told me that story with such zest and humour, still laughing at the idea of the taxi guy shouting that at him.'

Into adulthood there were still occasional flashpoints. He would sometimes be referred to around Dublin, ignorantly, if not deliberately unkindly, as 'the spade singer'. He once went to the Revolution Club with his friend Tom Collins and was told, 'Sorry, no blacks.'

When these slights occurred he would generally not allow them to pass unchallenged. Skid Row drummer Noel Bridgeman remembers 'Philip losing the head one time in the dressing room of the Club A Go Go, because someone called him a "spade". He was very, very annoyed. He was very sensitive. Being black [in Ireland] was unheard of – and he was black, illegitimate and living with his granny.'

He had a lifelong intolerance of mockery. 'He couldn't bear being slighted or laughed at,' recalled Gale Claydon née Barber, Lynott's long-term girlfriend in the early 1970s. 'If you ever laughed at him, that was it: you were dead. He would turn away but you had wounded him.'[5]

He was a black boy in an almost completely white country. He had no idea who his father was. His mother was over the water. At times it hurt, but it also meant he could be whatever he wanted.

Established in 1939, the Christian Brothers' School on Armagh Road was reaching its peak occupancy of 1,500 pupils in the late 1950s and early 1960s. Among the more notorious boys in Lynott's year was Dublin gangster Martin Cahill, a career criminal whose exploits were dramatized – some might say romanticized – in

The General, the acclaimed film which won John Boorman the Best Director award at the 1998 Cannes Film Festival.

It was a tough environment and an imposing place. The old school building was generally reserved for older boys sitting their Leaving Certificates. The new school was for everyone else, augmented with five 'sheds' to cater for the overspill. These were great corrugated tin outbuildings, half-moon shaped, of the type often used for temporary military constructions. Each one housed fifty-two children, taught by one Christian Brother or lay teacher, and was insulated with wood panelling. Heating in these vast hangars was provided by a crude stove attached to a chimney going up through the ceiling.

The war-like feel of 'the sheds' was apt. The Christian Brothers were a religious community within the Catholic Church, a lay order of unordained men dedicated to religion and charged with administering the education of boys from the age of eight to eighteen. Though it would be both unfair and inaccurate to apportion blanket blame, varying degrees of physical, emotional and sexual violence were routinely practised, a dark legacy that has subsequently become a notorious stain on the reputation of the Church as a whole. The cause of much belated soul-searching in Ireland and elsewhere, the actions of Christian Brothers from decades ago have led to ongoing criminal prosecutions.

Even in the absence of the most heinous abuses, the schools could be harsh, unpleasant environments. Former pupils of Scoil Colm, immediate peers of Lynott, recall incidents of institution-alized corporal punishment and countless episodes of casual cruelty. The sight of boys vomiting with fear in the schoolyard immediately prior to entering the building was a common one. 'The Christian Brothers were religious Nazis,' says Martin Duffy. 'We were indoctrinated by them. They were very ferocious, completely brutal people. They had a thing called a "leather"; it was part of their uniform, a leather strap which they had complete authority to whack you with.' The 'leather' was administered to the hand and sometimes to the head – only five of the best if you were lucky.

Entering CBS at Second Class, Lynott was taught by Mr McEvoy, a bespectacled, ruddy-faced, short-tempered lay brother. At first, 'we thought we were great fellas because he had a broken arm so he never hit us,' says classmate Kevin Horan. 'But when he got the cast off he took his canes out. He had one of those canes with a hook at the end of it, and he wasn't the worst by any means.'

During his years at school Lynott came home with his fair share of bumps and bruises, but he escaped the worst of the brutality. His academic engagement was lacklustre and he was no more proficient in his studies than he had been in Moss Side, but he was bright, polite and had charm. 'He was a very pleasant chap,' says his schoolmate Hugh Feighery. 'He always had a great charisma about him, even as a youngster. Even the school teachers took to him.'

Even had he had been more interested, CBS was not an environment particularly designed to encourage creativity or original thought. The school curriculum was defined by a through-line of religious doctrine and support for Irish nationalism. It was an age dominated by Éamon de Valera, whose dedication to creating a truly 'Irish Ireland' throughout his multiple terms as both Taoiseach and President never wavered. At CBS, the emphasis was on a one-sided appraisal of the country's history, language and geography. 'You had one teacher, and he was the font of all knowledge,' says Liam O'Connor. 'It wasn't an academic environment. [Free-thinking] wasn't encouraged, it was learning by rote. History was basically the history of wars in Ireland. The good guys were the Irish and the bad guys were the Brits. That was it. Geography was different Irish towns and their main produce.' On the sports field, Gaelic football and hurling were played while football, or soccer, was firmly frowned upon as the pastime of English colonizers. Light relief came in the form of films shown in the school hall. These were usually religious epics dedicated to the life of Bernadette, or perhaps a showing of John Wayne in *King of Kings*, or, on special occasions, the slapstick of Laurel and Hardy.

It was a narrow and oppressive curriculum. 'It was propaganda,' says Martin Duffy. 'Philip received Irish history as heroic tales: English rule was evil, and the Irish were the heroes for breaking free from that. He would have been completely indoctrinated in all that.'

The CBS's preoccupations most certainly left their mark but the fall-out was not necessarily negative. The impact of Catholicism stayed with Lynott. In his early years he was attracted to the Church, and even considered becoming a Passionist priest. He went regularly to confession and attended the Crusaders, a religious youth organization, at nearby Mount Argus seminary. As the inevitable distractions of adolescence kicked in, his interest waned. He stopped attending Mass in London in the 1970s, but when he became a father and moved back to Dublin in the early 1980s, Lynott would regularly take his two daughters to the Church of the Assumption on a Sunday morning. 'I was born Catholic, reared Catholic, churched . . . everything,' he recalled. 'All this stuff that's been beaten into you just comes out. It just catches you when you're a kid. So now I look on it as a basic set of ground rules that are really important. I can say, "I'm breaking this rule here", but at least I have a set of rules to work off.'[6]

He jumped into the great pool of Irishness with greater enthusiasm than most, displaying the zeal of the convert. 'Irish history and mythology made a big impact on him,' Brian Downey told me. 'I know he had a huge interest in it, and that seeped into his psyche and became part of him. He wanted to be Irish. Perhaps because he was black, he emphasized that as much as he could to fit in. He became steeped in the tradition.'

Lynott was forever susceptible to the romantic allure of heroic struggle. Stories from the epic *Ulster Cycle* – a series of medieval sagas and legends woven together to provide a creation myth for the whole of Ireland – were ingrained from school, but also featured in more contemporary forms of entertainment. He loved comics and cartoons. Aged nine Lynott drew his own eight-page Superman strip: pictures *and* story. In Crumlin, there was a little shop on the Old County Road that sold Marvel and DC comics. He would snap up the latest editions, read them eagerly, and then swap with friends like Martin Duffy.

It was a passion that endured into adulthood. 'We used to love those Marvel comics,' says Frank Murray. 'Sometimes when we were coming home to his house late from clubs, we'd share his bed, and he'd get out a bunch of comics and we'd read.' A song from the first Thin Lizzy album, 'The Friendly Ranger at Clontarf Castle', took its title from the local landmark at the end of Castle Avenue, but its lyrics were partly inspired by a comic strip. 'That whole piece – "I'm damned"; "indeed, dear comrade"; "I'm being bombed"; scooping up all the beans and spreading them like stars – he got that from a DC comic,' says Thin Lizzy's original guitarist Eric Bell. 'He just borrowed it. He used to get Batman, Green Lantern, Superman, all those fabulous American comics characters. When we were on the road, we'd stop at a garage and he'd buy a handful of them.'

During his schooldays, Lynott was in the target audience for the CBS's own comic paper, *Our Boys*. An Irish alternative to the British *Boy's Own*, in its pages the great figures of Celtic nationhood were brought to life as comic-strip heroes. There were captivating tales of Fionn MacCumhaill, the mythic hunter-warrior, and Cúchulainn, the revered Irish mythological prodigal who cut a swathe through entire armies and his fiercest foes. He had no biological father and died young. Irish astronauts rocketed into space and Irish detectives rivalled Sherlock Holmes for cunning and ingenuity. The 1916 uprising and de Valera's Fianna Fáil were eulogized. Much of the material was written in Irish.

It all played a wonderful kind of havoc with Lynott's imagination, and eventually drip-fed into his writing. A song on the first album, *Thin Lizzy*, 'Eire' recounts first the exploits of the 'high king' Brian Boru, who vanquished some 10,000 Viking invaders at Clontarf in 1014. In its final two verses, 'Eire' turns to the heroism of Red Hugh O'Donnell and Hugh O'Neill, two Irish lords fighting against the English in the Nine Years War at the end of the 1500s. Both events would have been taught by the Christian Brothers, offered up uncritically as heroic examples of the Irish ridding themselves of foreign domination. At the end of the song, Lynott concludes dramatically, *'The land is Eireann / the land is free.'* The original lyric was written in Irish.

'Emerald', on *Jailbreak*, explores a similar theme of terrible but righteous vengeance. On 'Fool's Gold', Lynott told the story of another historical injustice, the Great Famine of the mid-1800s, and the desperate stream of migration that ensued. The title track of Thin Lizzy's 1979 album, *Black Rose: A Rock Legend*, not only stitched together some of Ireland's best-loved traditional songs, it tapped into the potency of *Róisín Dubh* ('black rose') as a nationalist symbol of resistance dating back to the sixteenth century.

Eamon Carr co-founded Tara Telephone, the influential poetry-and-music collective of the late 1960s, with Peter Fallon, and later formed the groundbreaking Celtic-rock group Horslips. 'Philip's grasp on [Irish history] wasn't academic,' says Carr. 'He was dragging in comic book sources as well as mythological sources. It was essentially school-book stuff, but he could tell a bloody good yarn.'

Lynott's grasp of the scale and storytelling power of these legends and fables infiltrated every part of his own writing. His best songs are defined by a combination of the romantic and the dramatic, which feels truly mythic. The blend of yearning, machismo and bravado throws back to oral histories handed down through the centuries, stories designed to be embroidered and embellished each time they are told. The characters are vivid, the sense of place palpable.

'I've always wanted to write contemporary Irish songs,' he told *Hot Press* in 1983. 'I want it so that when you look back and ask "What was Irish music in the 1970s and 1980s?", the answer will be, "Well, there was this geezer Phil Lynott".'[7]

His aim became to write fresh myths, mint new legends. According to the tenets of this philosophy, in its essence 'The Boys Are Back in Town' is as much a song of Ireland as 'Emerald'.

3

The Black Eagles was not Lynott's group, at least not initially.

The origins of his first band dated back to 1962 and the house of Mr Fox in Crumlin's Sundrive Road, where twelve-year-old Frankie Smith and thirteen-year-old Hugh Feighery were taking guitar lessons. It was the dawn of the beat boom. Pop stardom seemed within the grasp, or at least the imagining, of every working-class teen. Even in Ireland. Smith and Feighery lived nearby on Leighlin Road and were both pupils at CBS. Having struck up a musical friendship, they decided to form a band, recruiting Frankie's brother Danny on bass and Mick Higgins, from nearby Dolphin's Barn, on drums.

The traditional line regarding Lynott's involvement in the Black Eagles is that he was deployed as bait. The band's primary aim was to lure Peter Lynott – older, good-looking, and already singing and playing in local bands called things like the Zyn and the Mortals – into their ranks and Philip was recruited simply to sell the idea to his uncle. Feighery insists it happened very differently. Peter joined first as singer; Philip came later.

The five-piece called themselves the Eagles and began rehearsing in the back bedroom at 15 Leighlin Road, the family home of Frankie and Danny Smith. A former Army sergeant who duly ran the band like a military operation, the boys' father Joe Smith started managing the group. He built a box on the roof rack of his Simca 1000 to transport their gear to shows at the Apollo cinema in Walkinstown and the Oriel in Chapelizod. He also fostered a relationship with Joe Mac Productions, a local variety group which played in nursing homes and institutions on a charitable basis, and invited the Eagles to perform regularly around the area.

They quickly became reasonably proficient, but Mr Smith was ambitious for his boys. Every street in Dublin in 1963 and 1964 seemed to be spawning almost identical beat groups playing hits by the popular artists of the age, ranging from Elvis Presley to the Shadows, the Bachelors to the Beatles. How could the Eagles make a mark? At a brainstorming session after rehearsals one night, Smith said, 'We need an identity. There are too many groups around here, people don't really know who we are.'

It was at this point that Peter Lynott mentioned his nephew Philip. He was already a local star – tall, skinny, legs like drainpipes. He was growing into the long, doleful face, with its sleepy smile and big, heavy-lidded eyes peering out from under his brow, a melting look practised and perfected in front of the mirror at Leighlin Road and later unleashed to devastating effect at the dances and discos of south Dublin. There was something wonderfully cartoonish about Lynott, an air of Dennis the Menace mischievousness that stuck with him. The low, shoulder-shaking *hur hur hur* of a laugh deserved its own cartoon bubble over his head.

He couldn't play a musical instrument or write songs, but he could hold a tune and he loved music. He and Peter would listen to the top twenty on Radio Luxembourg every Sunday night in bed on the transistor radio that his mother had bought for him.

At Christmastime and family parties he needed little encouragement to perform a turn, despite being an essentially shy boy.

He spoke softly, and scrunched up his long frame to make himself appear less tall, less conspicuous. 'He could be self-conscious about things,' says Frank Murray. 'That continued into Thin Lizzy. You can walk out on stage and look at a crowd of 5,000, or 20,000 people, and you can still be shy. I can watch film of Philip and point out his shy body language. I can see certain stage traits he had and where they came from. Paradoxically, he had a lot of confidence about a lot of other things. You have to have that to get up and sing in the first place, and it takes a certain amount of self-confidence to start working, and to get through the bad stuff in order to get to the good stuff.'

He was a popular boy. Interesting and unusual things tended to happen around him. Martin Duffy recalls that on one rare summer day when the streets of Crumlin were hazy with heat and promise, Lynott peeled a strip of sticky tarmac from the surface of Leighlin Road and rolled it into his mouth. He had a naturally egalitarian streak which ensured that his friendships were always diverse. 'He didn't look down his nose at anyone,' says Michael O'Flanagan. 'He was a bit like Cassius Clay – "I'm the greatest, but that doesn't mean you're a pygmy."'

He seemed to offer something for everyone: a laugh and a dirty joke for friends at school; a touch of swagger for the tough lads; exotic good looks for the more adventurous girls; talent, knowledge and enthusiasm for the musos; a quiet, soulful side for the poets and introverts. 'He was three years older than me, but there was only a year between us in school,' says Martin Duffy. 'He was in the lower grade, and I was a bright nerd. Somehow we made friends, and there was mutual respect. There was something sensitive in there that I could relate to. He was a very open guy. I liked him a lot.'

And the girls already loved him. Why on earth *wouldn't* you want him in your band?

With Lynott's arrival, the group decided on a change of name. They were now the Black Eagles. 'You wouldn't have to be a genius to work out where "black" came from,' says Feighery, although in partial mitigation he points out that there was a popular DC comic book series at the time called *Blackhawk*, about a squadron of shadowy fighter pilots, which may have played a part. There were practical considerations, too. Long before the Californian Eagles of *Hotel California* renown entered the music scene in the early 1970s, there were at least two other bands with the same name: a US vocal group and a British band, active between 1958 and the mid-1960s.

For a brief period the Black Eagles had the unusual selling point of a nephew and uncle sharing lead vocals, with both Philip and Peter as frontmen. It wasn't an arrangement built to last. There was the space issue – six boys and their instruments crammed into the Smiths's back bedroom. More significantly, there was the financial aspect. When it came to dividing up the handful of shillings they got for each gig, they began to feel not everybody was strictly necessary to requirements. They also felt that Peter wasn't entirely committed to the cause. After a short time, Philip was the sole lead singer of the Black Eagles.

As the band developed, rehearsals moved from the bedroom of 15 Leighlin Road to the Feighery residence at 117 Leighlin Road. There were two tin sheds in the garden to accommodate the overspill of a family of twelve. The smaller shed, a cosy 12 x 12 foot, was cleared out to create a practice space. This caused a minor stir locally. Crumlin kids would come down to listen to the music, 'fluting around' outside the door as the sound of the Mersey, the Hudson and the Thames leaked out. 'I'd knock on their bell on the way back from the boxing club because it was very enjoyable to listen to,' says Kevin Horan. 'There was always a few kids hanging around, and usually some girls.'

From the start, Lynott approached the idea of being the lead singer in a band with dedication. 'Philip would insist every day after school, "Come on, I want to do a bit of practising, you get the guitar and I'll sing,"' says Feighery. 'We literally went to school and then went straight back to his place. This was outside the standard practice we would do with the band. He lived it. He got a high when he sang, although he was a very shy person.' Already, the notion of a career was crystallizing. He told Feighery, 'I'm black, I'm Irish and I'm a bastard – if I don't make it as a singer I'm never going to make it.' 'I knew I had something to offer,' he later said. 'I had a strong determination.'[1]

The Black Eagles provided him with the archetypal musical apprenticeship. Between 1963 and 1967 Lynott learned his stagecraft performing at tennis and bowling clubs, community centres, skating rinks, church halls, teenage dances and schools, and after hours in many of the myriad of local cinemas, where the stage would be so narrow they had to be careful not to fall off.

The devil's music made a pact with God. They played Father Browne's, St John of Gods and St Anthony's Hall. They had a regular Tuesday spot at the Grove Hall in Clanbrassil Street, and a Sunday-night residency at St Paul's Hall in Mount Argus, the tiny parochial church hall in Harold's Cross where Lynott's mother recalls first seeing her son sing on one of her visits home. 'It was a beautiful monastery, and at the back of it there was a church hall where they used to run little concerts for everybody,' she told me. 'I knew he wouldn't want me to go near him, and I snuck down there with my friend. The priest came out, he was like a Franciscan monk, and I stood behind him and I watched Philip come out on stage. I thought he was really good, and full of confidence.'

'I'd see Philip in halls around Mount Argus and I was very impressed that he had guys who could play guitar with him,' says Kevin Horan. 'He wasn't brash, but he wasn't as shy as the rest of us were, and he obviously had plans for himself. They used to do "Blue Suede Shoes" and numbers by the Kinks. I thought it was great.'

The repertoire was sixties orthodox, although Lynott would often push for something a little different: 'Still I'm Sad' by the Yardbirds rather than 'For Your Love'; 'Crying Time' by Ray Charles. Little slivers of innovation slipped in alongside 'World Without Love' by Peter and Gordon and the latest songs by Manfred Mann, Billy J. Kramer, the Rolling Stones, the Beatles, and anything else in the top twenty. 'We would just imitate,' says Hugh Feighery.

The Black Eagles would regularly perform on Sunday nights at Moeran Hall, a community building on the border of Walkinstown and Crumlin. 'All the various beat groups from Dublin would come,' says Frank Murray. 'Because they were local the Black Eagles were favourites, they played there more than a lot of the other bands. I liked the songs they were doing – the Yardbirds, the Who, some R&B, a lot of the choice pop songs of the day – and Philip stood out. In some kind of naive way, people would assume that because he was black he was a great singer.'

Lynott and Murray became fast friends, along with Paul Scully and Michael O'Flanagan, two other Walkinstown boys who had seen the group play at Moeran Hall. One night Lynott and Murray bumped into each other after a dance and 'started walking home together. We started to discuss music, and we talked for hours and hours. I remember we stood outside my house and it just poured out of us. We had a lot in common about music and movies. That established our relationship, and we became great friends after that. He was just a regular teenager. He liked being in a band. His interests were music, girls, and movies. He didn't think of himself as anything special.'

Although the Black Eagles were essentially a local draw rather than a top name in the city, they regularly played prominent gigs in Dublin and around the country, supporting showbands and national touring acts. A modern continuation of the old dance bands, showbands were slick, professional ensembles numbering at least seven musicians and sometimes more, almost always with a brass section. They played the popular hits of the day and had the bigger, better ballroom circuit in Ireland sewn up. Typified by acts such as Joe Dolan and Dickie Rock's Miami Showband, they had no great interest in playing original or especially innovative music. Their purpose was to dish up a reliable set menu for drinkers and dancers during a night out. It could provide a good living, if not a terribly creative one.

Typically, showbands would play for between four and six hours, up to six nights a week. To lighten the load, they would often hire a group to play for the first hour to warm up the room. 'One of the regular bands we used was the Black Eagles,' says Robert Ballagh. The one-time bass player in the successful showband the Chessmen, Ballagh is now one of Ireland's most acclaimed artists. 'I don't think Philip was remotely interested in the showband scene. Any young guy with creative energies had to gravitate to groups.'

Nonetheless, the dance-hall circuit was expanding rapidly; a young group could make decent headway swinging on the coat-tails of bigger bands. The Black Eagles supported Belfast R&B group the Mad Lads on a Sunday night at the Bastille Club, a small ballroom attached to the Cliff Castle, a hotel in Dalkey, just south of Dublin. It was the first time that future Thin Lizzy manager Ted Carroll laid eyes on Lynott and his band. 'They were excellent,' says Carroll. 'The Yardbirds, the Small Faces, a little bit of soul – Otis Redding and Sam Cooke. It wasn't like, "Wow, we've got to hire these guys as soon as we can," but they certainly took care of business. They were only youngsters, but they were quite professional.' Carroll had never heard of the Black Eagles, which in itself illustrates the limits to their fame. 'They got changed in the back of the Commer van,' he recalls. 'The back door opened and they all came trotting in with their instruments in their stage uniform.'

In common with most bands of the day, the Black Eagles cultivated a unified look. They started out with black polo necks and Cuban heels and graduated to more flashy attire. The first time Frank Murray saw them, 'Philip had a kind of sparkly jacket that seemed to come to his waist, like a Bolero outfit.' He would sometimes wear a single glove, pre-empting Alvin Stardust and Michael Jackson by several years. When Carroll first saw Lynott at Dalkey, he and the rest of the band were wearing 'black shirts and pale blue bell-bottom denim jeans with little brass bells sewn down the outer seams below the knee. Phil came jingling out of the van.' Later, he would adopt a pared-back mod aesthetic: button-down shirts, silk ties, tonic suits and Chelsea boots. Tom Collins recalls photographing Lynott for a feature in the *Evening Herald* about new bands. 'He had the strangest hairstyle,' says Collins. 'It looked to all intents and purposes like a helmet.'

Keeping up appearances was a major part of the job description, on stage and off. It was a philosophy Lynott subscribed to his entire life. Being the lead singer of the Black Eagles offered the kind of opportunities he could use to his advantage. One made one's own luck in Holy Ireland. Supporting showbands, Lynott was granted access to places that were otherwise off limits to regular under-eighteens. After he had played his set, he could head into the throng, soak up the attention and determine what fun could be found.

'He had mini-celebrity status – "Look, there's Philip!" – because he stood out like nobody's business,' says Feighery. 'We had a good craic for our age. We had a very quick puberty, shall we say? There was great opportunity. I'm not saying you were *riding* [having sex], but you'd get girls wanting you to [walk] them home, and you'd get a feel. You had a great little life. At the time we were well ahead of ourselves. He lived for music and he loved singing and he loved women. That was 95 per cent of the time.'

It was a rapid initiation into the ways of adulthood, and a certain lifestyle. Lynott fell in love with being part of a road band early in life. Like many first loves, he never quite got over it. 'I believe in the rock culture,' he said in 1976. 'That is, spending six months of your life travelling to gigs and the other six months playing.'[2]

The Black Eagles were already playing three or four nights a week in Dublin. Perhaps once during the week and once on the weekend they would be booked further afield: Tramore in Waterford; Salthill in Galway; Dundalk in Louth; or Monaghan. The roads were awful and there were no twenty-four-hour roadside amenities out in the sticks. They would visit an all-night restaurant in Rathmines on their return to Dublin for something to eat before arriving home at two or three in the morning. Then up for school after a few hours' sleep.

It was physically wearing, and Lynott's already lacklustre engagement with his studies fell even further by the wayside. Though not a dedicated troublemaker – by nature he was more of a people pleaser – he had little interest in school and would frequently 'act the maggot' in class to keep himself amused. One day he tapped Hugh Feighery on the shoulder and whispered, 'Did I tell you, Hughie, I'm Lady Chatterley's lover?'

The Chatterley trial was a cause célèbre of the early 1960s. Penguin Books, the UK publishers of D. H. Lawrence's classic and controversial 1928 novel, had recently been prosecuted in the wake of new British obscenity laws. Following the verdict of not guilty, a new edition of *Lady Chatterley's Lover* was published in 1961. The novel had been in the news, and although it certainly wouldn't have been on the CBS reading list, the unholy trinity of sex, profanity and notoriety ensured that it had popped up on Lynott's radar.

'I swear to God I had no idea who Lady Chatterley was, but I laughed,' says Feighery. 'One of the masters, Mr Carruthers, insisted that I share the joke with the class. He was one of the more lenient guys, rather than some of the Brothers who were vicious bastards. I resisted but he insisted, so I said, "Philip said he was Lady Chatterley's lover." Well! This was sacrilege in Ireland. A big to-do started and we were dragged into the headmaster's office. We were actually expelled from school. Philip and I were walking home and we really didn't care, we didn't see the seriousness of the situation, but at home my mother met us. She was a very strong woman. She marched us back up to the office, and she went in with Brother Blake, who was the head man. I don't know what happened in there, but when she came out we were back in school.'

Not for long, in Lynott's case. He left as soon as he was allowed, at the age of fifteen, and enrolled at Clogher Road Technical School, where he studied metalwork and woodwork for two years without any great enthusiasm.

Life in the Black Eagles was also changing. In 1965, Brian Downey joined the group on drums. A fellow Crumliner and schoolmate, Downey was eighteen months younger than Lynott. 'We had crossed paths a few times,' he told me, 'But I didn't really know Philip too well until much later.'

Downey's father was a drummer in the local pipe band, and by the age of thirteen his son was playing in local groups the Liffey Beats and Mod Con Cave Dwellers. Already a terrific drummer, he was the taciturn type. Quiet and solid. 'Brian hasn't changed since day one,' says Paul Scully. 'A proper Dub: straight talking, no airs and graces, what you see is what you get. I'd say at times it was Brian who held the band together.' He was the kind of musician easily overlooked from the outside, but who played an invaluable role within a band. 'Brian Downey wasn't a drummer, he was a musician who played the drums,' says Eric Bell. 'There is a difference.'

The Mod Con Cave Dwellers had supported the Black Eagles one night at St Paul's Hall, and Downey had impressed. Lynott invited him to try out for them. 'We were looking for a drummer who could play a drum beat independent of the bass drum and the snare, and the best way we could tell that was to play "You Really Got Me" [by the Kinks],' Lynott recalled many years later. 'Brian Downey had seen us a few times, and we'd seen him. He came down and the minute he could play that beat he had the job. Plus, he had tom-toms, which the other drummer didn't have.'³ Downey and Lynott became not just the rhythm section but the spine of Thin Lizzy – and great friends, although the hierarchy was established early on. 'In the Black Eagles, he became the leader because he had the personality,' says Downey. 'He had a fairly domineering personality to say the least, he had a sense for leadership, and his musical judgement was always spot on. He picked the best songs for us to play, he had a great ear, and that carried on into Thin Lizzy as well. He definitely was the leader, no doubt about that.'

Around the same time, Hugh Feighery also departed the Black Eagles, replaced on guitar by Alan Sinclair. Feighery and Lynott had been extremely close, but when the guitarist left the friendship dissolved abruptly. 'I was disappointed that I didn't get more support off of him,' says Feighery. 'We just drifted away from each other. We were thick mates from the age of eleven through to about sixteen, and those are pretty formative years.

You go through a lot of life experiences in those delicate years, and we did it together.'

In 1965 Lynott started seeing Carole Stephen, a fifteen-year-old schoolgirl from Drumcondra, a more prosperous area on the other side of Dublin from Crumlin. She had gone with friends to a Sunday afternoon disco at the Flamingo Club on O'Connell Street where the Black Eagles were playing. Lynott spotted her from the stage – pale, very pretty, red-hair in ringlets and a distinctive sense of style – but didn't make a move. When the show was over and Stephen had left, he passed on a message to Brian Downey's girlfriend, and later wife, Terri O'Leary, who was a couple of years above Stephen at Maryfield College.

'Terri came over at school the next day and said, "Philip, the singer, asked me would you come again next Sunday to the disco?"' says Stephen. 'Well, I did go, with my friends, and at the interval he came down, bought me a mineral, and asked me to dance. Then he said, "Would you like to come out with us next Wednesday?" He said *us*, so I thought he meant the band, but he actually meant with just *him*. Very Dublin. We ended up going to the movies, and that was the beginning of it.'

Stephen was attracted to his air of vulnerability, always more immediately apparent, it seemed, to women rather than men. 'He bent a little when he walked,' she says. 'He didn't have the confidence to walk tall. He wasn't able to. He was a very shy person until he got to know you. Even when he asked me out, he asked somebody else to do it!' She was also struck by his looks and his 'fabulous' singing voice. 'I used to say to Philip, "You should be singing this or that song, it would be fabulous for your voice" – all those soul ballads from the 1960s by the black American singers. The band knew it was me, giving out on what they should play, and it would drive them mad. He wasn't striving to be a pop star when I knew him, he just loved playing music. He was amazing on stage. They weren't flash places, but he was so charismatic, and such a wonderful voice.'

They made a fashionable couple. Lynott with his thrift-shop chic, crew-neck jumpers, sheepskin coats and button-down shirts; she with her home-made dresses fashioned from remnants and sewn up at the back, her hand-crafted jewellery and huge bracelets, covered with vibrant material and transformed into earrings. Beauty on a budget. Lynott was living off money sent by his mother and the cash he earned from Black Eagles' shows (although if Stephen came to see the band and couldn't get a lift home in the van, he would often hand her his share of his ten-shilling fee for a taxi). He didn't play guitar or bass and he wasn't writing songs yet, but his creativity found other outlets. When his girlfriend was ill with tonsillitis he wrote her a poem, and he made her an iron identity bracelet at college with her name on it – a sign, she says, that 'he clearly wasn't doing the work he was supposed to be doing'. It was a physical relationship, but there was a youthful innocence to it. 'We were going steady,' says Stephen. 'We went to the cinema a lot, there was nothing much else to do.'

It was grey time – the Swinging Sixties hadn't quite swung all the way over the Irish Sea – and Crumlin was a grey place. 'Dreary,' says Kevin Horan. 'There wasn't much money around and not many products available. We still had coupons for coal and milk and sugar.' As with many modern housing developments, there was plenty of sculpted greenery and a fussy sense of order – but someone had forgotten to sketch in the details. There was a bingo hall, a boxing club and a few pubs, but even the incurably romantic Lynott later struggled to poeticize it. Crumlin was: 'Green grass. A girl who used to live across the road. A gang of guys on the corner playing spinning the coin. Me gran.'[4]

It would be a couple of years before the nightclub scene in Dublin took off and the music venues became licensed. Peter Lynott took Philip to the pub for his first pint at the age of fifteen, but it was not a regular occurrence. 'I had my first drink with [Philip], in the Elbow Inn on Mary Street,' says Carole Stephen. 'I didn't know what to have, and he said, "Have a Bacardi and coke." Very classy! I couldn't finish it.' He would take the occasional cigarette, but he wasn't a dedicated smoker.

Cinema was Lynott's other true passion outside of music and girls. He was a regular at the Star in Crumlin, the Apollo in Walkinstown and the Kenilworth in Harold's Cross. He admired Vanessa Redgrave and Catherine Deneuve, and his favourite film was *Casablanca*. Movies presented an opportunity to imagine numerous paternal archetypes, as well as role models that he might aspire to emulate: the lothario, the gunslinger, the gypsy, the cowboy, the vagabond. If it's not too fanciful to suggest that the Johnnies, Randolphs and Rockies who would come to inhabit so many of Lynott's songs walked off the cinema screen and into his lyrics, neither is it entirely implausible that he plucked much of his own sense of deportment from the same source. He particularly loved Westerns. As a young boy he often dressed up in cowboy outfits to role play. It offered the same sense of release he later experienced writing songs and performing on stage.

'I can get as heavily into what I'm doing as when I used to be a kid playing cowboys,' he said in 1977. 'When you'd be completely wrapped up in killing millions of Indians and just living this whole trip out: hiding behind rocks and trees and sneaking off to imaginary places. Anybody can be anybody in rock and roll. It allows for all these people to exist within it and live out their fantasies. I mean, I certainly do.'[5]

His sensibilities were highly attuned to visual stimuli. Just as he was turning fifteen, in the summer of 1964, the Beatles's

A Hard Day's Night had screened in the Star Cinema. He went with Michael O'Flanagan. 'It was ground-breaking because it was just a load of guys acting the bollix,' says O'Flanagan. 'It didn't have a proper narrative and didn't set out to be serious. Philip was very taken with that.'

Lynott later proposed that the Black Eagles embark on their own mini-movie. The owner of a Rolleiflex camera and a Bolex D8L 8mm cine-camera, O'Flanagan was carving out a niche filming and photographing many of the Dublin beat groups of the mid-1960s. For this project he was enlisted as cinematographer. Lynott appointed himself director.

They shot mock fight scenes around several local landmarks: the old police station, the cottages of Crumlin Village, the open spaces of Mooney's Field. There was some rudimentary technical trickery involved in a shot in which the entire band appeared to enter a telephone box without anyone getting out. Later, the group was shown pounding on the door of a locked Moeran Hall. This smart and inclusive shot is the first example of Lynott knowingly finessing a crowd; when the film was shown some weeks later while the Black Eagles were playing at the venue, the place went wild. Another moment suggests a more poetic aesthetic at work. A stone is dropped into a puddle and we watch the ripples slowly disperse, a visual non sequitur denoting a change of scene.

Mostly his life revolved around music: playing it, listening to it, talking about it, dancing to it. On the nights when he wasn't performing, Lynott would be in the clubs and local discos. His time-keeping was the only real source of dissention at 85 Leighlin Road. 'Sometimes he was a little fucker,' recalled Peter Lynott. 'If we were to be home at eleven o'clock, he could stay out until one or two in the morning and we'd be waiting up for him. He was rebellious in that way, coming in late.'[6] Mostly, however, he was 'a lovely kid', according to Timothy Lynott. 'You never wanted to chastise him too much because he was so gentle.'[7]

After Frank Lynott's death in 1964, it was Lynott's older uncle Timothy who assumed, reluctantly, the role of patriarch. Timothy would insist that he be back by ten or eleven o'clock, and then sigh and summon up the required dose of censure when his rules were ignored. It is Lynott's uncle who is 'the father' in 'Dancing in the Moonlight', Thin Lizzy's breezily soulful hit of 1977, and one of Lynott's most charming hymns to his carefree teenage days. '*I should have took that last bus home, but I asked you for a dance,*' he sings, recalling one of any number of nights when his head was turned by a pretty girl. '*And my father he's going crazy, he says I'm living in a trance.*' By the last verse, predictably, the lesson has not been learned.

> *It's three o'clock in the morning*
> *I'm on the streets again*
> *I disobeyed another warning*
> *I should have been in by ten*

On occasions when Timothy was successfully duped or placated, Sarah would have to be negotiated. 'Sometimes when we were coming home late from clubs, we would sneak into his house at two in the morning and I'd stay overnight,' says Frank Murray. 'We'd have to wait until his grandmother went out the following morning, because he didn't want her to know he had me staying over. She'd worry that he was staying out late.'

Timothy Lynott was the only person at 85 Leighlin Road working full-time, in a flour mill, and he spent a good proportion of his earnings on music. 'I bought one or two LPs a week, but when I got them home Philip and his friends would spend all day listening to them.'[8]

Lynott was fortunate. His uncle had good, broad tastes, encompassing everything from Mose Allison to the Who, folk to blues, the Mamas and the Papas to Tamla Motown; and later, Creedence Clearwater Revival, Cream, Steppenwolf. 'Timmy had an incredible collection of music,' says Paul Scully. 'We used to mitch off of school and we'd go to Philip's granny's house and play vinyl all afternoon, just sit on the floor and listen to the music. It was pre-drugs, pre-sex, really, pre- any of that. We were just cool guys hanging out together, all obsessed with music.'

To Timothy's collection of albums Lynott began to add his own purchases. 'Philip actually got a copy of the first Mothers of Invention album, *Freak Out!*, the original with the blue cover, in 1966,' says Scully. 'Alongside that he'd be playing Frank Sinatra's Capitol albums. Sinatra would have been so uncool in those days because your parents would have been listening to him, but Philip didn't care if it was cool or not. He was absorbing influences from all over. He'd be playing Buddy Guy, B. B. King and Muddy Waters, the Byrds and that psychedelic West Coast sound. He was into the Velvet Underground when nobody had heard of them. He had the first Simon & Garfunkel record. He had hugely diverse and eclectic tastes. He had a great antenna. We were like sponges, and he was really open to exploring.'

Brian Downey was part of their social group, and he would also spend hours at Leighlin Road, cycling from his home on Cashel Avenue, often with an armful of his father's jazz records. Eddie Vinson's 'Kidney Stew Blues', Oscar Brown Junior's 'When I Was Cool' and other cool cuts were added to the melting pot of music.

They often hung around the Snack Bar, a little café wedged between a chip shop and the Apollo cinema in Walkinstown. Lynott would order a Fanta or a hot chocolate and shoot the breeze with his friends. It was the closest the area came to sophistication.

'There was always a group of hard "chaws" hanging around looking for a fight,' says Michael O'Flanagan. 'We were lower middle-class lads interested in music and film and stuff like that, but these lads were tough nuts. They'd walk past and pick a fight. Somebody would get a box, someone would get a kick. Some of these guys would carry a hatchet in their pocket. We were a bit scared of them, but Philip didn't give a fuck. He wasn't a bit afraid of them. He'd give them a dig back, no problem. There was that side to him, too. He could handle himself if it turned to a fight, but he didn't spend a lot of time fighting, and he didn't go around picking fights.'

In common with many local teenagers, Lynott tried boxing, going for trials in the National Stadium, a mile down the road towards central Dublin. 'I think people thought, "Hey, there's a black guy, he's probably a great boxer,"' says Frank Murray. 'He wasn't. He always told me it wasn't good, what happened in the stadium.' Lynott's priority was to preserve his looks rather than put up a fight, although the experience served to further clarify his options. 'There were two ways of making it back in Crumlin,' he recalled. 'You were either a tough guy who thumped everybody around and pulled the chicks that way, or you played in a band. Not wanting the bruises, and being a bit of a coward at heart, I decided to sing in a band.'[9] In doing so he found a means of continuing to indulge tough-guy fantasies and channelling his aggression without, at least most of the time, getting a smack in the mouth.

Later in Lynott's life there were claims made for his prowess as a footballer, even a suggestion that it might have provided him with an alternative career path. Peter Lynott recalls him playing in goal, but by all accounts he wasn't particularly good at the sport or terribly interested. 'He couldn't kick a ball to save his life,' says Frank Murray. 'Entirely uncoordinated. He didn't grow up following football or anything like that. He only caught the soccer bug when he started following Manchester United around the mid-1970s.' Peter Fallon and Jim Fitzpatrick once convened a local football team they nicknamed Energy Reserves, which would meet for a kick around in the local park. 'Philip wanted to come, but he turned up in his cowboy boots and new jeans, and he thought he might get them dirty,' says Fallon.

Lynott lived in the everlasting now of adolescence. It was not an age, nor an era, for soul-baring. Privately, Lynott did not discuss at all the years before he arrived in Crumlin, and only rarely would he talk about his parents and his unusual domestic set-up. In time the questions of who he was and where he originated receded into the background, for those who knew him and perhaps even for Lynott himself. 'I used to look at him and think, where did he come from?' says another friend from the 1960s, Fran Quigley. 'We would have thought that he was an orphan, but I'd never ask him. I can't remember anyone making such a conversation. Why would they? We were young, we just went with it.'

His youthful feelings towards his mother were ambivalent. 'Philip never got on with his mother in the early days,' says Hugh Feighery. 'He had a problem with her, in so much as he felt hard done by. Even though when she came to visit he'd get stuff that other kids wouldn't get, it didn't really compensate for the mental trauma it caused. He certainly had hang-ups about that . . . In his formative years he felt [abandoned].'

During Thin Lizzy concerts, Lynott would introduce 'Wild One' as 'a song about running away'. It's an Irish song, alluding to the nation's complex dance with exile, and in particular the fate of the Wild Geese, the 30,000 Irish soldiers who left to serve in continental Europe following the Treaty of Limerick in 1691. It would take a tin ear and a particularly hard heart, however, not to also hear it as a deeply personal song from a son to his free-spirited mother who had first run away from Ireland, and then – as the child in Lynott couldn't help but perceive it – from him.

Wild one, won't you please come home
You've been away too long, will you
We need you home, we need you near
Come back wild one, will you

How can we live without your love?
You know that could kill you
How can we carry on?
When you are gone, my wild one . . .

So you go your way wild one
I'll try and follow
And if you change your mind
I will be waiting here for you tomorrow

For I would beg for you
I would steal and I would borrow
I'd do anything, anything at all
To end this sorrow

The candour of his comments to Hugh Feighery was unusual. As he grew older, Lynott was far less forthcoming on the subject. 'I was only aware that his mother was working in England and his granny was looking after him,' says Paul Scully. 'I never questioned it. There was none of that modern idea of going to see a psychiatrist about your hang-ups or your long lost family. He may have internalized it, but there were no long conversations.'

Had his friends felt sufficiently emboldened to quiz Lynott, this is what he might have told them: his mother was still living in Manchester, and he saw her only rarely. Having endured a tough few years, in 1964 Philomena Lynott had begun what became a long, settled and loving relationship with a local man called Dennis Keeley, two years her junior. They set up home together in a flat in Didsbury, and in 1966 they took over the management of a rundown hotel in Manchester's Whalley Range district, two miles south of the city centre. The area was separated from Moss Side to the east by the busy Princess Road, where Lynott had attended school only a few years earlier.

At the time Whalley Range was a byword for seedy neglect, a red-light district typified by unkempt tenements and once-elegant Victorian villas converted into shabby bedsits. Its atmosphere of down-at-heel disrepair was later captured by Morrissey in the Smiths' 'Miserable Lie': '*What do we get for our trouble and pain? Just a rented room in Whalley Range.*' In the 1980s, the German singer Nico, once of the Velvet Underground, lived a rather diminished existence in the same area.

The Clifton Grange Hotel, at 17 Wellington Road, was a roomy Victorian house that had seen better days. It was less a conventional hotel and more bed-and-breakfast digs, aimed at long-term tenants who were known, only somewhat euphemistically, as 'show-business clientele' – cabaret musicians, nightclub turns, drag acts, strippers, showgirls, comedians and dancers. It was about as far from Crumlin as Philomena Lynott could have travelled – which presumably was the whole point.

In short order, Lynott's mother went from manager to co-owner to outright owner of the establishment, which she created in her own lively, eccentric image. Once she had settled and found her feet, from his late teens Lynott would visit and stay at the hotel. In the mid-1960s, however, there was still a distance – physical and emotional – and much left unspoken. Lynott saw Philomena perhaps once or twice a year, when she came over to Dublin, an event which had all the pomp and ceremony of a royal visit. She would stay not at Leighlin Road but at the homes of older siblings. Various younger Lynotts would get the day off school and be taken shopping for beautiful clothes that their parents would disapprove of. She would arrive with a fashionable item for her son – a good shirt, a cool leather jacket – and take him out for tea at the Coffee Inn on South Anne Street or Sheries Café on Abbey Street. Sometimes his girlfriend Carole Stephen was invited along.

'She was terribly interested in me, asking all sorts of questions,' says Stephen. 'She was lovely to look at – very tall, hair up in a bun, very elegant. She'd bring Philip something really nice, and he loved that, but he didn't really know his mother in those days. I wouldn't say she was vastly important in his life at all. He adored his gran, Sarah. He loved her and was always quoting her.'

His mother did not set him down to explain the exact details of his paternity. Cecil Parris was not a fully fleshed out figure in Lynott's mind. He didn't even know his name. Instead, he was drip-fed snippets of information, not all of it necessarily accurate. Lynott's feelings towards his father were a mixture of confusion, hurt, bitterness and defiance. 'I'd ask him about his dad and he'd say he didn't know who he was,' says Hugh Feighery. 'He'd say he was a seaman, that's all. Sometimes he used to say he was a black bastard. A big black bastard. That's what he was calling him, but it wasn't a subject that he would be too happy to be discussing. He had a complex about it to a degree, I would say.'

Entering his mid- and late teens, and into adulthood, Lynott became increasingly emotionally guarded. 'Most of the time he kept his feelings wrapped up,' says Frank Murray. 'I think his mother played a part in making him tough in that way; not to show his feelings too much, in case that was perceived as a weakness. He would say odd things about his dad, but never anything deep ... Phyllis didn't actually go, "Let me tell you a bunch of things about your father." She told him she didn't know where he came from, that they'd had a relationship and they'd split up.'

In the absence of hard facts, he formed a romanticized portrait of his father. He believed that he was originally from either Brazil or the Caribbean. He learned that he was nicknamed 'The Duke' and that he had charm and an easy way with women. 'It all seemed a bit exotic, and he liked that,' says Murray.

'We heard he was a tap dancer,' says Paul Scully, laughing. 'That's all we ever heard! This very exotic idea that his father was a Caribbean tap dancer who wore very snazzy suits, hence Philip was a very snazzy dresser. He built up these images, depending on what Phyllis had or hadn't told him.'

Those close to him felt that his paternity was a source of nagging curiosity, rather than a gaping absence. It would flare up from time to time. 'I think he went through stages with it,' says Frank Murray. 'I don't think he was looking for the father, I think he accepted the fact that he was in a great family situation. He was brought up in a really loving family, by his grandmother and his uncles.'

Lynott did not give the impression of being a young man living under a cloud of angst and abandonment. He was heartbroken when his grandfather died, but otherwise he was a young man who appeared to be having the time of his life.

'Philip was a very, very happy guy, and a very funny person,' says Frank Murray. 'He was one of the funniest guys to be around, and it was infectious. Life was just funny for us. We were all very quick-witted, everyone was great with one-liners and nobody took anything too seriously. There were lots of verbal put-downs, and someone would shoot back with something equally barbed.

'We never moaned about being depressed, or about having broken up with our girlfriend. Everything was a laugh. The "sixties" had come along, we'd got out of the sepia 1950s, and life was Technicolor. There was a great sense of freedom and discovery. We were finding out about writers, musicians . . . and film-makers, broadening our horizons. That was enough to keep anyone busy.'

4

In September 1967, Lynott received an unannounced house call from Brendan Shiels. Known to one and all as 'The Brush' in honour of his bold cultivation of long hair and moustache, Shiels was the former bass player in the Uptown Band, a Dublin flower-power outfit which served as a breeding ground for several significant Irish groups. Other members of the band went on to play in the Chosen Few, Granny's Intentions and Elmer Fudd.

A straight-talking twenty-two-year-old from Cabra West in Dublin, Shiels knew what he wanted – fame; money; respect – and wasn't shy about grabbing it. He was also 'an extraordinary bass player,' says Eric Bell. 'He was into virtuoso stuff. Really knew what he was doing.' Shiels was on the lookout for a singer for his new group, Skid Row, to play alongside drummer Noel Bridgeman and guitarist Bernard Cheevers.

Lynott was a free agent. With a certain inevitability, the Black Eagles had fizzled out. One of their final shows was at Moran's Hotel in Dublin on 28 April 1967. 'It was really the stepping stone for us all to become a bit more experienced,' says Brian Downey, who went off to join a new blues band called Sugar Shack, having declined Shiels's offer to join Skid Row. 'We wanted to be the best beat group in the area, and I think we became that in the end.'

After imitation came the need for innovation, perhaps even a tilt at self-expression. While the commitment of the other Black Eagles varied – some had threatened to elope with their girlfriends; others to the Army – Lynott was not a dabbler. After the band ended, he had started up a short-lived 'West Coast' group called Kama Sutra but – rather contradicting its name – it was over almost before it had begun. He was waiting to make his next move when Brush Shiels showed up.

The Black Eagles had scarcely registered as a blip on Shiels's radar, but he had heard good things about Lynott from the Uptown Band's manager, Ted Carroll, the local impresario who had booked the group at the Bastille Club a year earlier. One night at Dublin club Sound City, another friend had tipped off Shiels about this 'spade singer' who – and this was the crucial part – 'looks great'.

Shiels and Carroll had duly attempted to recruit Lynott to the Uptown Band, but when they failed to make contact local singer Dick O'Leary was hired instead. The Lynott household had no telephone; on such prosaic domestic details potentially life-changing opportunities came and went. This time, having been unsuccessful in tempting another local singer, Peter Adler, to join Skid Row, Shiels was determined to get his man. One early autumn morning he took the number 22 bus from the other side of Phoenix Park and headed for Leighlin Road. 'When Philip opened the door I knew he was the man for the job,' he says. 'It didn't matter if he could sing or not, we could sort that out pretty easy. As far as I was concerned he couldn't fail.'

A born pragmatist, Shiels's snap judgement was all about the cover rather than the book. He needed a singer who looked the part and could front the band; the rest was mere detail. Lynott was surprised to be offered the job before anyone had even heard him sing. There was simply no time, says Shiels. 'The first thing

I told him was that things were happening, and we were going to be happening as well.'

When Lynott turned up to his first Skid Row rehearsal, Shiels was even more convinced that he had made the correct choice. Their prospective singer arrived wearing a beautiful dark-blue overcoat and green-tinted rectangular sunglasses, the kind that Jim McGuinn from the Byrds might wear to shield his eyes from the glare of the unyielding Californian sun. Their purpose was rather less pressing in autumnal Dublin, but that wasn't quite the point. 'I don't know where he would have got them,' says Shiels, still full of wonderment almost half a century later to have discovered a singer several streets ahead of the competition in the style stakes.

When Lynott did eventually open his mouth – to sing 'Hey Joe' – not everyone in the room was entirely sold. As the song finished, guitarist Bernard Cheevers called Shiels over and said, none too quietly, 'I reckon I could sing it better than that!' But Shiels was the boss, and for him 'that was the end of it. He had a sound. He was singing through Mickey Mouse amps, but he sounded right, he looked right, and right there and then he could do anything that Jimi Hendrix was doing. That's all I was interested in.'

The Jimi Hendrix Experience had impacted in Britain and Ireland earlier in the year, recalibrating what was and was not possible to achieve with guitar, bass and drums. Hendrix swiftly became a touchstone for Skid Row, and especially for Lynott. He couldn't even play guitar, let alone attempt what Hendrix was capable of doing with his instrument, yet he picked up on other parallels between himself and the American, noting his mixed-race heritage, his funky shyness, his cool stage presence and long, lanky frame. There was something of Hendrix's laconic mumble in Lynott's own singing voice, too.

Some early Thin Lizzy songs – among them 'Ray-Gun' and 'Old Moon Madness' – were explicit homages. In 1973, when Deep Purple's Ritchie Blackmore came courting Lynott to form a new band with Ian Paice and Paul Rodgers, the Hendrix connection was a major factor. 'It was like Hendrix number two,' said Blackmore. 'He looked like Hendrix, sounded like Hendrix.'[1] Lynott was aware of the link. 'At one time I made a conscious effort not to sound like Hendrix,' he said. 'It just happens I've got that kind of husky inflexion, so I thought, what the hell – people seem to like it. I wasn't consciously imitating him, although I've always thought his stage act was the perfect balance of showmanship and music.'[2] Soon his bedroom wall would be adorned with a huge poster of Hendrix, and he would grow out his smart, mod-ish 'helmet' into a wild, woolly Afro, à la Jimi.

Shiels was an equally devout follower, but from the beginning of Skid Row it was clear that Lynott's more esoteric musical tastes were not shared by his band-mate. 'The first time we met he was telling me about things I wasn't expecting, like Paul Simon's "I Am a Rock",' says Shiels. 'Then he starts on about Nico and the Velvet Underground. I had no interest in that. I was coming from somewhere else. Soul and rock, the Hendrix thing.'

Skid Row rehearsed at the home of Kathleen Quigley, who owned a sprawling tenement in Synnott Place, north of O'Connell Street. At the back of the house was an extension where, it seemed, every band in Dublin convened at one time or another. With no bespoke rehearsal studios in town, Mrs Quigley's home became the hub of the local group scene. It was a social service; no money changed hands. Two of her five sons knew Lynott well. Pat Quigley was a bass player in the Movement and would later play with him in Orphanage. Fran Quigley, his younger brother, became a friend and unofficial roadie for Orphanage and Thin Lizzy.

Drilled into shape at Synnott Place, Skid Row became very good very quickly. Their first rehearsal took place in September 1967. By February 1968 they were widely regarded as the best new group in Ireland. The trick was to mix virtuosity and a vivid stage presence with, in terms of musical choices, a savvy blend of the experimental and the familiar. Their repertoire was almost entirely covers. The Beatles's 'I Am the Walrus' and 'Strawberry Fields Forever', the Byrds's 'Eight Miles High' and 'So You Want to Be a Rock and Roll Star', and the Jimi Hendrix Experience's 'Hey Joe', 'Manic Depression' and 'If Six Was Nine'. They played the Animals's 'Sky Pilot', some Buffalo Springfield, a smattering of soul. Cheever owned a wah-wah pedal and Lynott had bought a Binson Space Echo effect for his vocals, the kind of technology that enabled the sound to weft, warp and phase in and out, keeping pace with the times as music started to become more psychedelic and the influence of the US West Coast scene drifted over the Atlantic.

It was a dawning age of visual as well as sonic experimentation. In America the Grateful Dead, Jefferson Airplane and the Doors were using liquid lights: slides of multi-coloured liquid ink heated by the lamp of a film projector to throw abstract, constantly evolving patterns behind the bands. Pink Floyd were attempting much the same thing in the UK. In downtown New York, the Velvet Underground were working with Andy Warhol and his Factory acolytes to create provocative film projections intended to shock and stimulate the senses just as much as the abrasively beautiful sound they were making.

Lynott, the sponge, picked up on these pioneering ideas and fed them into Skid Row. 'Philip knew what was happening, and he brought his own sub-culture with him,' says Brush Shiels. 'We put the band together, and the following week he brought Frank Murray and Paul Scully to me. They were our unofficial roadies.

The week after that he brought Mick O'Flanagan. He brought all the lads to the band who really made a difference. We were surrounded with people who had ideas, and that came from Philip. There was always an arty flavour to it.'

The liquid lights came courtesy of another friend, Gregory Brown. In the prevailing spirit of the age, he preferred to be known as Ashtar. O'Flanagan handled the film content. 'Philip knew all about the Velvet Underground and what they were doing with projections,' he says. 'I'd never heard of them, but Philip wanted me to do the same for him.' One portion of footage showed the Pope visiting Jerusalem intercut with images of the assassination of John F. Kennedy in Dallas. This was back-projected while the band played 'Sky Pilot'. Performed at the Catholic Young Men's Society Hall, such transgressions made the front page of the *Evening Herald*, under the headline: 'GROUP PERFORM BLASPHEMOUS SONG AT LOCAL DANCE'. 'Me ma wouldn't talk to me for three days,' says Shiels. 'It was quite progressive for the time.'

'They were really at the forefront of experimentation, and at the time Ireland was very conservative,' says Paul Scully. 'They even did a little mini-opera and performed it at the Moulin Rouge club in Dublin. Myself and Frank, who were the crew at the time, had to dress in white coats with stethoscopes and come on as doctors. I seem to remember amputation was involved. They used to fake fight on stage. Phil would walk off and then come back on, and the audience was so gullible they would believe it.'

This was a routine based on a scene from the film *The Defiant Ones*, starring Sidney Poitier and Tony Curtis, where the pair – one black, the other white – break out of jail and then turn on one another. Skid Row tried it out at one of their first major gigs, at University College Dublin, during a version of Jimi Hendrix's 'Manic Depression'.

'Beforehand, I cut Philip's shirt down the back, so it was just barely holding together, and we had handcuffs on,' says Shiels. 'Bernard was playing guitar with his teeth, and we came out like we were locked together, and then I ripped the shirt off him and [threw] my bass at him. The audience jumped up on stage to separate us – it was that good. So right from the start we had that dramatic thing. We got plenty of publicity right away. We could play, but we could do this other thing as well. Philip had that all his life. He knew how to put on a really good show.'

Lynott later recalled that he was 'totally into image in those days'.[3] It was part of the job. 'He was a brilliant frontman,' says Noel Bridgeman. 'A great presence, and a great mover without the guitar. We were very popular, we became a big band very quickly, and Philip had a lot to do with that. He had a great personality. He laughed really easily, he was very bright and alive and great company. Fantastic to work with onstage. Totally into the music.'

Though some distance from the strutting, crotch-splaying frontman he became, Lynott could throw the necessary shapes. 'He had a natural rhythm, sinewy and flowing,' says Shiels. 'He had no problems out the front. He lived the part day and night, he never slept. He was up for it, from day one.'

People would recognize him as he ambled down Grafton Street, and they would nod and say *howya*. He felt part of something. To paraphrase another hero, Bob Dylan, he could feel that something was happening, even if he wasn't yet entirely sure what it was.

'Dublin was a very small town,' says Michael O'Flanagan. 'You could put your arms around everybody.'

It was a city by name but still a village by nature. Dublin's cultural life force pumped out from the heart of St Stephen's

Green, down Grafton Street and over the river to O'Connell Street, and along South King Street, Merrion Row and Baggot Street. This was Lynott's stamping ground. 'Things moved fast from the Black Eagles to when Phil joined Skid Row,' says Frank Murray. 'The Black Eagles were just a bunch of kids from Crumlin, but when he joined Skid Row it started to happen. It was more of a hanging-around-town scene.'

He was finished with college. For a short while he experimented with gainful employment for the first and only time in his life, working as a turner and fitter at Tonge & Taggart, a local foundry in East Wall which made the cast-iron manhole covers and flood mouths which adorned Dublin's roads. He was paid two pounds and five shillings a week, he got his hands dirty and had to wear overalls. 'He hated it, absolutely hated it,' says Carole Stephen. 'I don't think he was cut out to have a job. He was definitely destined for better things.' Lynott tended to agree. The arrangement didn't last long. 'He was lined up to be a draughtsman,' says Frank Murray. 'Then he started making money with Skid Row. It wasn't a lot but it was as much as you could make as a draughtsman, and it was more fun.'

Unyoked, Lynott made the most of his freedom. No matter how late he went to bed, he emerged magically bright-eyed at dawn, looking immaculate and eager to embrace what the new day offered. He is remembered as a bundle of energy and ideas. He would catch the bus into town from Crumlin; or walk; or hitch a lift on the back of Michael O'Flanagan's Honda scooter, his long legs jutting out comically like bat wings.

He hung out at St Stephen's Green with a group which included Frank Murray and Paul Scully; John Hodges, a DJ at the Moulin Rouge club, a converted church in South Great George's Street; and Stevie Bolger and his younger brother Seamus, better known as 'Smiley', who was also a DJ. They created their own makeshift approximation of what they knew to be happening at the time in Haight-Ashbury and the King's Road. Only a few years later Lynott was already fondly mythologizing it. 'During the hippie days when I was starting to get into singing we used to buy a five-bob bottle of wine and sit [on the Green] just getting wrecked,' he said. 'You used to meet these tourist chicks all the time. You'd say, "I'd love to show you around, but I've got no money." So they'd go, "Oh it's okay, I've got money." So that was it. You were *in!* I wasn't a gigolo . . . but it was pretty fucking close.'[4]

The Green wasn't just about women. Bands in town from Limerick, Cork or the north of Ireland would congregate there. Musical connections could be made, hot tips traded, tastes verified and confirmed. If the Green wasn't happening, Lynott might take a spin to the Picture House on South King Street or wander down to the Grafton Cinema, near Trinity College, which showed a continuous loop of cartoons, newsreels and comedy shorts. He loved cartoons the same way he loved comics: for their colour and invention, and for the quick-fire and often anarchic leaps of imagination.

He mooched around the stores and flea markets, rummaging through the wares and chatting up the shop girls. Just walking down Grafton Street was an event in itself. Not yet pedestrianized, it could take Lynott half an hour to stroll from the top to the bottom. 'He was a showman,' says Jim Fitzpatrick. 'He would *promenade* up and down Grafton Street – that's the only word to describe it. He loved the attention.'

As musical and fashion tastes rapidly evolved, his wardrobe somehow kept pace accordingly. Before the Dandelion Market opened in April 1970, finally bringing the delights of tie-dye T-shirts, loon pants, cheesecloth shirts and sheepskin coats to Dublin's massed ranks of fashion-starved youngsters, there was precious little on offer for a sharp-dressed man. Jeffa Gill had come over to Dublin from Birmingham Arts College in 1965 to work on a design project, and ended up staying to help set up a boutique in Upper Leeson Street called The Happening. A machinist would make up her designs to order, but just as often people would drop in to chat, read books and play chess.

'Fashion-wise, there wasn't much at all,' she says. 'You had to make your own trends because you couldn't buy them. They didn't exist. There was a great shop called McBirney's on the Quays, where you could buy fabric and remnants. Philip stood out because he was very cool, very stylish. He loved dancing in the clubs, and he moved beautifully. He ranged down Grafton Street, arms and the legs flapping in and out. He always had an entourage, one or two guys from his area that hung out with him.'

He was inventive. He trawled the flea markets for vintage gear that could be given a fashionable twist. Frank Murray's girlfriend, Ferga, later his wife, was a fashion student at Grafton College. She would make the band custom-made bell-bottom trousers or even suits. Lynott swung from kaftans to white mackintoshes, suits to a full-length leather coat, patterned woollen jumpers to sunglasses and, recalls future Thin Lizzy manager Brian Tuite, 'a pair of ladies' boots with high heels. Charisma oozed out of him.'

It's fair to say that Crumlin had seen nothing quite like it. 'My mother started to complain that there were all sorts of funny people coming up the path to the door, dressed in these way-out outfits,' said Philomena Lynott, who was, nevertheless, happily encouraging his experiments from afar. 'I was bringing him all kinds of stuff from England, and he'd buy all this old gear. Evening dress wear from the flea markets, a grandpapa shirt with a studded collar . . .' He persuaded Brian Downey to travel to Manchester with him, primarily so they could get their hair cut at a fashionable salon.

His partner in crime, sartorially, was John Hodges. When Hodges died of leukaemia in 1969, aged only twenty, Lynott was 'heartbroken,' says Michael O'Flanagan. 'We had a wake at Slattery's in Capel Street and Philip was very upset. I'd never seen him like that, so emotional. He and John were very close. They were both like male models.'

Lynott moonlighted as a model during this time and for a period afterwards. He appeared in an advert for the new Wimpy restaurant, which opened in 1968 at 80 Lower Dorset Street. Propped up at the counter, his back to the camera, he turns his long, lean, unsmiling face to the lens beneath a strapline which promises, 'After the show it's the place to go'. He fitted the bill as the face of Dublin's coolest new musical scene-setters, although pragmatism may have played its part. The new Wimpy – 'Enjoy your meal in comfortable and artistic surroundings to mood music' – was a stone's throw from Synnott Place, where most of the groups rehearsed.

He was on the cover of *Hitsville '68* beat magazine with model Millie Jackson, and was used several times for *New Spotlight* by photographer Roy Esmonde – whose work appears on the first two Thin Lizzy albums – as the token boyfriend in female fashion shoots for the magazine. 'He would come up to my studio on Parnell Square,' says Esmonde. 'He'd come in with a little bag with multiple pairs of trousers and then go strolling off down Grafton Street with some new style.' Later, in 1971, Lynott frolicked in a pastoral scene with model Niki Adrian to advertise the wares of Dublin's Drury Lane Boutique. A year later he was holding hands with Pat Harrison as she sported a variety of mini-dresses from Cinderella Boutique.

When the shopping and parading was done, the nearby Coffee Inn was a regular late-1960s meeting place, an archetypal Italian café with red booths and Formica tables. Lynott would nurse a chocolate or, if funds were available, have a slice of pizza or a plate of pasta – 'spaghetti bollock naked', he called it. When his order arrived, he would mark his gratitude by saying 'tanks and armoured cars'. The downstairs restaurant at the Switzer department store on Grafton Street was another favourite place to spin out a few hours.

Dublin was a drinking city, and much of its business was conducted in the pubs clustered around Grafton Street. The Bailey on Duke Street was always a favourite. Once frequented by the young James Joyce, it had more recently been the haunt of poets Brendan Behan and Patrick Kavanagh, often vociferously drunk and combative; both had only lately departed, ravaged and much diminished by their alcoholism. *The Ginger Man* author J. P. Donleavy was also a regular.

The Duke on Duke Street and Bruxelles on Harry Street, outside of which a statue of Lynott now stands, and the nearby pubs of McDaid's and Kehoe's were all regular meeting places. Neary's was always a particular favourite of Lynott. It backs on to the stage door of the Gaiety Theatre, and over the years everyone from Phil Silvers to Peter O'Toole would roll in. Lynott's tipple of choice was a pint of Smithwick's, the creamy bronze ale brewed in Kilkenny. He disliked Guinness, though he related to the iconography of an Irish classic which, symbolically, it seemed to him, mixed black and white.

Pubs were for daytime and evenings. Nights were for the beat clubs. Dublin was a hive of live-music venues, dotted north and south of the river, among them the Countdown Club; the Club A Go Go; the Moulin Rouge; Flamingo; the 72 Club; Sound City; Eamonn Andrews's TV Club and Dublin's answer to the Cavern, Number Five. Most only had a 'mineral bar' – soft drinks only – though some circumnavigated the licensing laws by serving alcohol from teapots. The priority was music and social interaction. People came from across town to listen, see and be seen. Friendships were cultivated and scenes cross-fertilized.

To everyone involved, it was a time of great promise. 'It was a very small clique of people in Dublin then,' says Paul Scully. 'All we wanted to do was be around music and musicians. There was a lovely warmth, like a naive painting. Great stuff comes out of naivety, because you haven't got any value judgements.'

'People were poverty stricken and religion stricken,' says Noel Bridgeman. 'Music was like another world. It was a great escape. A brilliant release.'

The presence of Carole Stephen at Skid Row shows would infuriate Brush Shiels. He was determined to present his lead singer as footloose and fancy-free. 'I said to Phil, "I don't want to see Carole at gigs,"' he recalls. 'I said, "If we ever see her at the gigs again we're fucking you out." His job was to look at all the women, click with the chicks and concentrate on them. We had more women in our gigs than we had fellas, which was very unusual. The women loved him, it was as simple as that. That's why he got the job.'

Stephen laughs. 'It didn't bother me or Philip. He would come down to see me at the interval and dedicate songs and things like that, and I know Brush used to go mad.'

Their relationship was ongoing, but not without difficulties. It turned heads and challenged social prejudices. Stephen came from a middle-class family and had stayed on at Maryfield College to take her Leaving Certificate. On more than a couple of occasions Lynott was spotted lurking outside at the end of the school day, waiting to pick her up. 'The nuns were giving out about it for weeks, this black boy waiting for Carole Stephen,' she says. 'I was kind of shocked. I think people were afraid.' He very rarely ventured to her family home in Drumcondra. Stephen's father was a colonel in the Irish Army – 'he was a great father, we loved him and were all so proud of him, but he had a roar' – and was unaware of the relationship. He may not have approved. 'You would feel that Phil wouldn't be the first person he'd want to see,' says Shiels. 'In a band and, well, all the rest of it . . .'

They were up and down, on and off, for a couple of years. 'It was volatile with Carole after a while,' says Frank Murray. 'They were two volatile people.'

'We split up a few times, definitely,' says Stephen. 'He was very jealous, and when you're young you don't want someone to be jealous of you when you're not doing anything, just out dancing or having fun. One night we were out in Temple Oak, my friends and I would go there every Saturday, and Skid Row were playing that night. Somebody had asked me to dance, and Philip came down off the stage and interrupted.' At another Skid Row concert, he kicked out at a Coca-Cola bottle which had been left on the edge of the stage. It smashed against the wall, narrowly missing a girl in the audience.

Acute and irrational jealousy would be a recurring feature in all of his most significant relationships with women. He seemed wary of leaving himself emotionally exposed, and was capable of seeing rejection and betrayal even when it wasn't there. As far as Stephen was concerned, when they were going out together it was an exclusive relationship.

'It would be fair to say Philip was in love with Carole,' says Michael O'Flanagan. 'If we understood love in those days. They didn't split up because he was having it off with other women. They split up because she was going to have a baby.'

In December 1967 Stephen became pregnant. Early in 1968 she told Lynott that he was going to be a father. 'Philip wanted to run away to his mother,' she says. 'He said we could stay there. We hadn't a fiver between us, it was out of the question, but that was his suggestion.' Instead, she 'gave the problem over to my father, and he took over. Our family doctor put my dad in touch with a Catholic association, and they organized everything. I was very thin, and I felt I was getting a bump very early on, so I went to a home for unmarried mothers.'

Stephen spent most of her pregnancy at the Manor House mother-and-baby home, part of a convent run by the Sacred Heart Sisters in Castlepollard in County Westmeath, some sixty miles north-west of Dublin. The convent was surrounded by acres of lawns and fields, a self-contained world. The young women in residence were not allowed outside of the grounds for the entirety of their stay.

The cover story for Stephen's sudden absence was that she was on an extended visit to a school friend who had recently moved to Germany. Only her mother and father knew differently – and Lynott, although he had no further contact with his girlfriend or her family during that period, and indeed had no idea where she now was. 'She disappeared off the scene suddenly, we didn't see her again and nobody asked any questions,' says Michael O'Flanagan. 'It wasn't common knowledge. The kind of place Ireland was then, you could be having quintuplets and nobody would ever find out. Everybody knew there would be more to it than what was being told, but you didn't ask many more questions.'

The convents could be terrible places. The abuse meted out to young women and their children is now well-established, and Manor House was not exempt from these transgressions, but for Stephen 'it wasn't the worst place, and I didn't have an awful time at all. I did not have an unhappy time down there. The unhappy time came when I had to give my baby away. I only had him for a couple of days. My sister was getting married and I had to be home.'

Macdaragh Lambe, as he is now known, was born in Castlepollard on 25 August 1968, five days after Lynott's nineteenth birthday. His father's name is listed on the birth certificate. In accompanying documents given to the adoption agency he is described as 'studying for his exams and interested in singing and music'.

Five days after the birth, the baby was handed over to the Catholic Protection and Rescue Society of Ireland (CPRSI) in Dublin. During the period when the CPRSI was attempting to arrange an adoption, the infant was looked after at a mother-and-baby home in Blackrock, and was also temporarily cared for by two foster families. He was formally adopted into the Lambe family at the age of eleven months and grew up in Newbridge in County Kildare, twenty-five miles outside Dublin.

Mother and son would not see each other for some thirty years. Lambe sought out his true parentage in 2000 following the death of his adoptive parents and has been reconciled with his birth mother for more than a decade. 'We clicked very quickly, and we have built a good relationship,' he says.

Lambe now lives in Headford, twenty miles outside Galway, and works in the music events industry. He has two young children. Although he and his father would never meet, as he grew into adulthood the physical resemblance was so acute that Lambe became accustomed to 'people pointing in the local pub or wherever. Most people mentioned it. When I found out it all made sense, it answered a lot of questions in my head very quickly.'

A matter of days after the birth, in late August 1968 Carole Stephen returned to her home in Dublin. The relationship with Lynott was over. Contact had ceased completely, until one day she spotted him by chance in town, hanging out with Eric Bell and Gary Moore. When he saw Stephen he walked over. 'The two of us went to the cartoon cinema, and I told him everything,' she says. 'We sat at the back of the cinema and sobbed. It was a really sad time. We were in bits, we had to wait till it was dark until we came out. In terms of our relationship, there was no going back. I had to knock it on the head. We met up [again] a couple of times, but there was no mention of the baby. I blocked a lot of this out for a long time.'

Lynott told no one about the child. 'He never said anything to me, which was unusual, because at that time he told me everything,' says Frank Murray. 'I remember Brian Downey saying to me, much later on, that he reckoned Phil had had a child with Carole. This was in the mid-1970s. I said, "Nah, you're joking me, he would have said something." But he never did.'

'His son was never talked about,' says Paul Scully, but Lynott dropped hints and left clues in interviews and songs over the years, brief and cryptic though they were. In a short and otherwise banal 1969 chat for the 'Beat Up' column in the Irish magazine, *Woman's Way*, amid the usual fluff about his taste in females and his favourite bands, Lynott suddenly lets his guard down. 'Do you know what else I'd like to do?' he says. 'Adopt a kid. Now why can't single people do that? I'd like a kid and I'd be good to him and look after him and give him a good life – better than he'd have in an orphanage and no pun intended!'[5] The child is not abstract; he has a gender. Lynott couldn't help but be aware that he was reprising, at least in basic outline, the patterns of his own upbringing. Much later, he told Thin Lizzy manager Chris Morrison: 'My father left when I was two weeks old. Sounds like my kind of fella.'

On 'Brought Down', from Thin Lizzy's 1972 album *Shades of a Blue Orphanage*, Lynott sings that '*my baby had a baby by me*' and – as though time-stamping the emotion to the late 1960s – namechecks Irish freak-folk band Dr Strangely Strange on the outro. The following year, he wrote 'Little Girl in Bloom' for *Vagabonds of the Western World*.

> *Little girl in bloom*
> *Carries a secret*
> *The child she carries in her womb*
> *She feels something sacred*
> *She's gonna be a mammy soon*
>
> *When your daddy comes home*
> *Don't tell him till alone*
> *When your daddy comes back*
> *Go tell him the facts*
> *Just relax and see how he's gonna react*

It's a wonderful song, and when it was released in 1973 it intrigued everyone who knew him well. 'There's no other song [of his] like that,' says Frank Murray. 'I always thought it had something to do with him and fatherhood, even though it's about a woman.' Though refraining from outright revelation, it draws heavily on personal experience. The pregnant girl could be Carole Stephen, but it could also be his mother. Caught in the middle is Lynott, both child and man; abandoned baby and absent father. 'I just wept when I read the lyrics,' says Macdaragh Lambe. 'It's a very poignant one for me.'

It was 'Little Girl in Bloom' that finally forced Lynott's hand, prompting him to confide his secret. By 1974, Jim Fitzpatrick was not only working with Lynott designing Thin Lizzy album covers, he was also illustrating, alongside Tim Booth, Lynott's first volume of poetry, *Songs for While I'm Away*, essentially a collection of his earliest lyrics. Fitzpatrick asked his friend to describe the girl in 'Little Girl in Bloom' in order that his simple line drawing of a nude, pregnant female figure would be accurate. 'I remember saying, "Has she long hair?"' says Fitzpatrick. 'And he told me about sitting in the back of the cinema, crying with the girl, and that he had a kid. That's why the girl has long hair in the book. But he didn't tell me anything more. I didn't even know her name. If he didn't tell anyone [else], it wasn't because of secrecy. It was pain.'

5

'Philip struck me as a guy who had an eye for the main chance,' says Eamon Carr. 'He was a bit of a hustler, in the best possible way. He was as smart as Bowie was at that age.' Even while gaining recognition with Skid Row, Lynott was acutely aware that there was more out there, a whole city of ideas to be accessed and absorbed. His wandering eye remained vigilant. He struck up relationships with some of the most vibrant creative enclaves around Dublin.

There was more than a degree of calculation in this: Lynott would always weigh his enthusiasms against an awareness of how to play the angles and ride the streams. Yet he was also driven by an innocent curiosity and a genuine desire to learn. Above all, he wanted to do *everything*.

One of the most important friendships he cultivated during this period was with the psychedelic folk band Dr Strangely Strange and its benignly bohemian circle of associates. Ireland's answer to the Incredible String Band, Dr Strangely Strange formed in 1967 around the nucleus of Tim Booth, Ivan Pawle and Tim Goulding, a group of arts graduates in their early twenties. Pawle, an Englishman, had achieved considerable kudos in his social circle thanks to the dubious honour of having a glass of vodka hurled at his head by Brendan Behan in the Bailey, not long before the rampaging Dubliner expired.

The Strangelys and their coterie of artists, musicians and arts students congregated in a quasi-communal house at 55 Lower Mount Street, directly east of Merrion Square in central Dublin, near the Grand Canal. The woman who rented the property, Patricia Mohan, was known as Orphan Annie, and so the artistic flophouse at no. 55 was christened the Orphanage. As the name suggests, it was both home and ad hoc HQ to a floating band of waifs and strays.

There was food and heat, and a bed for those who needed one. Some tenants were permanent, many were transient. 'She was a very generous hostess, shall we say?' says Robert Ballagh, who drifted in the same circles. 'There were many parties. For anyone who either hadn't a place to go after the pub or felt too tired to make it home, there was always a bed for them in Mount Street. Philip laid his head down a good few times in the Orphanage.'

The kitchen, dominated by a huge fireplace, served as a communal sitting room, and became yet another of Dublin's many de facto culture cafés. Lynott sniffed it out early on, becoming a regular and welcome presence. One of the Orphanage mainstays was Annie Christmas, a young woman who harboured a tenderness for Lynott, which was reciprocated. She may have been the reason that the boy from Crumlin first came calling. 'I have an image of Phil and Annie dancing together,' says Tim Booth. 'She was a great, vivacious, big-built woman. A very good cook, very maternal, and she took Philip under her wing to an extent. She looked after him. She would always sigh when his name was mentioned.'

'He and Annie Christmas together was a lovely thing,' says Ivan Pawle. 'It was like yin and yang, but they were briefly an item. It was beautiful, really. He was still a teenager and she was in her early twenties.' It was not an exclusive deal. 'He was a very attractive man,' says Booth. 'Ladies would be in and around all the time, usually different ones.'

His effect on the opposite sex was immediate and reliable, although there was a sense that after the raised emotional stakes of his relationship with Carole Stephen, and the drastic fallout, Lynott steered clear of close attachments. 'He kind of stayed loose after that,' says Frank Murray. There was no shortage of girls, but they were not serious relationships. 'Oh my God!' says Paul Scully. 'If shagging was a sport then he would have been Ronaldo. God almighty, from day one he was a magnet for the ladies.' Later, there was a darker edge to Lynott's womanizing; it became compulsive. For now, it seemed a joyful expression of youth, opportunity and freedom. 'In those very repressed days, with young Catholic girls coming out of their first experience of sexuality, it was a really exciting time,' says Scully.

'Women adored him,' says Noel Bridgeman. 'Those dark eyes, tall, skinny legs, and that semi-lost look. He brought out their maternal instincts. He was very shy and defenceless, you had the feeling that he was very, very vulnerable, and he had to develop some kind of armour to protect himself.' It was, perhaps, easier for an incurable romantic with a thin skin to swagger through a field of willing 'chicks' (as Lynott invariably called women until the very last) than contemplate an alternative path of greater emotional risk. 'I'm very bad at saying what I mean,' he later acknowledged. 'I used to be very honest when I was young. I'd crack up and say "I love you", but it didn't hold the chicks . . . When I saw it didn't work, it made me very hard on the outside.'[1] Or, as he later sang in 'A Song for While I'm Away', '*I swore when I was younger / No one would win my heart.*'

Beneath the bravado, he could be easily wounded. 'Phil was very insecure,' Gary Moore told me in 2010, only a few months before his sudden death at the age of fifty-eight. 'Nothing like a chip on each shoulder for balance.'

Dr Strangely Strange were working on material that would end up on their 1969 debut album, *Kip of the Serenes*, produced by Joe Boyd. In these slightly more rarefied circles, Lynott's limited musical experience was not considered top of the list of his attributes, at least not at first. They just liked him.

'He was diffident,' says Booth. 'A nice young man. He had started playing the guitar a little bit, but not in the same way that we did. He played chords, we were more finger-pickers, much more folky. We used to just have a laugh and hang out. He was only young, and he was nice looking, and intriguing, because he was very Dublin and yet, if not black, then certainly coffee coloured. Yet it didn't seem to make a hair of difference to him, and it certainly didn't make a hair of difference to us.'

As Skid Row progressed, Lynott's place in the Orphanage hierarchy shifted at least a couple of notches. 'They did a version of "I Am the Walrus" in Dixon Hall in Trinity College which just blew me away,' says Booth. 'The song had only recently come out, and I thought, "How do they know how to do that?" It sounded really like the [Beatles] recording. It was a very good cover and they did it effortlessly.'

Early in 1968, a fifteen-year-old prodigy moved to Dublin from his home city of Belfast, driven south by the unrest fomenting on his hometown streets and his parents' disintegrating marriage. Gary Moore was filling in with Belfast trio the Method, who had travelled down to Dublin to play a residency at the Club A Go Go. Brush Shiels went to see them and, impressed, instantly invited Moore to join Skid Row. Bernard Cheevers had been offered a full-time job as an electrician with Guinness, and was leaving the band. In any case, Moore was clearly operating at a considerably more advanced level. 'They didn't play blues, they played all this West Coast stuff, so I was a bit apprehensive, but I joined anyway,' Moore said. 'It was a good way for me to get away from home. I was having a lot of trouble with my father at the time.'

He returned to Belfast to tie up any loose ends, and a week later arrived back in Dublin. The next morning, Lynott met Moore in town, bright and early as ever, and gave him a tour of the city. Or at least, *his* city: the clubs, cafés, music stores, record shops and pubs. 'We went for a Chinese meal,' Moore recalled. 'His suggestion. He knew I wouldn't like it so he got to eat mine! We went to the Moulin Rouge that night and picked up a couple of girls, and it was really cool and funny.' So began an intense and often combative friendship, inextricably interwoven with music, which would last, with significant cooling-off periods, for the next seventeen years.

Moore was not only a great blues guitarist in the mould of his idols Peter Green, John Mayall and Jeff Beck, but a terrific all-round musician. He could play harmonium, mandolin, bass and fiddle, and he was a fine mimic, turning his hand to numerous styles, including folk. He featured on the second Dr Strangely Strange album, *Heavy Petting*, released in 1970, and for a while stayed in the 'second Orphanage', a large house rented by Tim Booth in Sandymount, down near the seaside.

He joined Skid Row in time to play on their first single, which was also Lynott's first time in a recording studio. 'New Places, Old Faces' was written by Shiels and released in 1968 on Song, a local independent label. It's a gentle, pleasantly plodding folk-inflected track, with prominent tin whistle from Johnny Moynihan of Sweeney's Men, one of several templates for the 'Johnny' persona who crops up in many Thin Lizzy songs. Shiels's lyrics are a poignant domestic sketch of a working-class family forced out of their home by a compulsory purchase order. '*We've had good times here, me and my old dad,*' Lynott sings, carefully and with feeling, affecting the air of vaguely Elizabethan gentility in vogue at the time. There are no drums. The overall feel is reminiscent of the Rolling Stones's 'Ruby Tuesday' and 'Lady Jane'.

The presence of Moore in Skid Row and at the Orphanage ensured that the bond between Lynott and Dr Strangely Strange grew ever tighter. When Skid Row played in Carlow, seventy miles south of Dublin, Lynott lobbied hard for his friends to join them as their support act. The mutual incomprehension felt by both the band and the audience delighted him. 'Philip would be like a ringmaster, and he loved the idea of these two musical forms trying to talk to each other,' says Tim Booth. 'Occasionally there would be gigs in one of the beat clubs, and Philip would ask us to play an interval spot. We would perform this folky music to all these trendy mods.'

He was flushed by the success of Skid Row, 'but he was kind of divided,' says Ivan Pawle. 'He had this very strong romantic feeling which that band didn't necessarily serve.'

His eventual departure from Skid Row in 1969 was, perhaps, inevitable but traumatic nonetheless. Part of the problem was the old saw: musical differences. Cream and the Jimi Hendrix Experience loomed large in Shiels's mind. He became infatuated with the idea of Skid Row becoming a power trio. The introduction of Moore had radically expanded the possibilities of what they could do musically. There was an increasing number of instrumental solos. Words like 'interplay' were being bandied about. It was all getting rather *busy*. 'Skid Row were absolutely amazing musically,' says Eric Bell. 'Just unbelievable. Three guys on Dexedrine, you know, playing super-fast, very complicated music.'

The trouble was that Lynott, at heart, was a melody man. He liked songs with tunes that said something and cut through emotionally. Band and singer were heading in opposite directions.

In the mid-1970s, Lynott discussed this clash in sensibilities in the abstract, but it was clear which band he was talking about. 'That whole weird thing rock went through when the arrangements dominated . . . was very harmful . . . because although there are a lot of good musicians, musicianship and melody don't always have to be the same thing. There's a lot of false focus. The very harmful stage of the whole thing was when the bands just got up and just let it float . . . put screens and films on and hoped the audiences were tripping and that they'd get off on it.'[2]

In another interview, he put it more succinctly. 'I wasn't really needed anymore. I knew I was in line for the bullet.'[3]

Matters reached a head in June 1969, when Skid Row were booked onto RTÉ's music programme *Like Now!*, recorded at the Top Hat ballroom in Dún Laoghaire. Television was a step up. At 85 Leighlin Road, family and friends gathered around their sets to watch Skid Row perform 'Strawberry Fields Forever'. According to Michael O'Flanagan, the performance was 'a disaster' – particularly the vocals. Photographer Roy Esmonde, briefly a manager of Skid Row, remembers, 'I told Brush he should get rid of Philip, because he was singing flat.'

Whatever he may have sounded like live, 'New Places, Old Faces' and a Skid Row demo tape dating from 1968 give the lie to any suggestion that Lynott's voice, in general, wasn't up to muster. Recorded in Avon studios in Dominick Street, 'Living in the Shadow of a Shady Neighbour' is heavy and Hendrixian, while 'Notion in Motion' is smoother and snappier. Written by Shiels, both are relatively wordy, but Lynott sings them with verve and panache. The unique tone and style of his singing voice is already easily identifiable. He may not yet have had the confidence to fully forge his own vocal identity, and he may have slipped off-key from time to time on stage – but he could certainly sing.

Nevertheless, Shiels insists that 'Phil was having trouble pitching, and he was starting to jump around more, starting to look more like Roger Daltrey.' He tried to improve Lynott's breathing control by 'sticking his head in a bucket of water. I'd heard that could help, but it didn't work. It turned out his tonsils were really bad. I looked down his throat one day and there was this fucking golf ball halfway down. His ma said she would bring him over to Manchester and get the job done.'

While Lynott was in St Joseph's Hospital having his tonsils removed, Skid Row were already making plans to get rid of him. 'Philip wasn't even on the plane and we were practising [without him],' says Shiels. 'That was the end of it. When he came back I had to tell him. It's like being the manager of a football team. "You've been great for us up till now, but . . ."'

In January 1969, Shiels had spent a week – gratis – honeymooning at the Clifton Grange Hotel with his new bride Margaret, with Lynott tagging along for good luck. Now he was firing his friend in the doorway of Bruxelles. 'He took it very bad. It was fucking brutal, actually. Couldn't have been worse. Like a death in the family. He had his family, but the band was like another family, and he loved it. Just as everything was going terrific the family was letting him down. It was almost a form of rejection. Abandoned again. He was very upset, he got very emotional.'

For Noel Bridgeman, the sacking 'was like being kicked out of his house again,' although he adds that 'there was a little bit more to it all, I think. Brush knew that Philip had other things to do, but being young and insecure he maybe didn't have the necessary courage to make the leap into the unknown. It was comfortable in Skid Row. The band was very popular and Philip was very popular. I think Brush pushed him and said, "Go off and just do it." And he did.'

At the time Lynott was crushed, but he wept in private. In public, he readied himself for the next move. He and Shiels remained on good terms. As part of what might be termed the redundancy package, Shiels promised to teach Lynott to play bass. When their mutual friend, Robert Ballagh, left the Chessmen, he had sold his Fender Jazz to Shiels for £36. It ended up in the hands of Lynott, who played the instrument well into the Thin Lizzy days. Five days a week for the next few months, Lynott would take the bus from Crumlin to Cabra West and spend hours practising bass with Shiels. 'He got over his hurt inasmuch as he was playing pretty good bass in a fortnight, and in the back of his mind he was going to fuck me up. I could feel it. It was like, "I'll show this guy."'

Determination, resilience and a positive work ethic often get lost amid tales of rock and roll misadventure. Lynott had impressive reserves of all three. Michael O'Flanagan – whose projections were considered by Skid Row to be integral to their live show – would occasionally cry off when the band were playing some of Dublin's more volatile venues, like the CIE bus drivers' social hall, which guaranteed three fights a night as a bare minimum. 'One time Philip turned on me and said, "You only turn up when it suits yourself," and, more or less, "Shut up and mind your own business." He wasn't short of voicing his opinion in a forceful manner. He was sensitive to people's feelings, except when he was having a row with you. That would be different!' 'He was very sensitive,' says Noel Bridgeman, laughing. 'On the other hand, he was very insensitive.'

His sacking from Skid Row added another layer. It hardened him. In future years, Lynott was rarely reticent when it came to making hard decisions about getting rid of band members. 'You'll find that a lot of the guys who played with me got much tougher afterwards,' says Shiels. 'Things have to be done. You could honestly say it was the best and worst thing that ever happened to him. He was going to show everybody that he could do this thing, and he did. I was kind of surprised when he got bigger than me. I really was. It didn't suit me at the time.'

Other factors fed into Lynott's split from Skid Row. He was growing older and asserting his own tastes. Brush Shiels was a solid type. He married his childhood sweetheart in 1969, shunned drugs, liked football and kept fit. Lynott had no problem with any of that, but he leaned towards a more adventurous social scene. 'I noticed that Phil was taking something,' says Shiels. 'I don't think it was acid, it was something that could keep him going day and night. I didn't fancy that.'

Hugh Feighery recalls that while he and Lynott were in the Black Eagles and still at school, Lynott experimented with the time-honoured method of squaring the eternal circle of long nights and early mornings. 'Around that time Philip went in for pep pills,' says Feighery. 'He used to ask me to take them and I never did. Not that I felt any burden, but a pint used to do it for me and I used to smoke like a trooper. When he'd taken a dose of them, he was a different guy. He had this brash, didn't-give-a-shit attitude. He needed these things. Apart from the energy surge, I think it came from a complex of not feeling good enough about himself.'

Lynott told producer Tony Visconti years later, while working on *Bad Reputation*, that 'my mother turned me on to smoking spliffs when I was 13'.[4] There may be an element of poetic licence in that, but Philomena certainly had her bohemian side, and Lynott's visits to Manchester in his later teens could be eye-openers. The Clifton Grange was a home from home (and in some cases, an *actual* home) for scores of battle-hardened musicians, and Philomena was liberal enough when it came to accommodating the tastes and habits of her core clientele.

On 'Clifton Grange Hotel', from the first Thin Lizzy album, Lynott commemorated the establishment with a poetic twist, portraying it as an oasis of tolerance peopled with kindly, eccentric characters. One of these was Percy Gibbons from black Canadian trio the Other Brothers. Gibbons lived in a room in the attic, which was solemnly locked when he went on tour and ceremoniously reopened when he returned. He and Philip formed a friendship, in the mould of mentor and apprentice, playing songs together, writing, talking. The Other Brothers evolved into Garden Odyssey Enterprise, whose 1969 single 'Sad and Lonely' is a minor psychedelic wonder. For a short period there was some talk of Lynott joining its ranks.

His visits to Whalley Range provided an alternative education in the ways of show business at ground level. Back in Dublin, he was privy to a very different set-up at the Orphanage, where the drug scene was more ritualized, if relatively sedate. 'One has to say, there was the dope,' says Ivan Pawle fondly. 'Philip was attracted by that, that's perhaps one reason he came around to see us . . . I remember I once handed him a joint made out of five papers, I was quite proud of the fact that I could do a five-skinner back in the day.'

'The refreshment of choice in the Orphanage was a bit of Lebanese or Black, occasionally some Thai sticks,' says Tim Booth. 'Always very mild, soft drugs, and the odd tab of pretty good acid. We didn't take anything else at that stage, but we did smoke a lot of dope. Philip would smoke dope with us, but I never took acid with him.' They were a generous, nurturing crowd. When the young Gary Moore took to ingesting large quantities of amphetamine sulphate, they 'had a word with him,' says Booth.

The stimulus offered by Dr Strangely Strange and their associates was not merely chemical. They opened up a world of new experiences on Lynott's doorstep. 'Some nights you might wind up reading poetry in a bar with Pearse Hutchinson or Peter Morgan, and we'd go back to people's flats with a six-pack of beer and Luke Kelly would be singing ballads,' says Eamon Carr. 'It didn't happen all the time but when it did it was memorable. That would have been the kind of milieu that Philip was involved in.'

At the Orphanage he would rub shoulders with Robin Williamson of the Incredible String Band, one of the Strangelys's key influences. Williamson often came over from Edinburgh to stay with them, and 'Philip was *very* enchanted by this,' says Pawle.

'I remember going in there once, and someone said, "Oh, be quiet, Robin is upstairs meditating,"' says Paul Scully. 'I'd never heard the word "meditation" in my life! Philip was getting into folk music at that time, he was playing a lot of acoustic guitar. The commune was all exotic-looking women and men, hippie types, living together. Dr Strangely Strange had a big influence on him. They were very arty and had gone to university.'

Lynott was an affiliate member of the gang, leaning in from the fringes. He would join them in Toner's on Lower Baggot Street, a favourite haunt, close to the Orphanage and the College of Art. At the time the pub was still under ownership of the Toner family, who felt an almost patrician concern for the Orphanage crowd. Every Christmas they sent a quarter tonne of coal to the house, accompanied by a crate of Guinness, a bottle of whiskey and a bottle of gin. 'It was a hang-out for artists, writers, musicians and poets,' says Robert Ballagh. 'There was a regular crowd of us who hung around together, had shared interests, and Philip would have been a junior member of the club. He was part of all that. He was very young, but he was accepted. It was a very creative, optimistic time. We thought we could change the world.'

The venerated figures of the future were the youthful, questioning agents of change in the Ireland of the 1960s. People who went on to become some of the country's most acclaimed poets, artists, publishers and editors were making their first notable footprints on the landscape. At Sinnott's on South King Street, the likes of Leland Bardwell, Eiléan Ní Chuilleanáin, Hayden Murphy, Peter Fallon and Pearse Hutchinson would get up to read their work. There was no ceremony. It was a snug space, warm and scuffed, like a family sitting room. To wash down the poetry, there would be generous amounts of acoustic music and strong drink.

Dr Strangely Strange played at Sinnott's frequently, and on occasion Lynott would tag along, though it's unlikely that he ever stood up and performed anything himself. 'I don't recall him doing it,' says Tim Booth. 'I think he might have been a bit overawed to read his lyrics, or poetry, in front of people who really did have a craft. People who became very highly regarded Irish poets were trying out their wings there.'

Fallon agrees that 'he was more of an observer, but the literary side was very important to him'. He was dipping into the rich well-spring of Irish writers: Brendan Behan, Flann O'Brien, W. B. Yeats, J. M. Synge, Patrick Kavanagh, James Joyce. 'He'd often have an old book of poetry under his arm,' says Ballagh. 'He was genuinely interested in, and influenced by, the poetic heritage of Dublin.' He regularly spent time at Slattery's in Capel Street, another informal hub of poetry and acoustic music. Here, Pawle recalls, 'Philip did get up and read his stuff, I'm almost 100 per cent certain.'

He certainly performed with Tara Telephone. An influential poetry and music group formed in 1969, Tara Telephone were modelled on the Liverpool Scene and the Scaffold, the affiliation of northern English poets and musicians that included Roger McGough and Brian Patten. The Liverpool Scene were much beloved by John Peel, who produced their first album and played them often on his radio shows. They created a considerable stir in the late 1960s, finding fertile common ground between the rock firmament and populist poetry.

Tara Telephone established a similar set-up in Dublin. At their performances, poems were read with musical backing – guitars, bongos, viol – or set to a melody and sung. They were inclusive affairs, and there was often room for a folk group, a ballad singer or a band. Tara Telephone also ran a poetry magazine, *Capella*, which published work by Beat pioneer Allen Ginsberg, as well as John Peel, Marc Bolan and Mike McGear.

Having caught the imagination of underground Dublin, Tara Telephone were hired for spots on local radio, and even appeared on *The Late Late Show*, Ireland's most popular peak-time television chat show. 'We got an attentive audience, because by the late 1960s something called "the sixties" was actually starting to happen in Ireland,' says Peter Fallon. 'Poetry was part of the cultural mix, and the audience were receptive to it.'

Lynott's antenna twitched at this development. 'We were mentioned in despatches quite a bit, and he was hip to that,' says Eamon Carr. 'He was aware that there was a thread from these deadbeat kids in Dublin to these Liverpool guys, and two steps from there to John Peel. In his mind, what we were doing had some validity in the rock school, and that was partly what he was tapping into. He was conscious of what was going on around him, he was so connected, and he was trying to find his place and his voice. So he was definitely curious as to what we were at.

'It was a spirit of innocence and adventure, because none of us really knew what we were doing. It was partly about stardom for Philip, but a lot of it was about communication.' When Lynott asked Carr and Fallon, 'What's the scene like, man?' they told him to come along and perform. Eventually, he took them up on the offer. On Tuesday, 11 November 1969, he came to a Tara Telephone gathering at the rather grandly named Arts Society, in reality a scruffy room in a mews building at the back of Trinity College. He was accompanied by Brush Shiels and Gary Moore. 'They had acoustic guitars, and I believe that was the first time he played his own songs in public,' says Fallon. 'He had aspirations towards the more poetic line, and he thought that this would be the kind of company that would be attentive, receptive and gentle.'

Lynott had been making concerted attempts to write for the past couple of years. Indeed, those who saw the Black Eagles in their later days recall an original song called 'In an Institution', long lost in the mists of time. While still a member of Skid Row, the band had performed the occasional original number, invariably written by Shiels, who hadn't generally encouraged Lynott's efforts to follow suit. 'It was my band and I didn't give a fuck what he was doing,' he says. 'We wrote one together, but that wasn't great. We were just starting to get a feel for it.' This was 'The Photograph Man', a derivative slice of psychedelia which Skid Row performed in concert a handful of times and even recorded, and which Michael O'Flanagan describes as 'very pathetic all together. It was just a poor piece of writing.' He insists that the fact that he believes the song to be an unflattering portrait of himself has not skewed his judgement.

By the end of Lynott's tenure in Skid Row, it had become obvious that the group was not a comfortable place for a budding writer. He found a more nurturing environment among the bohemian circle of Dr Strangely Strange and Tara Telephone. 'There was a kindred spirit, because he was taking his writing seriously and most of the bands around him weren't,' says Eamon Carr. 'It was always very casual, but I think he might have been looking for validation and encouragement.'

Aware that the gauntlet had been thrown down by his contemporaries, Lynott had started, rather shyly, revealing some of
his own work. Perhaps picking up on the accentuated feyness
that characterized the lyrics Marc Bolan was writing with
Tyrannosaurus Rex, and almost certainly trying to impress the
more mature members of his social circle, his early efforts were a
long way from 'The Rocker'.

'I often used to call down for him in the mornings, and we'd
listen to a few records before we went into town,' says Frank
Murray. 'One day I remember he said, "Hey, I've written this
song." He sang it to me, and it was one of those Incredible String
Band-y kind of things – and *bad*! That was the first time I was
aware he was writing.'

This may have been 'The Death of a Faun', an early com-
position which he also played to Tim Booth and Ivan Pawle.
'Delightful!' says Pawle. 'It was a lovely little song. Very innocent,
dripping in the poetic. I remember thinking it was somewhere
between *L'après-midi d'un faune* [the nineteenth-century poem by
French writer Stéphane Mallarmé] and Dave Davies's "Death
of a Clown".' More likely it was inspired by tales of Oisín, the
great mythical poet of Ireland and son of Fionn MacCumhaill,
who narrates much of the *Fenian Cycle* and whose name literally
translates as 'little fawn' or 'young deer'. 'It was the first thing
I'd heard him try to compose,' says Pawle. 'He had that very soft
side to him, always, but he had to project the hard-rock image
increasingly when he got into the machine of it.'

'He was intrigued by what we were doing, and we were kind
of intrigued by his early songs,' says Tim Booth. 'You could see
there was something there, but they weren't great.'

Life experience also played its part in his evolution. He felt
he had things he wanted to get off his chest. The break-up with
Carole Stephen was a catalyst for delving further into his own

emotions. 'Naturally the first thing that inspired me to write was being blown out,' he said later. 'My ego was hurt and I thought, "I must write and tell the world what has happened to me. I owe the world this story." That was it and I got really carried away at one stage. I even started thinking "I'm a genius, this is art! I must get it out." I found that the more I worked on the lyrics as poetry, they became a better craft for the songs.'[5]

A serious point lay beneath the self-deprecation. He realized that everyday thoughts and ordinary experiences could be alchemized into the poetic and universal, a trick he turned with great success on a new song, 'Dublin', which cast a richly melancholy spell over his hometown. In 'Chatting Today', reminiscent of Bang-era Van Morrison, he left behind his deadening day-job at the Tonge & Taggart foundry – *'man, my mind it nearly drowned'* – and found freedom on the railway. On the even more directly personal 'Saga of the Ageing Orphan', the archetypal orphan observes his closest family members (Uncle Peter and his 'mama', Sarah) growing older and drifting further away from him.

He played his songs on acoustic guitar to Brian Downey, who was impressed. 'They sounded really great. A couple of them ended up on the first Thin Lizzy albums.'

At the Arts Society, Lynott was touchingly nervous, pacing around outside the building as though weighing up whether to hit or run. 'What is it like?' he asked Carr, who replied, 'It's just a bunch of people sitting around; nobody is going to eat you.'

The crowd consisted mainly of students, dressed in torn jeans and tatty pullovers. In their midst, Lynott cut a remarkable figure. 'It was as if Sly Stone was about to go on stage at Woodstock or something,' says Carr. 'Scarves and all of that. It wasn't a backroom pub vibe at all! When he came in, all the heads turned. I can't remember the repertoire, he did three or four things [very likely including 'Dublin' and 'Chatting Today'] and people hung

blin, 1969. *(Roy Esmonde)*

(*left*) Lynott's father, Cecil Parris, pictured in his twenties. (*Courtesy of Barry Keevins*)

(*below*) Bringing home the bacon at the Biz with his mother, Philomena Lynott. (*Chalkie Davies*)

The fledgling Black Eagles, circa 1964, rehearsing at the Smith residence, 15 Leighlin Road, Crumlin. *Back row, left to right:* Danny Smith, bass; Michael Higgins, drums; Philip Lynott, vocals. *Front, left to right:* Frankie Smith, Hugh Feighery, guitars.
(Courtesy of Hugh Feighery)

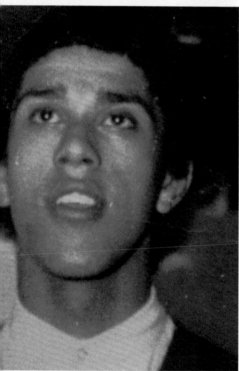

enes from the life of a budding pop star.
urtesy of Carole Stephen)

The first incarnation of Skid Row, 1968. *Left to right:* Noel Bridgeman, Brush Shiels, Bernard Cheevers, Philip Lynott. *(Courtesy of Michael O'Flanagan)*

(*above*) At the wedding of Brush and Margaret Shiels, January 1969, with Gary Moore also in attendance. *(Courtesy of Michael O'Flanagan)*

(*left*) Carole Stephen, late 1960s. *(Courtesy of Carole Stephen)*

(*right*) Macdaragh Lambe, aged three. *(Courtesy of Carole Stephen)*

Portrait by Roy Esmonde, 1970.

onlighting as a model for *New
light*, with Niki Adrian, Dublin,
1. *(Roy Esmonde)*

(*above*) Performing with Thin Lizzy at the disastrous Open Air Festival at Richmond Park, Dublin, 4 September 1970. (*Roy Esmonde*)

(*right*) 'Tin Lissy' are offered terms by Decca, November 1970.

(*Courtesy of Brian Tuite*)

Taking a break from recording Thin Lizzy's debut album at Broadhurst Gardens, London, January 1971. Ted Carroll is pictured third from the left at the back. *(Courtesy of Brian Tuite)*

in Lizzy at the time of 'hiskey in the Jar'. *Left right:* Eric Bell, Philip nott, Brian Downey. *urtesy of Ted Carroll)*

CCA F13402 c/w broken dreams

Tim Booth's inventive ad for Thin Lizzy's 1973 single, 'Randolph's Tango'. *(Courtesy of Ted Carroll)*

With Jim Fitzpatrick (*left*) and Peter Fallon (*right*) in Neary's, Dublin, August 1974, celebrating the publication of *Songs for While I'm Away*. *(Tom Collins)*

'*How can I leave the town that brings me down / That has no jobs, is blessed by God.*' Taking the air in St Stephen's Green, Dublin. *(Chalkie Davies)*

on his words. He made a huge impression on everybody, it was brilliant. The next day he was in the bar, telling everyone, "Oh yer, I was reading poetry in Trinity College last night." It was like, I've ticked that box.' He ticked it at least one more time, returning to the Arts Society in May 1970, accompanied by Eric Bell, to play a few more of his own song-poems.

He was learning the ground rules of being a star. Number one: act like one, even in a shabby room full of arts students with a potter's wheel in the corner. Lynott made a similar fuss over his entrance on another night in 1969, after arranging in advance to sit-in on a couple of songs at the Club A Go Go as the guest of local soul singer Ditch Cassidy. The venue had no dressing room. Instead of standing at the bar and waiting to be called up to sing, Lynott insisted on hiding out of sight under the serving hatch in the tiny cloakroom closet, his knees around his ears, before springing out to make his entrance.

'There was always the swagger, even walking into a coffee shop on Grafton Street,' says Peter Fallon, 'But there was always this wry, knowing smile, too, as though he were saying, "I know I'm not fooling you, I'm not even fooling myself, but I have to do it." But it worked, and it was brilliant. The best of him was brilliant.'

Only a few years later in the hard-rocking 1970s, keen to disassociate Thin Lizzy from what he regarded as the trad-rock millstone of 'Whiskey in the Jar', Lynott downplayed the significance of this period. 'The folk circuit . . . was a great thing to get into on your day off. Take out the acoustic guitar. You'd get free booze, crisps and plenty of chicks.'[6]

At the time he wasn't so off-hand. 'Philip was very, very drawn to the Dublin arts and creative scene,' says Tim Booth. 'He didn't necessarily understand what people were trying to do, but he knew that it was a territory where he could go, and we could path-find for him to an extent.' He was fighting on several fronts at once, hoping one of them would provide a breakthrough. Lynott stitched himself into a rich cultural tapestry that mixed music and poetry, art and literature, the traditional and the contemporary, old and new Dublin. In doing so, he was part of something quietly revolutionary.

Both Paul Scully and Noel Bridgeman echo James Joyce's description of Ireland as a 'priest-ridden' country. 'It was,' adds Bridgeman, for the avoidance of doubt, 'a fucking nightmare.'

'It's hard to explain to anyone who didn't live through it how imbued the Catholic Church was in every single thing we did, from the government down,' says Scully. 'They had so much power. The whole sixties thing was a huge revolution in hindsight. People were really coming out of their shells. There was no arrogance in it. We were just teenagers fighting against whatever was in front of us. It was never articulated, but we had a sense that we were a group of like-minded people. We all felt part of something that was going on.'

They harboured a genuine respect for much of Ireland's traditions, for the legacy of the writers and artists who had come before them, but it ran parallel with a passionate desire to move the story forward, to give expression to a more modern voice. The old orders which shaped outdated attitudes to sex, work, family and religion were up for question. Without being explicitly political, Lynott and his circle were questioning the orthodoxies of the time with every show they played, every song they wrote, every poem they produced.

It was not easy on the margins, but it fostered a sense of solidarity. 'It was a difficult time to try to forge any type of alternative career, which was why we all stuck together,' says Eamon Carr. 'We instinctively knew that in order to do anything we had to do it en masse. The writers had to work with the musicians, who had to work with the poets and the artists. We were all very like-minded.'

It was all a long way from Crumlin, and only made possible by the unique configuration of the times. A greater degree of class migration was suddenly possible in Ireland, or at the very least in Dublin. People were mixing outside of their allotted zones.

Lynott was certainly moving in interesting circles. One minute he might be chatting intimately to some hard case working on the door of the Green Rooster café in O'Connell Street; the next, he would be hanging out with Eimear Haughey, the daughter of Charles Haughey, at the time the Minister of Finance and later the leader of Fianna Fáil and three-time Taoiseach. For a black, working-class boy to be exchanging artistic concepts with some of the brightest minds of Trinity College – the most prestigious and exclusive university in Ireland, and renowned throughout the world – was indicative of a significant shift in the social tectonics.

'Music broke down barriers,' says Paul Scully. 'We would never have met students with degrees like Dr Strangely Strange otherwise. Even Philip moving from Crumlin to live in Clontarf [in 1970], going from a modern housing estate to these beautiful red-brick Georgian houses overlooking the sea, is part of the same thing. In a way the music drove him to do that, and the whole social mish-mash influenced the music as well.'

It was a life-changing period, and it illuminated the musical path Lynott chose to take after leaving Skid Row. His next band was called Orphanage – a name freighted with obvious significance. As well as casting back to his own childhood and its echo in more recent events, the name acknowledged the influence of Dr Strangely Strange and their coterie on Lynott's progression. It was also a dry joke on his current circumstances. Formed in the autumn of 1969, Orphanage consisted of Lynott, ex-Black Eagles drummer Brian Downey, Pat Quigley and guitarist Joe Staunton, formerly of local band Macbeth. They were all musical outcasts.

'Brush had thrown Philip out of Skid Row, said he couldn't sing,' says Pat Quigley. 'My band, the Movement, had broken up. Brian Downey had been in a band called Sugar Shack, they'd broken up. We were all sitting in the pub, and Phil said, "Why don't us guys get together? We're a gang of bloody orphans!" It was the name of the Strangelys place, but it also worked for us.'

Lynott could have walked into any number of successful local bands or taken an easy ride for good money on the showband circuit, although more than one person has suggested that his colour may have barred him from taking that route. Instead he wanted to form a group that not only accentuated his own gifts as a more melodic writer and singer, but fused all the elements in the air around him, uniting the rockers, the poets and the traditional musicians. 'The whole idea of the band was that there was always a nucleus of four members and we'd have three other musicians travelling with us,' Lynott later remembered. 'It was a musical orphanage . . . a nice idea.'[7]

Terry Woods, the mandolin player in Sweeney's Men and later a member of the Pogues, joined the band at several concerts. Gary Moore and Dr Strangely Strange were often involved. Local guitarist Joe Alexander would be on the fringes. Fran Quigley recalls the Chieftains's Paddy Moloney taking part at one Orphanage show at the Trinity Ball. 'The object was that people could come and have a blow with us and not have to be in the band,' said Lynott. 'At that time, a lot of folk artists were getting interested in electronics, and we thought we were the band that could help them out in that respect. It didn't work out that way.'[8]

Orphanage didn't quite click, but it was an imaginative idea. They would swing from Chuck Berry classics to Bob Dylan's 'Lay Lady Lay' and 'I Shall Be Released'; the Lovin' Spoonful's

'Daydream' to Eddie Floyd's 'Knock on Wood'; traditional folk to early Free; Sam and Dave's 'Soul Man' to the Beatles's 'While My Guitar Gently Weeps'.

'The Orphanage period was an experimental one for him,' says Eamon Carr. 'They were quite distinct from Skid Row. It would have been [more like] the softer side of Lizzy. West Coast and dreamy, that's how I remember it. It was very loose, slightly whimsical and meandering, with a pastoral feel. Almost like early Fairport Convention. There was a fluidity to it, it didn't have a rock and roll edge, or the great, sharp focus of early Lizzy. It didn't actually make a huge impression.'

'It was a strange band,' says Pat Quigley. 'It was a mixture of rock, heavy metal and hippie stuff. A real mixed bag.'

For Lynott, Orphanage felt like a more natural, satisfying fit after Skid Row. He could dial down the decibels, add more light and shade. Pat Quigley was a more direct bass player, and his style was as much of an influence on Lynott's development on the instrument as Shiels's. 'When Brush took off on the bass he didn't know how to come back,' says Quigley. 'He was all over the place, like a lead guitar player. I played melody. Simple playing. Once you got the right leg pumping on the floor you couldn't lose. I taught Philip how to play bass. I'd say, play what you're singing, and that's what Thin Lizzy songs did.'

Orphanage were together through the end of 1969 and into early 1970, doing the rounds, playing most days of the week in Dublin and further afield: Limerick, Cork, Kerry, Connemara. 'At a few places we might stay overnight,' says Pat Quigley. 'We were after anything in a skirt. The craic was great. Philip was always laughing, always looking forward to gigging. We were all young mad bastards.' When they performed at a history-themed banquet at Bunratty Castle in County Clare, they ended up dressed in medieval costume, fencing around the venue.

Orphanage were paid up to £50 for some shows, pennies for others. They made some recordings at Dominick Street studios, a mixture of covers and originals, including 'Chatting Today' and 'The Friendly Ranger', a blues called 'You Fool, You', and another new song called 'St Stephen's Green'.

It was a step down in status after Skid Row. His former band were going from strength to strength without him. They had released two more singles, and had fallen in with Fleetwood Mac manager Clifford Davis. After staging a 'farewell' Dublin show in October 1969, at which Lynott showed up with Orphanage to perform and, according to Smiley Bolger, 'blew them off the stage', Skid Row moved to London. They released their debut album *Skid*, on Columbia in 1970.

Although Orphanage had no such success story to tell, the band were significant beyond their immediate impact and relatively short lifespan. It was the first time Lynott began to play an instrument on stage, strumming an acoustic guitar on 'While My Guitar Gently Weeps'. At the age of twenty, he was finally performing some of his own original material. Both developments became non-negotiable red lines in the formation of his next band, which was called Thin Lizzy.

6

Eric Bell was an East Belfast boy who, at twenty-two, had already played the field. He had been a member of numerous bands, including the Deltones, Shades of Blue and the Bluebeats. For a short while in 1966 he had played guitar in Van Morrison's Them, not long before Morrison left Britain for the United States.

Another blues aficionado in thrall to Jimi Hendrix, by the summer of 1969 Bell's freak flag was barely fluttering at half-mast. He had left Belfast and its raw R&B scene and moved south to Dublin, earning a decent living playing polite pop and restrained rock and roll in the Dreams, an eight-piece Dublin showband fronted by John Farrell, the former singer in Pat Quigley's old group, the Movement. The Dreams had scored several Irish top-twenty hit singles – among them 'I'll See You There', 'Baby, I'm Your Man' and 'The Casatchok' – in 1968 and 1969.

Bell was experiencing mainstream success and earning good money, but he felt something was missing. The Dreams offered no outlet for his more expressive tendencies. He was told what to play. If he dared add some feedback to a track, or attempt a particularly inventive solo, his band-mates would mutter, 'Knock it off, Ravi Shankar.' His hair was moderately long but neatly combed. The band dressed conservatively in smart suits and wore their shirts tucked in. Commercially, the Dreams were on a different plane to Orphanage. According to the cultural battle lines of the day, however, they were firmly on the wrong side. Bell was a terrific and versatile guitar player. He was a bluesman who liked a joke, a drink and a smoke. He was sensitive and a little wild. He looked at the Dreams and saw the square root of square.

Bell saved up his weekly wage of £35 until he could afford to quit the band. 'I was fed up with the music we were playing,' he says. 'I was trying to form a rock trio, and I started going around Dublin looking for bass players and drummers to form a three-piece band. Everybody I asked wasn't interested, and my money was running out. I thought I'd made this horrendous mistake. I was very impulsive in those days.'

One night while Bell was doing his rounds, he bumped into keyboard player Eric Wrixon. Another Belfast man, and another former member of Them, Wrixon had recently been working in England with his band the Trixons. He and Bell knew each other socially, and ended up having a few drinks and sharing a tab of acid. They walked down to the Countdown Club, where Orphanage happened to have a booking that night.

'I didn't even know there was a band playing,' says Bell. 'We just went to the club because we knew the owner and he'd let us in for nothing. Orphanage were playing things like Bob Dylan's "It Takes a Lot to Laugh, It Takes a Train to Cry", and they were excellent at it. I don't think they did any of Philip's songs, and he wasn't playing bass at the time, he was just singing. He had a bit of [stage presence], but it certainly wasn't honed. He was a good-looking guy, and he wore this kind of kaftan on stage and did these Egyptian dances. He was certainly working at being a frontman, and I was really knocked out by Brian's drumming.'

During the break, Pat Quigley and Joe Staunton wandered off to get a drink. Lynott was alone with Downey in the changing room when Bell entered – unannounced, if not entirely unknown. Gary Moore was a mutual friend and, though they had never met, Lynott and Bell were aware of one another by reputation. At some point during the conversation, the Northern Irish guitarist progressed from asking whether Lynott knew any musicians who might be interested in being in a band with him, to walking away with a commitment that the three people in the room form a new group.

Brian Downey was sceptical but was persuaded by Lynott, who joined with Bell only after setting out two very explicit conditions. Lynott would be the bassist, and the band would play some of his original compositions.

The following Monday, he visited Bell's flat in Manor Street with a reel-to-reel tape containing three of his songs, performed acoustically. They were 'Dublin', 'Chatting Today', and either 'Diddy Levine' or 'Saga of the Ageing Orphan'. Rich, poetic, melodic. 'Oh man,' Bell recalls. 'They were so good. I knew right away I could put my guitar style into them. That was that.'

On 1 January 1970, *New Spotlight* magazine announced that Eric Bell was leaving the Dreams to form an as yet unnamed new band. Eric Wrixon would also be joining on keyboards. For the first few months of their existence, Thin Lizzy were a four-piece.

Their early rehearsals took place in a basement below the Band Centre shop, Mrs Quigley's Synnott Place tenement and Temple Oak Tennis Club. They tested their strengths, poked at their limitations. 'We discovered that Eric Bell was a really, really good guitar player,' Brian Downey told me. 'I knew that Eric played in the Dreams showband, who were a huge pop group in Ireland at the time. It was only later that I found out he played with Van Morrison and Them in Belfast.' In contrast, Lynott's bass-playing was, according to Downey, 'pretty raw to say the least. He was just feeling his way. In the early days we mostly just played blues jams.'

A bond of friendship quickly developed. 'When I first met Philip he was a fabulous guy,' says Bell. 'A real man's man, an eye for the women. He loved clothes. Very poetic. Great company, full of life, yet very soft spoken. A really nice guy.'

Orphanage didn't so much break up as slowly disperse, like smoke in the wind. They had outstanding dates to fulfil and the lines of demarcation became hazy. When they played the Tabu Club in Limerick in January, Bell came along for the ride for a rare overnight stay. After the show Lynott, Bell and Downey started working up a number for their new band. 'As far as I'm concerned that was one of the first Thin Lizzy rehearsals, in Ryan's Hotel in Limerick,' says Fran Quigley, who was there as the roadie. 'I was tired, and after the gig I went up to my room and there they were. Brian banging away with his drum sticks on the side of the bedside table, Philip with the bass guitar, unamplified. They were working on a number. It was three o'clock in the morning, but they were intent on getting going as quickly as possible. They were already discussing the music they were going to play.'

On 4 February 1970 Orphanage played at Dublin's Liberty Hall on a bill that included Tara Telephone. Less than a fortnight later, on 16 February, Thin Lizzy made their debut.

There were no recriminations. In those days, bands came and they went. 'I said to Philip, "Don't mind me or [Joe] Staunton, get yourself a band,"' says Pat Quigley. 'I had a day job, I was on a career drive, but Phil and Downey had nothing to lose. There was no hard feelings, nobody hated anybody or anything like that.'

Quigley's younger brother Fran stayed on as part-time crew, swayed by Lynott's obvious quality and apparent professionalism: 'Philip came to me at one of the Orphanage gigs out in Finglas – dive of a place – and said, "I'm forming a new band, will you be our roadie? The deal is that I'll give you 5 per cent." That impressed me! I was still at school, but he really had his head together. He had a big mind, he thought like a star. In his head he *was* a star. The way he walked, the way he talked – he had "something", that's the phrase everybody used. He had the ability to inspire people. Even when he wasn't on stage he was on stage, he was selling himself the whole time. He was just made to be successful.'

The buzz around town was: Philip Lynott has a new band. They're going to be very cool.

The road to Wembley Arena, Madison Square Garden and Sydney Opera House began in a school hall in Cloghran, a dot on the map north of Dublin. The first Thin Lizzy gig was little more than a live rehearsal, a chance to throw something out there to see what might stick.

They had toyed with calling themselves Gulliver's Travels but couldn't quite commit to it. In the end they took their name from a cartoon model robot in the *Dandy* called Tin Lizzie – 'the metal maid'. It was Bell's idea. 'Nobody liked it, nobody wanted it, but for some reason we used it,' he says. It was, in part, a local in-joke – the hard 'T' sound of the Dublin pronunciation of 'thin' and 'tin' is essentially identical, a phonetic quirk which resulted in the band being billed as both Tin Lizzie and Thin Lizzy, and assorted variations on those spellings, for at least two years. The announcement on 21 February 1970 in the *Evening Herald* about this new 'local super group' named them as Thin Lizzy, but they were called Thin Lizzie on the sleeve of their first single, 'The Farmer'.

They could have chosen any number of songs for their debut. Between late 1969 and early 1970, Lynott made several recordings with an assortment of musical friends and acquaintances. It's striking how many options he had available to him, and how many creative urges he was seeking to serve: poetic folk singer; rootsy singer-songwriter; blues-rocker; pop singer. He and Bell would even play around the pubs together for a few pounds. In time, he would channel all of these identities into Thin Lizzy. For now, they existed independently of one another.

He appeared alone on RTÉ's *Like Now!* to perform a new piece called 'The Friendly Ranger', which at this point was literally half the song it became. On another occasion, Eamon Carr and Peter Fallon accompanied Lynott to Avondale Studios for an exploratory session. 'He'd got a promise from the Irish branch of a label [most likely EMI Ireland] to put together a compilation album,' says Carr. 'We turned up at this little voiceover studio. Gary Moore was there with his acoustic guitar, and a couple of ballad singers from [a cappella vocal group] the Press Gang. I don't remember what we did, there was a lot of fucking around. I don't think anything was ever used.'

A friend of Lynott's called John D'Ardis had opened a small eight-track studio on Hagan's Court, just off Baggot Street, called Trend. Looking to establish credibility in the market place, he offered Thin Lizzy some free studio time at Trend if they spread the word. Several early Lynott songs were recorded here by an embryonic version of Thin Lizzy, in what would now be called 'unplugged' recordings: Lynott and Bell play acoustic guitars, backed by Downey on bongos, and Wrixon on flute and piano.

Gary Moore may have also appeared on some of these tracks, which are uniformly lovely, particularly two charming songs never subsequently recorded or officially released. The enormously catchy 'It's Really Worthwhile' has a good-time Mungo Jerry feel. It's sweet and warm, an easeful country-blues with campfire harmonies and some witty lines:

> *She was very faithful until she met a boy called Jim*
> *It was he who said to her, 'Don't give out, just give in.'*
> *And only the guilty can tell you that it's a sin.*

'Mama and Papa' resurrects the refined, amusingly affected anglicized vocal style Lynott used on Skid Row's 'New Places, Old Faces'. Musically, it's a jumpy psychedelic-folk number; lyrically it's a hippie pastoral, with much talk of *'waterfalls'*, *'valleys'* and the *'Lady tree'*. A first draft of 'The Friendly Ranger' begins with the same words as the version recorded for *Thin Lizzy*, but includes an extra stanza, while the last two verses of the released recording are absent. The tentative melody is almost unrecognizable and there is no mention of Clontarf Castle in the lyric or the title, presumably because Lynott was not yet living in that part of Dublin. 'Saga of the Ageing Orphan' is graced with Wrixon's piano, but otherwise closely resembles the recorded version, as does the haunting 'Dublin'.

'In the context of what was going on around him, those recordings were very different,' says D'Ardis. 'Philip had a vision even back then. He could have had an earlier career doing that kind of material and morphed into a rock career later. He was such a fantastic songwriter.'

The song Thin Lizzy chose to release as their first single sounded like the work of another group entirely. 'The Farmer' was a loping country-rock song heavily influenced, both musically and lyrically, by the Band. Whereas in the Band's 'The Weight', *'Luke's waitin' on the Judgement Day'*, here Lynott affects a moonshiner Southern drawl to sing about *'Reverend Luke way up north in Tennessee'*.

It's a pleasant song and Lynott sells it well, but he sounds like someone trying on another man's clothes for size, while the B-side, 'I Need You', wasn't a Thin Lizzy recording at all, but rather an existing backing track created by John D'Ardis with another group of musicians. 'It was a kind of Blood, Sweat & Tears pastiche,' he says. 'I asked Philip if he would sing on it, because he had a very soulful voice. He had no problem with that, and Eric overdubbed guitar. That was the end of it for a while. Then they got a single deal with EMI to release "The Farmer", and they didn't have anything else finished to go on the B-side, so they asked if they could use that demo. It was never intended for release.'

'I Need You' is, unsurprisingly, an oddity, a rather dishevelled jazz-pop number in the vein of Georgie Fame and the Blue Flames, with warm organ and blasting horns. If nothing else, it offers an intriguing glimpse of Lynott as he might have sounded with the Black Eagles or early Skid Row, transformed into a finger-snapping soul man, belting out Ray Charles and Otis Redding.

Released as a one-off single on 31 July 1970 by EMI Ireland, the Irish arm of Parlophone Records, 500 copies of 'The Farmer' were pressed and only 283 sold, despite some local radio play and a concerted publicity drive which involved illegally fly-posting most of O'Connell Street. By the time the single was released Thin Lizzy were evolving again. Eric Wrixon had contributed organ and a roadhouse piano break to 'The Farmer', but before the track saw the light of day he was asked to leave – which is why he can be heard on the track but is nowhere to be seen on the vogueish psychedelic cover photo. Wrixon was the first Thin Lizzy member to be excised from publicity shots, though not the last. Money was too tight to stretch four ways, he was told, and the blend of personalities wasn't quite working out.

It was as a trio that Thin Lizzy began to gel. 'We used to jam on stage for about fifteen minutes, just the three of us, getting into this thing,' says Eric Bell. 'We tried new sounds every night. It was very natural, the interplay between us. It was magical when it started.'

They quickly gained a following. In June Thin Lizzy appeared in the top three in *New Spotlight*'s poll of best Irish bands. By autumn, the half-full venues they had played eight or ten weeks previously had queues snaking around the street. 'It was so exciting to see this new band taking off, and people just loving what we did,' says Bell. 'I think in a way we took it for granted. We started becoming a bit blasé about it, but by the same token we were genuinely surprised that this little buzz was starting to happen. Things just fell into place.'

'They were the best band in the land, because it was all about coolness and credibility,' says Fran Quigley. 'Whatever band Philip was associated with would have been the coolest band. He had the cool label. It was a small scene and you could make an impact pretty quickly.'

'Philip had a certain amount of pulling power,' says Frank Murray. 'People would be aware that this was his new band. Brian and Eric, too, had [recognition]. The public knew about these guys, they weren't a bunch of unknowns.'

In the beginning the standard Thin Lizzy set was the typical broth of shared influences: 'Street Fighting Man' by the Rolling Stones, songs by Spirit, Hendrix, Jeff Beck and the Flying Burrito Brothers, plus an occasional representative of Lynott's more off-piste tastes, such as Roger Miller's 'Little Green Apples', or a slow, spacey version of 'I Put a Spell on You' by Screamin' Jay Hawkins. When they travelled outside Dublin and played 'Dancing in the Street' by Martha and the Vandellas, Lynott would replace the original track's roll call of Detroit, Chicago, New York City, Baltimore and Philadelphia with Cork, Galway, Limerick and Kerry – equating the urban centres of black America with the provincial towns of white Ireland, giving everyone in the crowd a kick of recognition and symbolically fusing the twin elements of his own racial identity in the process.

'When we started off, we'd sing everybody else's numbers,' Lynott later recalled. 'Then, gradually, we introduced our own songs, dropping favourites as we went along, until half the set was original.'[1]

New rockers like 'Look What the Wind Blew In' joined 'The Farmer' and relative oldies such as 'Saga of the Ageing Orphan',

'Dublin' and 'Chatting Today'. Thin Lizzy started to become what Lynott had always craved: a powerful rock band that was also a platform for self-expression. 'When I saw Lizzy for the first time I thought, oh, that's interesting, they've tightened up the arrangements, they've tightened up the playing,' says Eamon Carr. 'They weren't quite a power trio, but they had the intensity of the Jimi Hendrix Experience. Stuff like "Look What the Wind Blew In" had an identity to it. Philip was already very solid on the bass. He wasn't Jack Bruce, but he was rooting it fine.' Before every Thin Lizzy show he would practise in the dressing room. At home, he spent hours at a time playing bass at the band's new communal house in Clontarf. 'He started becoming very proficient,' says Bell. 'He worked very hard at it.'

Lynott had left 85 Leighlin Road by the time Thin Lizzy formed. He rented a place in Kenilworth Square in Rathgar, and later stayed at 111 Anglesea Road in Donnybrook. These were areas befitting a budding local rock star. 'Kenilworth Square was pretty posh,' says Peter Fallon. 'He really liked that address.' As the band began to gel, he was taken with the idea of creating a headquarters. Groups such as Traffic, the Band and the Grateful Dead had pioneered the idea of living communally, the better to immerse themselves in music and forge a collective identity.

'We were in a pub one night, and Philip said, "Do you fancy getting a house together?"' says Eric Bell. Within a week Lynott had pocketed the keys to the upper floor of a large, red-brick Victorian villa at 28 Castle Avenue in Clontarf, a distinguished coastal suburb of south Dublin. Bell moved out of his flat on Manor Street in May 1970, and the two men started living together in one of Dublin's prime residential areas. The rather austere castle sat at the end of the road. The cricket club was across the street, the sea a stone's throw away.

The Castle Avenue flat was spacious, with a large living room, a ramshackle kitchen, one bedroom and a quirky conservatory – a Victorian 'plant room' – built on the side of the building on the first floor, where Eric Wrixon stayed for a time prior to leaving the band. Today, the property is worth at least 4 million euro, and has listed building status. In 1970 its elegance was a little rougher around the edges, but still – Crumlin boys didn't usually end up with plant rooms in Clontarf.

These were, Bell recalls, 'magic days. We shared a room at this point, there were two beds. Every morning we'd wake up, I'd go and make the tea, and Philip would roll this big joint. Then I'd come back in, get back into bed, and we'd pass the joint back and forth and put on *Astral Weeks* by Van Morrison, and just fly away. It was like that every morning. Incredibly creative, looking back on it. We had a television, an old black-and-white thing, and it was only on twice, I would say, in about a year. The record player was permanently turned on and hundreds of different records were being played, all day and all night. We were just surrounded completely by music, all the time.'

It worked its way into their bones. The hardy perennials were Jimi Hendrix, Van Morrison, Bob Dylan, Jeff Beck and Frank Zappa, taking their place alongside new progressive blues-rock bands such as Free, Spirit and Spooky Tooth. But there was room for everything: jazz, crooners, Chicago blues, cowboy songs, Irish traditional music, soul, the sepia-tinged Americana of the Band.

Castle Avenue wasn't a bachelor pad for long. First, Bell's girlfriend, Eleanor, moved in. Then Lynott met Gale Róisín Barber, an eighteen-year-old dentist's daughter from Belfast who had finished her A-levels earlier that summer. One of Barber's friends had socialized with Thin Lizzy after a recent show up north, and secured an open invitation for anyone passing through Dublin to come and visit the band in Clontarf. Barber 'wanted to escape from Belfast'[2] and shortly afterwards headed to Dublin, where she tracked down Lynott and his friends drinking in the Bailey one night. She found him shy, handsome and charismatic.

Soon she was lodging in the plant room, wrapped up in a sleeping bag and earning her keep as the flat's head cook and bottle-washer. She and Lynott became an item on the night of his twenty-first birthday party, a rowdy affair which lasted until morning. He looked lonely as the party wound down and dawn broke, Barber recalled. She later discovered that he had been with four other women the previous night.

'Gale was beautiful, and a really smart girl,' says Jim Fitzpatrick. 'Small, dark-haired, wore glasses. Beautiful face. I loved hanging out with her. She was a fascinating woman, really interested and intelligent. For a while they had a great relationship.'

Although they would remain a couple for several years, Lynott didn't tend to advertise his relationship status and, like Carole Stephen before her, Barber's presence wasn't encouraged at gigs. They rarely went out together as a couple, except to the cinema, where darkness offered anonymity. When Philomena came over from Manchester to visit her son at Castle Avenue, Barber was asked by Lynott to leave for a few days, although the two women later got on extremely well. Any discussion about his early childhood was off-limits.

Girlfriends were just the start of the influx. Castle Avenue soon became the after-hours destination of choice for every rocker, roller, chancer, dealer and freeloader in Dublin and its environs. The house rapidly went from a dishevelled kind of domesticity to a surrogate Orphanage, only significantly rowdier.

'It ended up with about fourteen people living there,' says Bell. 'People just appeared out of the wallpaper and next minute they were on the floor. Some of them had sleeping bags in the kitchen, on the staircase. Groups would be doing gigs in Dublin at night then they'd drive to Castle Avenue, and arrive about two o'clock in the morning. We'd hear "beep, beep" and look out the window, and there'd be about two or three transit vans with all these fucking weirdos and hippies, all coming up into our flat. We'd have about thirty or forty people in our house, guys out of bands, roadies, managers, women, groupies. We'd have big parties every night.'

Even today, the escapades of the 'Clontarf Cowboys' retain a mythic aura. Frank Murray remembers Castle Avenue as 'a crazy place'. Paul Scully recalls 'wild all-night parties, but it was all good fun, nothing horrible. It was like student days, almost, though we were more students of life than students of books.'

It was a time of great promise, fuelled by an exploratory hedonism. Lynott was already smoking dope daily, and to this staple he added hallucinogens and greater quantities and variations of alcohol. Sometimes at Castle Avenue a plastic bin was filled with any and every type of available drink, and the contents drained. He discovered that he had a remarkable constitution for excess. 'We used to drop lots of acid and mescaline together, get out of our heads,' says Eric Bell. 'The next minute the whiskey bottle would come around. No glasses, just the bottle. "Aw Jaysus, you can't hold your drink, man." All that crap. Macho stuff. Pain in the ass. But what I did notice is that we'd all be absolutely destroyed, and then some guy would come up at 1.30 in the morning from a record company or magazine and go over to Philip and start talking to him, and Philip could just pick himself up off of the floor and start talking business. It was incredible.'

Not everybody was as comfortable with Lynott's expanding repertoire of chemical distractions. It caused a divide among some of his old Dublin posse, which became more pronounced as the years went on. 'I never really got involved, I stayed away from all that,' says Brush Shiels. 'They were doing what they were doing, and we were kicking a football. Away he went.' Fran

Quigley remembers feeling uneasy at elements of life at 28 Castle Avenue. 'I went down there many times and hung out, but then I'd leave because the dope would be coming out and I was a very straight character.'

At least one of Lynott's friends suspects that he had his first experience of heroin around this time. Heroin and cocaine were practically unheard of in Ireland in the 1960s, but not entirely off the radar. 'I believe he got into using heroin at a very young age,' says Noel Bridgeman. 'I wasn't aware of it then, but looking back I could see the signs of it. I remember the dealers at Clontarf, after he had left Skid Row and I was down there.'

Lynott was friendly with Jimmy Faulkner, a well-known guitarist who played in the Jingle Jangle Band and later with local soul singer Ditch Cassidy in his Freak Show band. Faulkner remained a popular musician until his death in 2009. He was a wonderful guitar player, and also a heroin user. 'It was a small scene in Dublin then, a very closed shop,' says Bridgeman. 'I worked with Jimmy for quite a number of years, and now and then he let slip that when he and Philip hung out together as young fellas in the early days they took it.'

Lynott's flatmate and chemical comrade in arms at the time, Eric Bell, doubts whether he was taking heroin during this part of his life. 'He would have told me,' says Bell. 'Jimmy Faulkner was a good friend and a very good guitar player, and yes, I think he was [taking heroin]. There were a few people we knew who were. Another guy we knew, a great slide blues player, was into heroin as well, but they kept it very hush-hush. They didn't flaunt it. Maybe Philip had taken it. It's possible, but he never mentioned it.'

Drugs were strictly recreational. Lynott was above all focused on making music. In Castle Avenue Thin Lizzy truly became a band, and Lynott became a songwriter capable of serving its needs. He composed on a nylon-string guitar, experimenting with ideas, which he and Bell would then develop together, exploring riffs and chord sequences. Brian Downey was still living with his parents in Crumlin, but before long he was in Clontarf every day. When Lynott had the bones of a new song, the three of them would work it through again and again, Bell and Lynott on acoustic guitars and Downey playing the drums on his lap.

As the songwriting evolved, Thin Lizzy's live set gradually began to jettison most of the unoriginal material. Many of the tracks on their first album were written at Castle Avenue. Lynott pulled inspiration from all around him. 'Eire' and 'The Friendly Ranger at Clontarf Castle' drew on scenes from local history. The former recounted High King Brian Boru's vanquishing of the Vikings in the Battle of Clontarf in 1014. The latter was completed at Castle Avenue by the addition of two verses, in which Lynott name-checked the landmark at the end of his street.

He wrote a song for Gale Barber, 'Look What the Wind Blew In', indulging his life-long love of secret codes and clunky puns. Playing on the unusual spelling of his girlfriend's first name, the lyric outlined her impact on a man inclined to run from the strength of his own feelings.

> *Many lovely ladies*
> *I have felt, touched*
> *And I was not afraid*
>
> *I took them out dancing*
> *Out romancing*
> *And I was not afraid*
>
> *Then somewhere from the north*
> *This Gale I knew just flew in*
> *And I am afraid*

Lynott took his lyrics seriously. 'He was great for working and working and rewriting,' says Jim Fitzpatrick. 'He'd have notebooks with loads of stuff. I can testify to the trouble he went to really get the lyrics right.' For a long time the endeavour paid handsome dividends. The concluding verses of 'The Friendly Ranger at Clontarf Castle' were written as a poem, and are rather beautiful in their crafted capturing of joy and sadness and all the in-betweens.

To feel the goodness glowing inside
To walk down a street with my arms about your hips, side by side
To play with a sad eyed child till he smiles
To look at a starry sky at night, realise the miles

To see the sun set behind the steeple
Clontarf Castle, no king, queen or knightly people
A coal fire, and it's pouring rain
To wave goodbye to a very good friend, never meet again
Little thoughts bring little memories of you to me

'I always thought he was a gifted songwriter – he had that naturally – but the guy worked his bollocks off,' says Eric Bell. 'He would go out and run about with all these chicks, but behind it all he was working on songs all the time. He used to carry a gypsy bag with him and he'd have a book in there of lyrics. You'd be sitting talking to him and the next thing he'd pull the book out and start writing in it furiously, then put it back again and go, "Sorry man, what were you saying?" He really worked incredibly hard all the time. If it wasn't his singing, it was his lyrics, or it was his bass-playing, or it was his image on stage. The whole package.'

The idyll at Clontarf couldn't last forever. Such a respectable area would only tolerate an open-all-hours hippie commune in its midst for so long. One day there was a knock on the door at no. 28 and through the reefer haze and across the generational divide Lynott was handed a petition signed by more than fifty local residents, demanding that they move out. It scarcely registered. 'Looking back on it I couldn't blame them in the slightest, but you know when you're young and you don't give a shit, you don't see it that way,' says Bell.

Eventually, the lease lapsed and Lynott took a one-bedroom flat with Gale Barber, who was now working in an accounts office in Mountjoy Square. His days in Dublin were drawing to a close; the city was throwing out heavy hints that it was time to move on. On 4 September 1970, Thin Lizzy played at Ireland's first outdoor music festival, held at Richmond Park, the home of local soccer team St Patrick's Athletic. Mungo Jerry, riding high with their folksy hit single 'In the Summertime', were top of the bill.

The previous weekend, a tatterdemalion army numbering some half a million had made the trek to see Jimi Hendrix, the Who and the Doors at the third Isle of Wight festival. (It was one of Hendrix's last performances; he died on 18 September 1970, and Lynott and Bell held a 'wake' for him in the Bailey.) In the lead up to the Dublin Open Air Pop Festival, an agitated local press had been full of spook stories about the event happening on their doorstep. Private-security personnel, guard dogs and floodlights were being deployed to ward off 'hooligans' and 'a lunatic fringe element'. In the end, less than 1,000 people attended Ireland's first gathering of the clans, and the event was swiftly written off as a catastrophe. Even Lynott, resplendent in full-length leather coat, stack-heeled boots and two-toned bell-bottoms, couldn't save the day. 'I've been to more interesting wakes,' was one young attendee's verdict, reported in the following day's *Irish*

Times. The underlying message of this aborted attempt to kick-start 'the sixties' in Dublin as a living concept was clear: as a cultural hothouse, Ireland had a long way to go.

Thin Lizzy had recorded a single. Their gigs were sold out almost everywhere they played. They were featured regularly in the papers and magazines. At the end of October they appeared on RTÉ's *Like Now!*, the scene of Lynott's downfall with Skid Row fifteen months earlier, and received a positive response. Ireland had offered what it had available. The best thing the country could do for them now was conjure up an escape route.

They found one courtesy of Brian Tuite. Until now, Thin Lizzy had been managed by Terry O'Neill, a friend from Lynott's Skid Row days. Smart and inventive – 'imagine a young, Irish Del Boy,' says John D'Ardis – O'Neill was also broke and inexperienced. He was on the lookout for a partner to alleviate the workload and the financial burden. O'Neill approached Brian Tuite, the former manager of local band Granny's Intentions and the owner of Dublin's main music-equipment shop, the Band Centre. Tuite had already been tipped off about Thin Lizzy by Fran Quigley, who worked in his shop. He contacted Peter Bardon, who ran a successful agency that booked showbands all over Ireland. Bardon agreed to put up capital, but only on the condition that Terry O'Neill relinquish any claim on the band.

In the autumn of 1970, Tuite and Bardon took over the management of Thin Lizzy for a nominal sum, remembered by most parties to be in the region of £200. 'More of a thank you fee than anything else,' says Bardon.

Both men had other, bigger irons in the fire. For Bardon Thin Lizzy was always strictly business but for Tuite, the more hands-on of the pair, it was a matter of heart as well as head. 'The big thing at the time was bands writing their own material,' says Tuite. 'Phil said, "We've got twelve songs at the moment that we'd be happy enough to record." I thought, yeah, I've heard that crap before, but when I listened to the stuff he was writing I liked it very much.'

Almost the first thing Tuite did was to seek out a record deal. He was good friends with Frank Rodgers, a Dubliner now working in London as an A & R man with Decca. Rodgers' father was Louis Rodgers, a powerful dancehall promoter who brought major American country acts like Hank Locklin over to Ireland. Frank's sister, Clodagh, was a successful singer, actress and TV personality who went on to represent the UK in the 1971 Eurovision Song Contest with 'Jack in the Box'.

Tuite arranged for Frank Rodgers to see another of his acts, the white soul-singer Ditch Cassidy, with a view to Cassidy earning a deal with Decca. Rather than use Cassidy's regular band, Tuite secured Thin Lizzy a spot at the same audition as the singer's backing group for the day. 'I said to the lads, "Listen, Frank's coming over to hear Ditch, but he's not going out of here without you . . ."'

Watching Cassidy sing that afternoon in an empty Zhivago's nightclub, Rodgers found himself intrigued by the trio. Although Lynott was just playing bass, Rodgers could feel the star quality. 'I could see the potential,' Rodgers said. 'Because of Phil. Everything could be hung around Phil . . . He had *it*.'[3]

Afterwards they repaired to a nearby pub and Rodgers offered the band an album deal with Decca on the spot. (Cassidy drew the short straw, and was signed up for a single on Decca subsidiary Deram.) 'Before Frank left we had shaken hands on a deal,' says Tuite, although Rodgers ensured that he and other Decca personnel saw the band play again before anything was signed, this time performing their own songs at their own concert. He departed even more convinced that 'I had something that was going to make the company money.'[4] It wasn't just about Lynott's looks, but his abilities as a songwriter. According to Tuite, '"Look What the Wind Blew in" was the one that swung Frank, but he really thought the cross section of songs would make a good LP.'

Tuite travelled to London to meet Decca's head of A & R, Dick Rowe, the man who had turned down the Beatles and signed just about everybody else, including the Rolling Stones, Tom Jones and the Small Faces. The paperwork was drawn up on 12 November 1970, and on the first day of December Decca officially signed 'Tin Lissy' to a one-year recording contract, with the option of extending the deal by two further periods of one year in September 1971 and September 1972. All going well, they were committed to delivering three albums to the company. The advance was £500, with a further £500 to be paid after the album had been completed.

Lynott left for London with the band and Brian Tuite on 3 January 1971, the morning after a Thin Lizzy show at the Afton Club in Dundalk. On the boat to Holyhead, he spotted John Peel at the bar. Never one to miss a hustle, and aware that Peel was good friends with Peter Fallon, he was bold enough to introduce himself. 'Philip went over and started speaking to him, and said, "Oh, I'm in a band called Thin Lizzy, maybe we can keep in touch?"' says Eric Bell. The permanently abashed Peel mumbled his assent. 'He liked the nerve of it,' Lynott remembered. 'So we had one contact.'[5] It was a good one. Within ten months Peel would be booking the group for a session on his Radio 1 show; within six years he would be writing the introduction to Lynott's second volume of poetry.

The meeting with Peel on the ferry was regarded as an omen, a laying on of hands from the hippie-prince of Britain's underground music scene. They arrived in London with a powerful sense, says Eric Bell, that 'everything was happening'.

They booked into a guesthouse in Sussex Gardens, within striking distance of Decca's studios in Broadhurst Gardens, West Hampstead. The following morning, a Monday, they began recording the first Thin Lizzy album. By Friday evening they were done. 'We got up at nine in the morning, [went] into the studio, played from about ten or half ten to eight or nine, then clocked off and went back to the guesthouse,' says Brian Downey. 'Then we did it again, for the whole week.'

They were working with American producer and songwriter Scott English, who had co-written Jeff Beck's hit 'Hi Ho Silver Lining' and Amen Corner's 'Bend Me, Shape Me'. English was Decca's choice. He 'wasn't a bad producer,' says Brian Tuite, who is credited on the album sleeve, only half-jokingly, as 'Referee', 'but he thought he was better than he was. Philip fell out a bit with him because Scott wanted to turn down the bass. It got to the stage where I was up in the control room and Scott would say, "Go down and tell the bass player to turn down." He wouldn't use the [talkback] mike because Phil wouldn't do it anyway. So I'd say to Philip, "The Bearded One wants you to turn down the bass," and he'd say, "Tell that fucking Yank to piss off." He knew full well the mike would be open.'

The only outside player involved was the respected musician and arranger Ivor Raymonde, brought in to add mellotron to 'Honesty Is No Excuse'. Raymonde went away impressed. 'Ivor said to me, "Who wrote that song?"' says Tuite. 'I told him it was Phil, and he said, "That fella has some talent, let's hope he doesn't spread himself out too much." He said, "He'll write something like 'My Way'."'

The symphonic, soulful pop of 'Honesty Is No Excuse' is Lynott at his most directly expressive, both proud and troubled by his own knockabout ways, and facing up to the end of youthful innocence. It has an uncharacteristic elegance and simplicity. *Thin Lizzy* is an engaging ragbag of material, much of which reflects the circumstances in which it was recorded. 'We were permanently stoned,' says Bell. 'Scott English was this jovial American guy, a nice big bloke. He had this enormous bag of grass in one of the drawers in the studio. He brought it out, threw it on the table and said, "Help yourselves, boys!" That was it. I can't actually remember recording the first album. I didn't know anything until the end of the record, it was just a haze. Smoking a bit of dope and playing music went hand-in-hand for us. We were just that type of band at that point in time. It seemed to work for us, we got ideas. There was a lot of things on that album that were completely ad-libbed.'

The songs had been bedded in through a year of live performance. If the album has a defining characteristic, it's of an early 1970s jam-band expressing their musicianship through a thick smog of reefer vapour. 'The Friendly Ranger at Clontarf Castle' finds Lynott's meandering cross-stitch of comic-book quotations and poetic melancholy set adrift. 'Clifton Grange Hotel', the starry-eyed portrait of his mother's *'refuge of mercy'* in the heart of Manchester's red-light zone, is similarly lacking in form, while 'Return of the Farmer's Son' is a workout rather than a song. Promising melodies flare up then fade, diverted by arrangements that are by turn overly busy and disjointed.

It's a typically flawed first album from a band not yet sure how to get the best out of either their songs or their sound, and as a result attempting to do too much at once. Thin Lizzy were still in clear thrall to their idols. Jimi Hendrix is all over the derivative space-rock of 'Ray-Gun', written by Eric Bell, while there are echoes in Lynott's vocals of many of the singers he admired, among them Hendrix, Rod Stewart, Van Morrison and Joe Cocker.

The record offers only glimpses of the honed power to come. 'Look What the Wind Blew In' is oddly sparse – the pitfalls of a trio laid bare – but still packs a punch, particularly when muscle and melody fuse on the *'run boy, run'* section. 'Eire' is strong and original, Lynott's tale of Celtic heroism elevated by Bell's highly atmospheric guitar overdubs. He had originally sung the words in Irish, but Decca balked and asked him to re-record the vocal in English.

Throughout, a distinctive lyrical sensibility adds extra depth and dimension to the sometimes wayward music. The best of the songs on *Thin Lizzy* draw in the listener with their vivid characterizations, evocative street scenes and fragmented, secular confessionals. In the early days of the band, Lynott was striving to create a music that combined the dream-like lyricism of Van Morrison's *Astral Weeks*, drawing powerfully on the pull of memory and place, and the open-ended, ambitious ebb and flow of progressive rock.

'Remembering Part 1' and 'Diddy Levine' are the most striking examples of this attempted fusion – epic in scale, with distinct musical sections. The latter is one of several domestic mini-dramas Lynott wrote between 1969 and 1972. The narrative is convoluted and at first appears tenuous, burdened with shifting time frames and apparently random characters. On closer inspection, the song directly questions the extent to which Lynott might have agonized over his childhood.

'Diddy Levine' begins in the *'later Forties'* and spans twenty years. The titular female has a young child and is living with a man whom she then leaves – *'and with the child in her arms she went looking for a fling'*. She turns down two marriage proposals. *'Through all her mother's lovers'* the child keeps the maternal surname. *'Inheritance, you see,'* Lynott concludes, *'runs through every family.'*

The word 'father' crops up in four of the album's ten tracks. 'Saga of the Ageing Orphan' is another patchwork of images pulled from the family scrapbook. It's very beautiful, an overt expression of Lynott's gentler folk side. His voice is pitched low, the music is empathetic and almost subliminal, with Bell's fluid acoustic guitar work recalling Jay Berliner's quasi-classical guitar lines on Van Morrison's 'Beside You'. The sadness is allowed the space it deserves, and flows through. *'We had come in search of one who evades us all,'* he sings, slowly, softly and precisely. *'Never heeds the call.'*

It is this quality that snags the listener almost half a century later: the ache of nostalgia and acute sense of loss, astonishingly keenly felt for one so young. *'I keep on remembering the old days,'* sings Lynott on 'Remembering Part 1', lending the album its theme. If he is not remembering the lost girl in the *'pretty dress with the zip up the back'*, he is recalling days at the old picture house; *'a happy home, a hand to hold'*; or *'father and I waving goodbye'*. He was still only twenty-one, and yet seemed to pine for an age that had not yet even passed. It's the same quality evoked in Seamus Heaney's poem, 'Glanmore Revisited': *'It felt remembered even then / an old rightness half-imagined or foretold.'*

PART TWO

Are You Out There?

7

Tin Lizzy. Tin Lizzie. Thin Lizzie. Tin Lissy. No matter how it was spelled, with a record deal and an album awaiting release, Thin Lizzy were now routinely billed as 'Ireland's top group'. They returned home immediately after recording the album in London. Gigging in Dublin and further afield between mid-January and mid-March, Lynott was already possessed of the giddy feeling that his horizons had been forever broadened.

These months were the last time he lived in Ireland for a decade. In the final weeks he stayed at 10 Eglington Terrace, in Donnybrook, the family home of Brian Tuite, which had been put up for sale and was sitting empty. He moved into the bedroom that had belonged to Tuite's infant son, adorned with teddy-bear wallpaper. 'Phil told me one day that after he'd taken some of the old magic grass, he woke up in the middle of the night and started talking to the little bears,' says Tuite.

The decision had already been taken to move to London permanently to coincide with the release of the *Thin Lizzy* album in April. That great Irish cultural cliché – exile – awaited him. He was ambivalent about it. 'To do what I wanted to do I had to leave Ireland,' he said later. 'It was a catch-22. I didn't want to leave.'[1]

'He liked London, but he felt that as a band they had been forced to go to England, which he thought was wrong,' says Jim Fitzpatrick. '[As such], he felt there should be a huge Irish input into every part of Thin Lizzy.'

Gale Barber was moving to London with Lynott. Former Skid Row manager Ted Carroll was also making the trip. Carroll had resolved to stop working with rock bands, planning instead to set up his own record shop, Rock On, in west London. After returning to Dublin in late 1970, however, he had been wooed into a change of heart by Brian Tuite and Peter Bardon. The pair had more pressing day-to-day business interests in Ireland, which prevented them moving to England to oversee the band. They needed somebody to manage Thin Lizzy in London. Carroll wasn't keen, but the offer of a partnership in the management company clinched it. That, and the music.

'They invited me to dinner and played me a test pressing of the first album and I was impressed with it,' says Carroll. 'I always liked Phil's singing, but I didn't know he could write songs, and I was very impressed with his lyrics. I thought he was very talented: great wordsmith, good singer, good melody writer. That's why I got involved with Thin Lizzy. In March 1971 I went into rehearsals and began working out an act, a mixture of original songs from the new album and some covers, just trying to get a running order, presentation, all of that.'

In the few weeks before they all left for London, Carroll observed the group dynamic. 'Brian was a superb drummer, and Eric was a great guitarist. They were the two really accomplished musicians in the band. Phil wasn't an outstanding bass player, he was getting by and improving all the time, but it was perfectly adequate and suited the band. His vocals, I think, were the strongest part of what he did. On a musical level they all worked together. Eric contributed a lot in terms of riffs and intros, but

Phil mostly wrote the songs on his acoustic guitar. The lyrics were all his. Phil was the leader. It was his band, but he had the greatest respect for Eric and Brian.'

London was the inevitable next step. In Ireland, the glass ceiling for creative rock groups barely rose above the vault of the Five Club. Although Thin Lizzy had recently broken through to the more lucrative ballroom circuit, ending the monopoly of showbands by virtue of their sheer popularity, they were still viewed as poor relations. There was no industry infrastructure to support a group with ambition. 'There was a very limited "cool" audience,' says Peter Bardon. 'If you wanted to make any headway you had to leave.'

Taking the boat from Dún Laoghaire had become a familiar rite of passage for the bigger Irish acts. In 1968, Limerick's Granny's Intentions had left for London, signing to Deram and later recording their sole album, *Honest Injun*, a record widely regarded as having some of the worst cover art in rock history. The People – featuring Henry McCullough – followed in their wake and became Eire Apparent, persuading Jimi Hendrix to both play on and produce their debut album. Gary Moore's old band the Method was in London, as was Skid Row, now plugging their debut album and setting their sights on America.

It was not an easy transition, as Thin Lizzy discovered. In the time between leaving Dublin and arriving in London, creased and crumpled from being crammed in the back of the van for eight hours, they went from being a group that mattered to a band that might as well have formed that morning. In effect, they had to start all over again. 'Nobody knew who we were,' says Bell. 'Before we left Dublin we were probably in the top three, if not the biggest band in Ireland. We left and went to London, and nobody cared. We were expecting VIP treatment, and instead it was, "Fin 'oo?"'

They started playing immediately. One might reasonably claim that they didn't stop for the next twelve-and-a-half years.

If life was lived on the road, then it must follow that home was the red Avis transit van that Brian Tuite hired for £175 a month and was, he says, 'doing a million miles a week'. Lynott sat in the front passenger seat, a position he maintained – even as the drivers changed and the vehicles progressed from vans to Fords, station wagons, limousines and Daimlers – for the rest of his life. 'Philip would never sit in the back, he was always up front,' says the photographer Chalkie Davies, who lived with Lynott in the late 1970s. 'He used the excuse of the length of his legs, but I think there was more to it than that. I don't ever remember him sitting in the back of a car.' Lynott never learned to drive.

They travelled the first of Tuite's metaphorical million miles on 23 March 1971, making their London debut upstairs at Ronnie Scott's Soho jazz club, and were paid £6 for the privilege. Fran Quigley had made the trip over with the band as a 'humper and hauler'. 'There couldn't have been more than twenty people in the room,' he says. 'I said, "Fuck it, I can't do this." I told Philip that night I had to leave. I could see it was going to be drudgery, poverty, struggling.'

So it began. Thin Lizzy were, as Lynott boldly declared in a press release the following year, 'a truckin' band. We always have been, and we always will be.' Over the next eighteen months they supported anyone and everyone, from the Faces, Status Quo, David Bowie, Eddie Floyd, Canned Heat and Uriah Heep to scores of long-forgotten bands and singers. Life became a blur of one-night stands conducted in pubs, clubs, hotels and college halls from Redruth, Cornwall, to the Isle of Arran. They played three or four times a week, zig-zagging across the country on 'dartboard' tours, which followed no conventional geographical logic, and rehearsed at least a day each week in between. Crowds varied from 20 to 120 people. They were rarely paid more than £10, and sometimes nothing at all. On more than a few nights they all slept in the van.

There was nowhere Thin Lizzy wouldn't go. They played a prison chapel, only realizing as they drove through the gates that 'the smell of dope in the van would have knocked you out,' says Eric Bell. 'We were all scurrying about trying to hide the dope in various parts of the van. We played on the altar. Philip looked at me, and I looked at Brian. It was like a fucking *Laurel and Hardy* movie. These 200 guys walked in, blue denim shirts and black slacks, and just sat there. No noise, total silence. We started playing, and we went down really well. Then they all walked out again, and that was it. We played all these crummy gigs for next to nothing. Our management had us out everywhere. We would be on with another five bands, bottom of the bill. Treated like Paddies from the boat. A lot of guys just looked at us like we were three idiots. I felt very insecure in England and London at that point. It got to me a little bit.'

Lynott, too, seemed inhibited. He had not yet overcome his natural shyness on stage. In Ireland, where he felt more assured of his place in the pecking order, this sense of reserve communicated itself to the audience as a rather stately confidence. 'Mr Cool,' says Brian Tuite, 'standing there lifting an eyelid.' In England, this apparently supreme detachment calcified into a chronic lack of self-belief, which undermined his stage presence. He was restricted by his bass, a difficult instrument to play while singing, let alone posing, but even between songs he seemed awkward and tongue-tied. He ummed, aahed and mumbled. Ted Carroll went so far as to prepare rehearsed lines for him to say to the crowd, which only seemed to make things worse. In the end, Eric Bell undertook the majority of the talking. 'He'd just stand there, play the bass and sing,' says Bell. 'None of his dramatic, legs apart type thing. It was all very laid-back – a poetic, serious musicianship vibe.'

His inability to meet the crowd's collective gaze made their shows an awkward experience. 'He was a shoe-gazer before his time, he would look down at his feet and only look up to sing,' says Ted Carroll. 'I kept on at the band about the importance of communicating. Find somebody and catch their eye and connect with them. It's important that you make contact with the audience.'

Their audience proved elusive. The debut album, *Thin Lizzy*, was released on 30 April 1971, having been remixed by a young engineer called Nick Tauber after Frank Rodgers had objected to the job Scott English had done. The album was not widely reviewed and was not a commercial success. Ted Carroll's notes from the time record that *Thin Lizzy* sold a total of 2,499 copies in the first five months. Of these, just over 1,800 were sold in Britain and Ireland, and the remainder in mainland Europe.

The only obvious inroads came courtesy of Radio Luxembourg. Canadian DJ David 'Kid' Jensen instantly fell in love with the record and played it continually. 'We would listen to his late-night show as we were coming back from gigs and he was playing a couple of tracks every night,' says Brian Downey. 'It became number one in his best albums of the year list.'

They followed it up in August with the *New Day* EP, four tracks recorded with Nick Tauber at Broadhurst Gardens. It comprised a punchy reworking of 'Remembering' from the first album, the stoned, rambling 'Old Moon Madness', and the rocking 'Things Ain't Working Out Down at the Farm', on which Lynott, memorably, somehow contrived to turn *'out'* into *'ow-ee-ah-yeet'*.

Significantly, *New Day* found a home for 'Dublin', Lynott's beautiful, sad and conflicted reflection on the city that formed him. 'Dublin' is short but captures the essence of the place: the pull of exile and the dragging counterweight of memory; the sentimentality and sweet sadness; the lack of money and opportunity; the fondly recalled local landmarks. It was written as a poem, and there is a charming recording of Lynott reading it as such, but it resonates more strongly when it is sung to music.

After our affair, I swore that I'd leave Dublin
And in that line I'd left behind
The years, the tears, the memories
And you in Dublin

At the Quays, friends come and say farewell
We'd laugh and joke and smoke
And later on the boat
I'd cry over you

How can I leave the town that brings me down
That has no jobs, is blessed by God
And makes me cry?
Dublin

And at sea with flowing hair
I'd think of Dublin
Of Grafton Street and Derby Square
And those for whom I care
And you, in Dublin

It's an important song, not just for Lynott but for Ireland. 'A lot of people at the time would think, why would you want to write about that?' says Brian Tuite. 'But that was the way he lived Dublin. That was the way he felt it. Everything he did had a personal touch to it.'

'Aside from things like "Molly Malone" and "The Auld Triangle", nobody really said straight up in a lyric: Dublin,' says Paul Scully. 'It was quite a revelation, and quite an intimate thing. We suddenly heard Dublin mentioned in a song with a strong Dublin accent, as opposed to Ray Davies singing about London. It was ours. Ireland always had an inferiority complex about England, we were always held down, so when Philip sang proudly and poetically about Dublin, that was quite an amazing moment.'

London was a breath of fresh air, an unbuckling of the belt. For all that Lynott loved Dublin, in the 1970s the city was dour and downtrodden. Its physical beauty was in a state of disrepair, while its burgeoning bohemianism was battling centuries of ingrained inferiority, censure and prohibition. In Ireland, Lynott had been at the centre of something still in the process of being formed. That was why Skid Row and Thin Lizzy were able to make an impact so quickly. It was also why they had had to leave. In London, he felt plugged into the mains of a genuine movement. The days moved at a faster lick, and for the first time in his life he could walk down a street without *everybody* staring. He was excited by the challenge.

'I'd always wanted to get to London – Carnaby Street and that,' he said later. 'The whole rock boom was still there in them days, '69 wasn't so far away. I was so pleased to get over and have a run-around. It was a lot better than I thought it would be, and a lot different. Much freer. It was great to walk into a youth environment where young people seemed to control it. The whole youth culture seemed to be very big, much more so than in Ireland, where you had to wear a tie to get into a dance. It seemed to cater for people like me, and I didn't feel as freaky as I used to. I could wear jeans and sit down on the ground and listen to music.'[2]

'That's what our life was,' says Eric Bell. 'Sauntering off to Hampstead Heath, walking about like hippies. I'd say about 80 per cent of all the people who walked past me in London had bell-bottom jeans, patchouli oil and velvet coats, and a big joint hanging out of their mouth. That was where the youth was at that moment in time. [It] seemed to be like a big revolution was starting, and we were part of that.'

Some London practices confused Lynott. He thought the Underground trains had to be hailed, like buses or taxi cabs. When he first arrived, 'me and Brian put out our hands to stop the train. We nearly lost our hands. We were really untogether on things like that. There was a lot we didn't know. But, at the same time, we were fairly cool. We weren't dum-dums.'[3]

During his first year there, Lynott rented a single-room bed-sitter on the third floor of a Victorian villa at 61 Hillfield Road in West Hampstead, an attractive tree-lined street of terraced houses which branched off from the main drag of West End Lane. Gale Barber lived there with him. 'Ted Carroll found it incredibly difficult to find us a place,' she recalled. 'At that time nobody would rent to either black or Irish, so we had a double dose of not being wanted.'[4] Lynott later described the difficulties he had finding somewhere to live in London as 'the hardest time I ever had being black'.[5]

The house was owned by an Italian couple. Their rules were strict and the facilities were basic, but the rent was manageable, at £7 a week, and the area convenient for Decca studios and the M1 motorway. Lynott liked West Hampstead, and stuck close to West End Lane until 1978, when he moved further west to Kew.

He was surrounded by an Irish diaspora comprised of bands, roadies, friends, girlfriends and assorted hangers-on which had settled in Hampstead and nearby Belsize Park. Everyone back home thought they were living the high life in London. The reality was rather less glamorous.

Paul Scully and Frank Murray were now working with Skid Row and living in Belsize Avenue, alongside Gary Moore, in 'one of those enormous old London houses,' says Bell, who also moved in when Thin Lizzy landed. 'There must have been about fifteen rooms, on three or four floors. Gary lived in the ground-floor flat with his girlfriend. Frank was upstairs with his wife, Ferga. Then I moved into this other room in the house with my girlfriend Eleanor, who was pregnant at the time.' Ted Carroll lived next door, at 31 Belsize Avenue. Brian Downey shared a flat at nearby Greencroft Gardens. Soon they were joined by another Dublin friend, Peter Eustace, who started handling the sound and lighting for Thin Lizzy, and their roadie and driver, Mick Tarrant.

They were forever on the edge of penury, although Lynott fared better than most. Like the rest of the band, his accommodation was paid for and he was given £10 a week to live on, but he had access to other revenue streams. The songs on the first two Thin Lizzy albums were published by Decca's in-house publishing company, for which Lynott received an advance of around £1,000. He would also, in the words of Frank Murray, 'tap up his mother if he ran short'. When he needed a new bass, it was Philomena who signed the hire-purchase agreement. 'He had more of a cushion than the rest of us, but we just accepted it,' says Murray. 'That was the way it was.'

Thin Lizzy were already coming to terms with the fact that Lynott possessed the kind of attributes that ensured he would be singled out as the main attraction.

'I suppose he had started asserting himself as the leader,' says Bell. 'I can remember one of the first times I got an idea that that was going to happen. After we had recorded our first album, one of our managers came up to me and showed me a rough plan of the cover. On the back there were some small photographs of me, Philip and Brian, but there was a huge one of Philip on the left-hand side on his own, [running] the full length of the sleeve. Ted said, "I hope you don't mind, Eric, it's because it looks so long and lanky." I suppose they were associating it with *Thin* Lizzy. I could see the sense in what he was saying, but a little part of me was going, hmm, Philip has got two photos on the cover, one of them huge, and Brian and I have one.'

He was not just the most charismatic, he was also the most engaged and hands-on. 'Philip was *very* organized,' says Ted Carroll. 'Sometimes very talented musicians are so wrapped up in the music they find it difficult to deal with other things. Gary Moore would be a good example of that. Phil was very together, a good communicator, and he basically took care of everything. Things were joint decisions, they discussed them in rehearsals and in the van, but he was running the show.'

Following New Year dates in Ireland and a long and rather dispiriting college tour of England in the company of Arrival and Barabbas, on 10 March 1972, the second Thin Lizzy album was released. *Shades of a Blue Orphanage*, a title which blended the names of Lynott's and Bell's previous bands, had been recorded in a rush with Nick Tauber. They were in a new studio, De Lane Lea in Wembley, Lynott having found the old Decca building somewhat stuffy. 'They were quite old-fashioned, it was a little bit like having Big Brother watching you,' says Tauber. 'They gave us a really tight budget. We were really up against it. We were doing fourteen-hour days, it was absolutely bonkers.'

Technical problems with the Cadac console left clicks all over the tapes and drove Lynott to distraction. More significantly, he found himself facing a perennial industry problem: following up a collection of songs that had taken years to write, with a second album written on the hoof. Thin Lizzy had little time to rehearse because they couldn't afford to stop touring. They asked Decca for a £1,000 advance to tide them over, but were refused.

'We ended up in the studio with really not much of a clue what we were going to do,' says Eric Bell. 'A lot of the second album was made up in the studio, there and then.'

The result was a regression. Older songs such as 'Chatting Today' were pressed into action, and several others – the meandering 'The Rise and Dear Demise of the Funky Nomad Tribes', the throwaway Elvis Presley pastiche 'I Don't Want to Forget How to Jive', the time-marking 'Call the Police' – are filler. 'Buffalo Gal' has a smooth, soulful melodicism, and 'Sarah', the tribute to Lynott's grandmother, offers further evidence that he would not be boxed in by genre, but even the better tracks were denied the opportunity to fulfil their potential. The 1977 version of 'Brought Down', on which Lynott added overdubs to the original 1972 recording, streamlines the song's latent power and potential into something truly dynamic. On *Shades of a Blue Orphanage* it sounds like a demo. Much of the rest of the album is similarly underwritten and underpowered. 'It sounds a bit naff, production wise,' was Lynott's later opinion.[6] 'A depressing time for the band. We just didn't feel it sounded like us, it lacked the balls, the energy.'[7]

8

During Lynott's first year in London, Thin Lizzy released two albums and an EP; twenty-three songs in total, of which eighteen were written solely by him, four were co-written with Eric Bell and Brian Downey, and one was written by Bell alone.

They form a body of work quite distinct from anything else he ever did. 'There is a real poetic sensibility in those first two albums,' says Eamon Carr, while Bob Geldof describes it as 'convoluted and quite arty. The first album opens with a long spoken poem. It was kind of hippieish, groping towards hard rock.'

The standard is patchy, but there is a quality that only rarely reappears in the band's later work. 'Although it was rock music, it was very melodic, and incredibly well structured,' says Midge Ure. The future Thin Lizzy guitarist and keyboard player was one of the few people who was impressed at the time by the first record. 'It set them apart immediately from what was going on then. Songs like "Diddy Levine" and "Dublin" are stunning.'

The seven-minute title track of *Shades of a Blue Orphanage* is another of Lynott's vivid Dublin vignettes, which surrenders to the bittersweet drag of nostalgia for the old town. He recalls the cinema where he watched Roy Rogers and Hopalong Cassidy, returns to St Stephen's Green, toasts old flames and absent friends. These are not happy, sun-kissed memories; they are *'true blue, Irish blue.'*

His early songs of and about Ireland are his most nuanced on the subject. Many of them were written while he was still living in the country. Once he left – although he was never far away, and it was unusual for more than six months to pass without him returning to Dublin – Lynott looked back with an increasingly romantic eye, falling upon often clichéd representations of Irish archetypes. James Joyce viewed his homeland from a distance with a vivid ambivalence; Lynott, particularly as time wore on, was happy to view it through the prism of rose-tinted spectacles. His Ireland was a fond fairy-tale, a shamelessly sentimental construct full of doughty working-class characters, gypsy lovers, mythical heroes, warriors, outlaws and wild women. He painted in the broadest of brush strokes.

The avoidance of complexity was not an accident. It was the entire point. Lynott wanted these songs to stand as bold assertions of Ireland's historic power and unique character. Like Van Morrison, he had no interest in offering contemporary social critique or explicitly political sloganeering. Comparing 'Róisín Dubh (Black Rose): A Rock Legend' and 'Emerald' with other depictions of Ireland in the 1970s, be they the Boomtown Rats's 'Banana Republic' or Stiff Little Fingers's 'Alternative Ulster', it's clear the extent to which Lynott ducked the issue of modern Irish identity. Even when the issue came up in interviews, he offered cosy platitudes. 'I'd like Ireland to become one nation, but then, we are,' he said. 'We seem to be all Irish when we're away from Ireland.'[1]

Gale Barber had grown up in Belfast, which in 1969 descended into the sectarian Troubles that would rip the city and the country apart for the next thirty years. She struggled to see the romance of it all. 'It used to annoy the life out of me,' she said. 'I'm from the north and, to me, it's a country full of idiots who really ought to have their heads banged together. But he just thought of everything as being wonderful.'[2]

'He avoided modern Ireland like the plague,' says Jim Fitzpatrick. 'Philip was a traditionalist, his version of Ireland was the idealized version. I remember when Bobby Sands died [an imprisoned member of the Provisional Irish Republican Army, Sands died on hunger strike in 1981], we had a really serious conversation and I took the piss out of him. He had a romanticized view of the Provos being the continuation of the great Irish struggle – whereas I saw them as being in the way.' On *Chinatown*, released in 1980, the back cover included the slogan 'Smash H Block', pledging solidarity to the campaign supporting the hunger strikers.

He was a product of his upbringing and his education. '[At school] we were only forty years away from the 1916 Easter Rising, and they were all heroes,' says Fitzpatrick. 'Philip kept that, and when he went away he became a lot more wistful, a lot more nostalgic. He read a lot of Irish history and a lot of books about Ireland. He was educated about how Ireland fitted into the whole of European history, but his idea of Ireland was more the idea of this romantic struggle against Britain.'

This approach also became a means of affirming his own identity. 'Irishness became very important to him, something he could hook on to,' says Tim Booth. 'It allowed him to have much deeper Irish roots than people might initially perceive from just looking at him. I think he was very glad to discover all of that, and learn about it, and be able to bring it up if anyone was to challenge his roots in any way.'

There was suss in everything Lynott did, and the way he packaged and presented his Irishness was no different. The hokey puns, the Celtic art, the ripe romance, the sentiment, the poetry, the creaky stage patter – 'Is there anybody here with any Irish in them? Is there any of the girls who'd like a bit more Irish in them?' – and the off-hand literary allusions combined, in time, to create an identity for Thin Lizzy that was distinct from any other band. 'He had a shining ambition, a very clear pathway that he wanted to take,' says Booth. 'He needed certain accoutrements to allow him to progress down that route, and the Celtic thing was part of it. He used it very well to brand Thin Lizzy. It was pure Celtic branding, done very cleverly, before anyone was really aware of the concept of branding. Philip *got* all that.'

Shades of a Blue Orphanage was released into a vacuum of indifference. 'Same old story,' says Bell. 'We're all wondering, "What the fuck are we doing? There's nothing happening."' Lynott was frustrated. Ted Carroll sent a terse memo to Decca, detailing a long list of complaints and bemoaning the company's lack of belief and threadbare support for the first two albums. Rather desperately, he pointed out the success they had had on the Luxembourg album chart. The truth was, neither record was strong enough to take the band to the next stage.

Succour of sorts was offered by touring. 'Gradually Thin Lizzy began to get more polished and gain more confidence,' says Carroll. 'They would get rebooked in the clubs; most of the promoters liked them. It took a while to build up a following . . . but gradually it started to happen.'

In 1972 they played their first European dates, performing in the Netherlands, Germany, Belgium and Switzerland. Life had slipped into a pattern, which continued, with only minimal evolution, until 1974, by which time Frank Murray had become Thin Lizzy tour manager, and a big, blond Scot called Charlie McLennan had been hired as their roadie.

They grew accustomed to vast amounts of travelling, followed by a short gig, often on a multi-band bill. Sometimes they drove back to London, sometimes they stayed overnight. A few drinks, a club, perhaps a girl, and to bed at three or four o'clock in the morning. In the hotels, B & Bs and boarding houses, they slept two to a room, at best. Then up again at eight to make last orders for breakfast. Miss breakfast, and they might not eat until the evening. Such was the fineness of their financial margins. Then back in the van, or the leased second-hand Ford Granada – prone to breaking down – and on to the next stop on the schedule. Repeat. It was the life Lynott had chosen, and it was better than working, but it was far from glamorous.

'We seemed to be constantly touring,' says Murray. 'There were never many breaks, we had to work in order to get wages. It wasn't like you could take three or four months off; it wasn't like there was a big kitty there to keep paying everybody. We spent most of our lives in a car. We had some dreadful drives between places. Getting from one gig to the other really sapped the energy out of us, but when you're younger it's fun. Nothing really bothers you. Actually, Philip loved touring.'

The lack of responsibility suited him. Pulling into town, playing his songs and heading off again at sunrise had a cowpoke romance into which he could easily buy. He loved the freshness of each day, he loved meeting new people, and he had the metabolism for it. He smoked dope more or less constantly, rolling joints in the front of the car on the road and passing them to Bell and Downey in the back. After the gig, it was time to go out carousing.

'Philip was the kind of guy who would drink and drink and drink,' says Frank Murray. 'He was a guy who liked to keep up with people. On the continent in those days you could drink later than you could in London. We used to go out clubbing, most of the time we'd drink local beer or vodka and orange. One night we went into a drinking competition deep in the sticks, somewhere in Germany. They took out this plastic bucket from underneath the bar. It seemed to be made of slops and fish, the smell off of it was dreadful. We had to take a mouthful each, which we did, then they had to take a mouthful. Then they said, "Again." So we did it twice. Silly stuff like that.'

Such escapades left no discernible mark. 'Philip would get up the next morning for breakfast and he looked like a million dollars,' says Eric Bell. 'Absolutely fresh. Showered, shaved, hair washed, clothes pressed. I don't know how he did it. Brian and I were crawling out of the bed, eyes out on stalks, and Philip's downstairs having a coffee. He had an incredible constitution, he just kept going.'

In their first eighteen months in Britain, any sense of ennui came not from the effects meted out by the lifestyle, but from the sense that he was banging his head against a brick wall. On 3 June 1972, Thin Lizzy played Peterborough and Liverpool on the same day. Even the normally upbeat Lynott began to despair. 'We'd finished the gig, and Philip walked into the changing room, threw his bass on the floor and just sat down, his hands between his knees,' says Bell. 'One of the roadies came in and saw this, and he says, "Philip, was it the sound? Was the sound no good tonight?" Philip said, "No man, for fuck's sake. How do you get off this fucking circuit?" The roadie went, "Oh, you need a hit record, mate." He walked out and Philip went, "Ah." We sort of knew that was the answer. Regardless of how good you were musically, or how brilliant your stage act was, if you had a hit record, you were seen by millions of people on TV. Overnight success. Until that happened we were just forever going round in this transit van, playing any club, any pub, any town, anywhere.'

In the band's under-appreciated, penny-pinched state, Ireland represented a land of golden promise. Simply *being* in London validated them back home, where they could earn up to £200 each night, at least ten times what they could demand in Britain and Europe. The influx of ready cash enabled them to clear some of the debt that had accrued since their last trip and to keep a modest amount of working capital in reserve, at the same time topping up their depleted sense of self-worth. Small wonder that regular Irish tours – two or three times a year – became a ritual.

When Thin Lizzy returned home in the first fortnight of July 1972, the talk in Dublin's bars, clubs and music press was of their next single being, according to the *Evening Herald*, 'a shake-up of a traditional Irish ballad'. After the failure of *Shades of a Blue Orphanage* to gain any ground, band, management and record company were scratching their heads. Changes were afoot. Peter Bardon had already cut his ties. Busy back in Ireland, and tiring somewhat of having to keep dipping into his personal finances to keep the band afloat from week to week, Brian Tuite was also in the process of stepping down as manager. 'All I did was pay the fucking bills,' he says, not unkindly. 'After six months they had turned over something like £5,600, of which £2,500 was owed to me. That was a lot of dough. I'd be sending money to them all the time.'

Tuite eventually got what was owed him. He passed on the reins to Chris Morrison, who took over as co-manager with Ted Carroll. A young Scot, Morrison had been a junior partner at Acorn, a prominent booking agency based in Soho that had Status Quo, Manfred Mann and the Equals on its books before going bust. 'I thought Thin Lizzy were fantastic,' says Morrison, 'But the finances were a nightmare. I had £1,000 savings and it had all gone by Christmas.'

The pair's first order of business was to secure Thin Lizzy a full release from their contract with Decca. 'Chris and I went to see Frank Rodgers,' says Carroll. 'We said, "Look, neither of the albums have sold very well, Decca don't seem very committed, why don't you just let us out of the deal?" Frank said, "There's another year to go, we've invested quite a bit."

So we agreed to do a single, and if it didn't do anything then they would let us go.'

The idea was to record a new Lynott song. 'Black Boys on the Corner' was his first concerted attempt to engage with his non-Irish roots. In part it was an expedient land grab for the fashionable Blaxploitation market. The rhythm of the song, established in the opening interplay between splashy cymbals and bongo drums, was influenced by Isaac Hayes's 1971 hit 'Theme from Shaft'. Lynott's semi-parodic spoken intro – *'Whatcha doin', maaan?'* – and the depiction of black kids shooting pool and rolling dice owed more to the current trend for gritty low-budget movies set in inner-city America than anything Lynott had yet experienced on the mean streets of West Hampstead. Yet the chorus was undoubtedly personal, and pertinent.

> *I'm a little black boy*
> *And I don't know my place*
>
> *I'm a little black boy*
> *Recognise my face . . .*
>
> *I'm a little black boy*
> *And I just play my bass.*

Swaggering yet also vulnerable, it reads like a terse telegram from the confused child who landed, alien-like, in Crumlin, and was forced to make the best of it. The subtext states, I'm here and I'm different, what are you going to do about it? More importantly, what am *I* going to do about it?

The music – dominated by Bell's juddering, ragged-edged guitar riff – conveys the coiled tension and simmering threat of an antagonistic street encounter. 'Black Boys on the Corner' is the first clear glimpse of the Thin Lizzy to come. Possessed of a lean power and a very clear sense of its own purpose, in little more than three minutes the recording made almost everything the band had released previously seem rather whimsical by comparison.

The song was, unsurprisingly, earmarked as Thin Lizzy's first single since 'The Farmer'. Taking a short break from touring, they rented an upstairs room at the Duke of York pub in King's Cross to rehearse in the afternoons. During a lull, Eric Bell started reading *Melody Maker* and Brian Downey rested behind his drum-kit, idly leafing through a newspaper. Lynott, eternally restless, picked up a six-string Telecaster guitar and began messing around at the microphone. 'He started singing all these stupid songs, just as a joke,' says Bell. 'We weren't paying any attention to him. At one point he started singing Irish songs, and then he started singing "Whiskey in the Jar". I was very bored, so I started playing guitar along with him. Then Brian started playing the drums.'

Lynott had known 'Whiskey in the Jar' forever. 'It was a song I used to do on the folk circuits,' he told *Sounds* in 1976.[3] A traditional Irish standard dating back to the seventeenth century, it was practically ingrained in the national consciousness. On any given night in the pubs clustered around Grafton Street and Baggot Street it would be hard to avoid. The Dubliners recorded it three times in the late 1960s, and more populist folk groups from around the world, among them Peter, Paul and Mary and the Seekers, had also reinterpreted it.

As with many traditional songs, the words were subject to tweaks and revisions in differing versions. In its broad outline, 'Whiskey in the Jar' appealed to Lynott for its fatalistic account of a marauding highwayman roaming the mountains of southern Ireland. The imagery is big and bold. The grain of romantic nationalism and anti-establishment heroism that runs through much of his Celtic writing is present in the theme of a free-spirited outlaw robbing a military man, Captain Farrell, of his money. The twist comes later, when the highwayman's lover, Molly, betrays him. The protagonist ends up shooting Farrell and is sent to prison, while the bold Molly makes off with the spoils.

As Lynott and the band were toying with 'Whiskey in the Jar' in the Duke of York, Ted Carroll walked in, listened and uttered the immortal words: 'That sounds like a hit.' None of them were convinced. The song connected to a version of Ireland they respected and appreciated, but one with which they did not particularly want to be directly associated. Lynott was eager to write a new kind of Celtic folklore, not lean on an old one. 'We were going to throw Ted out the window of the pub,' says Bell. 'One of the reasons we left Ireland was to get away from Paddy music. We couldn't relate to anything he was talking about.'

When the time came to record their new single, however, Lynott didn't have anything to offer as a B-side, so they agreed to try 'Whiskey in the Jar', recording the basic track in three takes at Decca's new Tollington Park Studios, in Islington. Lynott played around slightly with the melody and the tempo, in particular letting the chorus stretch and breathe. They used drums and two acoustic guitars, played by Lynott and Bell. No bass. No electric guitar, no solos. It harked back to the band's earliest recordings at Trend Studios. It sounded like they were busking.

Bell took away a cassette of the raw track and agonized for weeks. Eventually he came up with the atmospheric introduction, modelled on a pipe part he had heard on a tape of the Chieftains that Lynott had played in the car one night as they returned to London from a show in Wales. It had cast its spell during 'the twilight zone', that strange, disquieting period between two and four o'clock in the morning, when the world is lit by the orange glow of the motorway lights and the border between dreams and reality seems to dissolve. Later, he added the signature riff, the track's prominent melodic hook. These additions were overdubbed shortly before the single was scheduled for release. Without them it's doubtful whether Thin Lizzy's version of the song would have made the same headway; with them, it burst out from a smoky snug bar and became accessible to a rock audience. In the end there was still no bass, and it *still* sounded like a demo.

Despite the apparent serendipity of its creation, the recording of 'Whiskey in the Jar' may not have been quite as off-the-cuff as it appeared. As ever, Lynott had his ear to the ground. Just as he was aware of what was gaining currency in New York and London, he was plugged into what was happening in Ireland, where his friend Eamon Carr was now enjoying great success as the drummer with his band, Horslips. Formed in 1970, Horslips had caused an almost immediate stir by fusing traditional Irish songs, air and jigs to an instrumental rock aesthetic, in the process essentially creating the template for Celtic rock. They released their debut single, 'Johnny's Wedding', in March 1972, and their debut album, *Happy to Meet – Sorry to Part*, followed on CBS later in the year.

Musically, Horslips were a more intricate affair than Thin Lizzy. Intellectually, they were more consciously conceptual, committed to uniting Irish history and tradition into a defined creative identity. But the general idea of using traditional music in a modern rock context may have suggested an alternative route for Lynott to explore. 'We were enormous, biggest album of the year, and Philip was very conscious of that,' says Eamon Carr. 'He was well hip to what was going on in the folk scene in Dublin, he had absorbed it and he kept those links alive. He had a grasp of traditional music and folk music early on. He was on a parallel track to us, in a way, but "Whiskey in the Jar" was so different to the rest of what they were doing and what they were about.'

When Decca boss Dick Rowe heard Thin Lizzy's two new tracks, he made an instant decision about 'Whiskey in the Jar'. 'He said, "No way is this going to be a B-side, this is the A-side,"' Brian Downey told me. 'That was down to head office. We had no say in the matter.'

Part of the procedure of turning 'Whiskey in the Jar' into a hit involved editing the song for radio, cutting it from 5:50 to 3:40 (although the single still featured in the full length version). 'We cut out one of the verses, because there were four verses in the five-minute version, and some of the solos,' says Nick Tauber. 'Philip was amazing. He didn't mind doing things like that. He was very business-like. He knew we needed a three-and-a-half song for the radio, they were never going to play five minutes.'

The pragmatist in him thought back to Liverpool: *How do we get off this fucking circuit?* Bell – more of a purist – wasn't so sanguine: partly because Lynott didn't tell him that his solos were being cut, and partly because he bristled against what he regarded as a retrograde move away from original, blues-based rock. 'Eric felt we were selling ourselves out by doing an Irish song,' says Brian Tuite. Privately, Lynott had similar reservations, but he also realized it was a chance to sell himself *in*.

'Whiskey in the Jar' was released on 3 November 1972 to no great fanfare. It sold a total of eighteen copies in the first twenty-four hours. The same day, Thin Lizzy embarked on a month-long tour with Slade, at the time the biggest band in Britain. Slade had been stirring up a convincing approximation of Beatlemania on the back of three number-one singles over the preceding twelve months, their Droogy threads and roughhouse Black Country brio the 1970s equivalent of mop-tops and lovable Scouse wit. American glam-rocker Suzi Quatro was also on the bill. Like Thin Lizzy, she was a relative unknown, still several months away from her commercial breakthrough with 'Can the Can'.

After all the one-night stands and patchwork tours, this was an opportunity to play large theatres in front of crowds numbering several thousand each night. But it was a test, too – of material, of mettle, of presence.

The tour opened at Newcastle City Hall. 'There was about 3,000 people there, the balcony was stuffed,' recalls Eric Bell. 'It was like a football crowd, loud and pissed. People singing "You'll Never Walk Alone", scarves everywhere. All they were interested in were Slade, they didn't give a shit about us.'

The atmosphere was hostile, almost gladiatorial. As soon as Thin Lizzy shuffled on, Lynott was subjected to catcalls and racial abuse. Some of the crowd threw objects at him. The band started into 'Slow Blues', an as yet unreleased new song which was all touch, all feel. As an opening number it proved a catastrophic misjudgement. It quickly became apparent that it would take more than mellow mood music and eyes-tight-shut virtuosity to convert Slade's wildly partisan audience. As the uproar from the crowd grew louder, Lynott shrunk into himself. He had no idea what to do or how to respond. From the wings Suzi Quatro watched a trio that had no discernible leader or clear point of focus. 'Phil wasn't even up front, they were just a three-piece band,' she says. 'He was shy and almost apologetic on stage. I got the sense he found it quite intimidating.'

After only three songs Thin Lizzy retreated ignominiously to the dressing room, defeated and depressed. They were followed there by Chas Chandler, the manager of Slade, and former manager of Jimi Hendrix.

'Chas Chandler walked in and went, "What the fuck was all that about?"' says Eric Bell. '"You are here to wake the crowd up, not to put them to sleep. If you don't pull your socks up you're off the tour." He was looking at Philip as he was saying this, and then he walked out and slammed the door. Philip was on the verge of tears. It was the first time I'd ever seen him really dejected. He was floored completely. His hero's manager had just told him he was crap. Philip really, really took it to heart.'

The following day, Thin Lizzy had a solo date booked before the next Slade concert in Oxford, and they used it to radically rearrange their set and their attitude. 'Philip got everyone there early and rehearsed all their rockers,' says Chris Morrison. 'He learned lessons very quickly.' The adjustment helped, but the tour remained a challenge. They got on well with Slade and Quatro, but the shows were tough. 'The fans were very non-responsive,' Quatro recalls. 'Thin Lizzy had a hard time, they had to battle every night.'

The tour was 'a real turning point' for Lynott, says Bell. 'That's when the change started. Philip started for the first time really looking at how very successful English bands handled the crowd. How to keep them interested and how to sell it.'

Thin Lizzy had supported David Bowie earlier in the year at the Electric Village in Bristol, and they had played with the Faces more than once. Alongside Rod Stewart and Bowie, Slade's ebullient leader Noddy Holder was another master at harnessing the energy of a crowd and using it as fuel for a genuine *performance*. Lynott watched all three from the crowd or the wings, studying their physical stage craft.

'He realized that you had to put a little bit of showmanship in,' says Eric Bell. 'That's what the people wanted, otherwise they might as well sit at home and listen to the music. They wanted visuals as well. Philip started slowly realizing this. Every now and again after that first night in Newcastle I'd look around and I'd see him throwing a shape that he'd never done before. He used comic book poses: the guy standing up on top of a rock in the sunset shaking his fist up to the heavens, shouting, "I swear I'll do this" – that kind of thing. Or putting the bass between the legs, pointing out at the crowd. Then he'd realize what he was doing and he would go back to being shy Philip again. But he knew that that wasn't going to be quite enough to do what he wanted to achieve.'

It was a beginning. Lynott did not become the supreme performer of *Live and Dangerous* fame overnight, but an incremental process of transformation was underway. Years later, he told Sean O'Connor of Irish band the Lookalikes that he had practised for hours in front of a mirror with his guitar to get the poses right. 'Phil *became* that showman figure,' says Suzi Quatro. 'He wasn't [built] that way. Noddy and I are both in your face, and he looked at that and wanted to take that on, but I don't think it came naturally to him. The rocker guy was not the Phil I knew.'

He was looking for ways to connect, despite the restrictions of playing bass for the duration of every show. Holder wore a tall, wide-brimmed top hat adorned with mirrors, which reflected and fragmented the spotlight, sending it beaming back into the audience. At first Lynott experimented with a small circular mirror dangling from the machine head of the bass, then he refined the idea and came up with a chrome scratch-plate. Screwed onto the body of the guitar, the mirror enabled him to tilt the instrument to catch the lights and dazzle the crowd, pinpointing individuals out in the darkness. It was a long, silver thread binding the band to the audience, and one of the most significant developments in Thin Lizzy building a rapport with their fans.

He also made changes to his playing style. As a fellow singer-bassist, during the Slade tour Suzi Quatro told Lynott '"you're not a bass player, you're a frustrated guitar player". He didn't argue with that. Even his stance was more like Hendrix. He was in a trio at that time, he had to fill in a lot of spaces.' By the time Thin Lizzy recorded a promo clip for 'The Rocker' in 1973, Lynott was taking a different approach to his instrument. He adopted a more aggressive stance – crouching and prowling, legs apart – and raised his arm dramatically above him in the air between notes. He stopped using his fingers and started using a pick. His playing became more rhythmic and direct, grounding the songs and streamlining the sound of the band. 'He never thought of himself as a great bass player, but if you listen to the records he was super,' says Noel Bridgeman. 'Phil was the rock everybody sat on. He never gave himself much credit for the fact that he didn't play like Jaco Pastorius, that was his insecurity again, but Phil was a fabulous bass player and drove the whole thing along.'

Each change was made as part of a concerted response to the realization that Thin Lizzy needed to develop a much sharper cutting edge if they were to have a fighting chance of winning over larger audiences. Before the tour began they sneered about Slade being a pop group who dressed in silly clothes. Up close, they were the loudest, most dynamic rock band they had ever heard. They didn't mess around with moody intros, atmospheric spoken word pieces and extended jams. Lynott noticed that, too.

When the tour reached the Free Trade Hall in Manchester on 15 November, Philomena Lynott came to see the show. She and her son were now thoroughly bonded. They had forged the close and loving relationship that remained until his death. Too much had occurred, however, for a conventional parental relationship to exist. They would always relate on a slightly different frequency. 'I think it was a pleasant surprise to her that Philip became the person he became, and she kind of lived her life through him,' says former Thin Lizzy manager Chris O'Donnell. 'I wasn't comfortable with it. It wasn't a mother-son relationship, it just wasn't. There was no discipline: "Oh, it's harmless, it's just a bit of puff." She was blind to the obvious, and always in his defence.'

'There's no doubt he adored her,' says Jim Fitzpatrick. 'When they started to spend time together she was an amazing mother and he was an amazing son. If anything she was too liberal with him. I would have put manners on him, especially when it came to drugs, but you can't blame her for Philip's nonsense.' Lynott was fond of her partner, Dennis Keeley – 'a great guy, I hope my father was like him, I really do'[4] – who regarded himself as a friend rather than a stepfather figure of authority.

After the Manchester show, Thin Lizzy, Suzi Quatro and her band stayed the night at the Clifton Grange Hotel. Quatro wasn't terribly impressed. 'The room was cold and damp, that's what I remember,' she says. 'But it was free of charge, and we were on a shoestring, so we said, yes. His mother was a very nice lady, very eccentric.'

The hotel was a must-stop fixture on the tour itinerary each time they ventured into the north-west. If they were playing Liverpool, often they would drive straight to Manchester after the show and stay there. By the early 1970s, the Clifton Grange had established itself as a unique part of Manchester's social landscape, and was known locally as the Showbiz or the Biz. The residents' bar was a tiny room adorned with photographs of Hollywood film stars, complete with fake autographs. The bar operated far beyond its legal remit, becoming an after-hours drinking club that rarely opened until two in the morning. It was, in the words of one regular, a 'shebeen'. Late-night callers walked up the steps at the back of the house to a door, and buzzed to get in. Dennis Keeley would be upstairs acting as lookout.

The clientele were drawn from a wide spectrum of society. Northern Irish football legend George Best was a regular during his days playing for Manchester United. Later on in the 1970s, other players from the club would regularly drop in. 'Philip started getting really into football then,' says Frank Murray. 'It was obvious he was going to be take Manchester United [as his team]. Philip was never going to be a guy who was going to follow a team who was going to lose.' He would eventually become a shareholder in the club.

In the Biz bar in the early hours, the renowned QC George Carman might graze elbows with Best, still out carousing as dawn broke on the morning of a game. Pop singers mixed with actors from *Coronation Street*, and the local CID would fraternize with the so-called Quality Street Gang, a loose affiliation of Manchester businessmen of dubious repute. Despite the myths that have sprung up around the gang over the years, many self-propagated, they weren't necessarily career criminals. In their official capacity, they ran car-sales pitches, pubs, scrapyards and bookmakers, and very few had serious convictions. But they undoubtedly operated on and often beyond the fringes of the law. They associated with genuine gangsters, and would not back down from trouble. They adored Philomena – they called her the 'Godmother' – and they became good friends with her son, too.

Lynott was an easy touch when it came to gangster chic, with its grimy glamour and macho code of ethics. He needed very little impetus to get the creative juices flowing, and the rough-house romance of the Quality Street Gang was filtered – not always verbatim, but in spirit – into several Thin Lizzy songs. The adrenalized swagger of 'The Boys Are Back in Town' was partly a tribute to the atmosphere in the Biz whenever the Quality Street

Gang descended. One of several templates for *'Dino's bar and grill'* was Deno's, a famous and rather fancy Manchester nightclub run by Denos Kitromilides, a Greek-Cypriot entrepreneur. It was often the last legitimate stop on the circuit before everybody piled back to Clifton Grange.

Though it was set in the American ghetto, 'Johnny the Fox Meets Jimmy the Weed' was initially inspired by Biz regular and Manchester villain Jimmy 'The Weed' Donnelly, while 'Waiting for an Alibi' drew on a favour owed to another family friend, Joe Leach, who at one point supplied Daimlers to Thin Lizzy, and was later instrumental in guiding keyboard player Darren Wharton towards the band. 'They were nice people, sweet and respectful,' says Chalkie Davies. 'You wouldn't have known [about their criminality] unless they told you. We would go to football with them.' When guns, hard drugs and ultra-violent gang culture hit Moss Side in the 1980s, the Quality Street Gang suddenly looked rather quaint.

Taking the temperature at the Biz became a ritual that continued throughout the 1970s whenever Thin Lizzy were within striking distance. The entire tour party would descend, accompanied by whatever guests were around, and see in the dawn. Money never changed hands. They often end up serving themselves at the bar. Graham Parker visited while touring with Thin Lizzy in 1976. 'It was a crazy place,' he says. 'It was like a speakeasy or something. Drinking and women and other stuff – it was wild. It was just this riotous party.'

'I can remember once Kid Jensen came over to see the band play, somewhere in the north-east, and we drove back to the hotel,' says Ted Carroll. 'We stayed up drinking in the bar, and when we decided to go to bed someone pulled back the curtains and it was broad daylight outside.' There was no hurry. At the Biz, breakfast was served whenever you woke up.

9

At the end of the Slade tour, which concluded in Bristol on 5 December 1972, Lynott sent a letter to Peter Fallon in Dublin. 'A wild time was had by all!!!' he wrote, enclosing a couple of publicity photographs of himself 'just in case the chick wants a photo of yours truly, if not, sell them!!! (for free)'. Wrapped up amid the charm and guileless, good-humoured vanity is the unmistakeable whiff of raw ambition. The man who had observed stardom up close every night for a month was suddenly hungry for a participating role.

Thin Lizzy ended the year in Ireland, where 'Whiskey in the Jar' was number one and would remain on the charts for seventeen weeks. They saw in the New Year at the Fillmore West, in Bray rather than San Francisco, played RTÉ's *Spin-Off* programme, and recorded an excellent session for Ken Stewart's radio show. Everywhere they went their hit single was heavily trailed.

Back in Britain, its trajectory had been stealthier. 'It was a sleeper,' Brian Downey told me. 'It took ages to get into the charts.' When it had first been released, radio play was slow except from their staunch ally, Kid Jensen on Radio Luxembourg. When the song was finally aired on Radio 1, courtesy of DJ Stuart Henry, Decca hadn't sufficient stock to satisfy demand. The record was lost in the Christmas rush, but Carroll and Morrison decided to re-promote it in the New Year with the help of a young booker called Chris O'Donnell, who had previously worked with Morrison at the Rik Gunnell Agency.

O'Donnell enlisted one of Britain's leading music publicists, Tony Brainsby, to drum up some interest in the band. Brainsby brought a touch of old-school patrician clout to Thin Lizzy. He represented Queen, Fleetwood Mac and Paul McCartney and lived at Atherstone Mews on Gloucester Road in South Kensington. 'If you put an R at the front and a D at the end,' he would say languidly, 'It spells "Rather Stoned".'

Brainsby assembled an only mildly hyperbolic press release, which included a picture of Lynott wearing a top hat, à la Noddy Holder. He had toyed with a demi-glam look following the Slade tour – a sprinkle of glitter here, a smudge of Gale Barber's mascara there – but he was more comfortable in denim, even if his jeans were carefully embroidered with colourful thread and patterned patches.

O'Donnell also hired an independent record plugger, Mike Beaton, to hype the single. Tim Booth was working in London as a commercial artist, and Lynott asked him to pitch in. 'I got a little noggin and put some whiskey in it, stuck on a little label and sent it round to DJs,' says Booth. 'Philip loved all that.'

Almost three months after its release, 'Whiskey in the Jar' finally broke into the singles charts on 20 January 1973. It rose to a peak of number six on 11 February, and spent a total of eleven weeks in the top forty. It reached number seven in Germany.

Lynott and the band were despatched on twenty-four-hour junkets to France, Spain, the Netherlands and Germany to perform on television and talk to the press. In Britain, there was a sudden surge of media interest. They were interviewed by *New Musical Express* and performed on *Top of the Pops* and the children's television staple *Crackerjack*. The latter had been hosted by Lynott's future father-in-law, Leslie Crowther, from 1960 to 1968, and was now presented by Michael Aspel. On the former they were introduced by Noel Edmonds wearing a tartan bow-tie. 'It really took us by surprise,' said Lynott. 'Suddenly we were flung into a new world.'[1]

Lynott was 'over the moon' at it all, says Bell. 'Completely, totally, absolutely joyful.' He relished the attention and recognized the opportunity it presented. The single may have been a 'fluke'[2] but it had saved their career. It bought them time, brought them attention and afforded them greater power in controlling their own destiny.

Once 'Whiskey in the Jar' had stuck, Ted Carroll and Chris Morrison immediately went to Decca to renegotiate their contract. Instead of parting from the label, they agreed a six-month extension on the original deal, which would encompass a new album and take them through to March 1974. Decca advanced the band £10,000 of the royalties accruing for 'Whiskey in the Jar', monies spent on paying off heavy debts. The company also agreed to make a budget of £5,000 available to help promote the next album.

Doors opened. Thin Lizzy started playing cooler clubs to larger crowds, but such developments further exposed the problems highlighted during the Slade tour. Audience expectations had increased exponentially, but the group struggled to keep pace. They did not yet have the music, or the showmanship, to deal with the step up in status. The crowd would surge forward when they played 'Whiskey in the Jar', but when Thin Lizzy failed to hold their attention they would retreat back into the shadows.

Before the single had even left the charts, Lynott was distancing Thin Lizzy from it. 'We don't want people to get the impression that we are a folk rock band who do nothing but up-date old

Irish drinking songs,' he said in March 1973. 'The flipside ['Black Boys on the Corner'] is really much more reflective of what we play on stage. We do all our own material apart from [that] one number, and it's all hard driving rock.'[3]

He was acutely sensitive to how the band were regarded critically, and suspected that the single could, in the long run, do more damage than good. The *NME* suggested that the Anglo equivalent of 'Whiskey in the Jar' would be a reggae version of 'Greensleeves'. Brush Shiels thought the record was abysmal and made no bones about it. Eamon Carr regarded it as 'a novelty'. 'It took them a long time to escape from "Whiskey in the Jar",' says Paul Scully. 'They ended up hating it.' The second incarnation of Thin Lizzy, featuring Scott Gorham and Brian Robertson, never performed the song live. A decade after its release, Lynott declared that the 'song has lived to haunt me'.[4]

'After the success of "Whiskey in the Jar" there was an awful lot of pressure on the band,' he said. 'People wanted us to record "Tipperary" rocked up, or "Danny Boy" rocked up . . . Everybody was coming up and telling us what we should be doing, and it wasn't going too well.'[5]

Rather than take the easy or predictable option, the next Thin Lizzy single was 'Randolph's Tango', an elegant, unashamedly romantic original which was, said Lynott, 'the result of a conscious effort not to record a follow up'.[6] It's a sharp, sweet song, a mini movie or short story compressed into four minutes. He has fun with his two protagonists – the sensuous *señorita* with a plan, and the swashbuckling *ranchero* forever two beats off the pace – whose star-crossed affair finally comes good. Tim Booth's ad campaign turned the lyrics into an illustrated cartoon strip. The single bombed, but the point was duly made that here was a writer of wit and substance, fronting a band which was far more than a one-trick pony.

And yet as much as Lynott professed his dislike at what 'Whiskey in the Jar' represented, from time to time he explicitly tempted lightning to strike twice. The singles 'Philomena' and 'Wild One', released in 1974 and 1975 respectively, were attempts to write original songs that echoed the Celtic folk-rock template of their breakthrough hit. Neither made any commercial headway, which was no loss in the case of 'Philomena', though more surprising in respect of the excellent 'Wild One'.

'Looking back, [the success of "Whiskey in the Jar"] must have been extremely hard for Philip,' says Eric Bell. 'Number one, it wasn't one of his songs, and number two, he didn't even play the bass on it. And it became a hit.' Not just a hit, but the definitive version of a song which had been around for more than 300 years. The tempo, melody, guitar hooks and lyrics on the Thin Lizzy version have become the standard. They are integral elements of subsequent recordings by Simple Minds, Pulp, Metallica and scores of other pop and rock artists. One wonders what Lynott would have made of it all.

Prior to touring with Slade, Lynott and Gale Barber moved out of Hillfield Road and into 2a Welbeck Mansions on Inglewood Road, less than half a mile south along West End Lane. It was a rented two-bedroom flat in the kind of elegant mansion block typical of London's more affluent districts. There was a security gate, a lobby with a marble floor and an elevator leading to the apartment on the second floor.

Thin Lizzy were still constantly on the verge of financial catastrophe, but for Lynott there had been a small but significant shift in status. In February 1973 Ted Carroll and Chris Morrison set up their own publishing company, named after a new addition to Lynott's homestead, a black kitten called Pippin. Carroll and Morrison owned 15 per cent each of Pippin the Friendly Ranger,

Music, Bell and Downey 20 per cent each, and Lynott 30 per cent. With publishing and performing money filtering through, he could afford to move. What extra money he earned was often ploughed back into Thin Lizzy in the form of equipment and stage clothes.

Domestic life was communal. Lynott lived at Welbeck Mansions until 1976, but he was almost never alone. He and Gale occupied one bedroom, and the other was open to anyone who needed it. Frank Murray, Brian Robertson, Nick Tauber, Smiley Bolger, Jim Fitzpatrick and a Nigerian engineer called Desmond all lived there at one time or another. Many more bodies could be found sleeping it off on the living-room floor on any given morning. Letters went home to his friends: 'call and crash any time' – an offer routinely accepted. The 'open-house' ethos was maintained until he died. 'Philip didn't really know how to be alone,' says Jim Fitzpatrick.

The parts of his life that existed away from the band generally revolved around listening to music, watching films and smoking dope – in letters to friends Lynott would sign off, 'Stoned Again, Philip.' They might go for a drink in the Black Lion on West End Lane, stop in at a café or falafel house, catch a band and go to the Speakeasy for a late drink. He'd go shopping for clothes on King's Road, and when summer came around, he cleared his daytime schedule to watch Wimbledon tennis on television. Arthur Ashe was his favourite. 'It's a good stoner sport, you just sit in the armchair,' says Frank Murray. 'I remember he insisted we drink Pimm's while we were watching it.'

It was a more worldly extension of the scene that had existed at 85 Leighlin Road when they were all in their teens. 'The guys were always in and out of the flat,' says Frank Murray. 'Collecting wages, discussing gigs, or just hanging out. They used to smoke a lot so they'd often come over and intend to stay an hour. Four or five hours later they'd still be there. We'd listen to a bunch of records and just shoot the breeze.'

Ted Carroll had set up Rock On records in 1971 at Portobello Road market. He had access to the best of all worlds of music. Lynott loved Capitol-era Steve Miller and Rod Stewart's *Gasoline Alley*, Neil Young's *After the Gold Rush* and old favourites like the Kinks, Buffalo Springfield and Jimi Hendrix. He was listening to Marvin Gaye's *What's Going On* and *Trouble Man*, Stevie Wonder's *Music of My Mind* and Sly Stone's *Fresh*. 'I remember hearing the first Eagles album with Philip at Frank Murray's house,' says Tim Booth. 'I think later that seeped into things like "Borderline" and "Cowboy Song". We all had the Flying Burrito Brothers and the Byrds.'

The impression he gave was of a man constantly on the move. 'He didn't like sitting still,' says Jim Fitzpatrick. 'He was either having sex, taking drugs or working.' Of these three, work took precedence. He thought about the band constantly – its sound, its image, the songs, the show. He was often in touch directly with the record company. 'Philip learned very quickly how to use the music industry properly,' says Nick Tauber. 'He was, with the exception of Freddie Mercury, the best worker of a room on the planet. He used to go down to the call centres where they sold the records and speak to all the girls, as well as the secretary of his A & R man, the secretary of the label's managing director. He knew how to work the business. He was an incredible asset, not only on stage, not only as a bass guitarist, singer and writer, but as a member of that brand. He knew how to make people like him and he knew how to make them feel easy. He was very smart. He knew what he wanted from the band, he knew what he wanted to accomplish in life, and he knew what he wanted from everyone else.'

He was writing all the time, often enlisting help from Gale Barber to fill in words or phrases. 'He was always looking for words that rhymed,' she said. 'We had a lot of parrying backwards and forwards with that, and with stanzas.'[7] When a new song had been whipped into decent shape, he would make an acoustic demo on the hefty reel-to-reel recording machine he now had at home, set up in the living room next to his TV, record player and stack of records.

Barber calculated that he was away 85 per cent of the time. When he returned he struggled to adjust and often seemed not to even try. She was now working in social services, dealing with people with significant problems. Lynott seemed to be afloat in his own bubble.

'The more Philip came home from tours, the less he would speak to his girlfriend,' says Bell. 'He'd just come home and go, "Oh yer, hello, I'm home." That was it. "Wash my clothes, make my dinner, let's go to bed." Then, goodbye – away again. That's the way it could get when you're away from home for maybe four weeks at a time. You come back and your girlfriend is there and she's very domesticated. You can't relate to it. You want to go back to the sleazy hotel rooms and sitting up to three o'clock in the morning with loads of people, smoking dope, and so on.'

'Phil was always playing the field discreetly,' says Carroll. 'At gigs he would nearly always pull. Girls were attracted to Phil and he was attracted to them. It was a given.'

'To some extent [the womanizing] is overstated,' says Frank Murray. 'Women would come up and talk to him . . . It was natural for lead singers in bands, especially one as easily recognizable as Philip. It didn't mean he had to go off with them all.'

During the inevitable Irish tour in the spring of 1973, much was made of Thin Lizzy's success in what a small piece in the *Irish Times* called 'the Great Big World Outside'. The paper's review of the band's show at the National Stadium noted their newfound dynamism, and also the change that had come over their lead singer. '[His] presentation is much improved. Philip Lynott no longer waves one leg awkwardly in the air as though looking for somewhere to put it down, maybe because the group have found their feet at last.'[8] Another piece, in *New Spotlight*, admired their 'superb light show' and mentioned the 'international acclaim' that had greeted the band since they were last back home.

They went into Tollington Park to record their third album with renewed confidence. On the heels of 'Randolph's Tango', another new song confirmed the progression in Lynott's writing. 'The Rocker' lays persuasive claim to being the first Thin Lizzy classic. From its explosive guitar riff to its roll call of tough-guy mannerisms, it's the sound of Lynott shrugging off his hippie robes. The tangible fact of having a hit seemed to encourage him to step inside a new, mythic persona, hanging with *'the boys'* in the juke joints, watching the *'chicks'*, *'looking for trouble'*.

The iconography is baseline rock and roll: sex, violence and motorbikes, although there's room for a reference to *'Teddy boy'* Carroll and his *'Rock On stall'*. What could be crude is highly effective. Henceforth, Lynott's lyricism became considerably more streamlined and character driven; emotion tended to be subordinate to building narrative atmosphere. 'He worked his way through the poetic thing, and he hadn't quite found his [style] until he hit on "The Rocker",' says Eamon Carr. And while it's possible to divine tongue-in-cheek humour in the song's heightened portrait, it presented a vision of the quintessential rock star, which Lynott would find himself increasingly striving to live up to.

Although not the hit it deserved to be when it was released, in punchy edited form, in November 1973, 'The Rocker' shored up Thin Lizzy's waning critical credibility. The sense of a creative breakthrough was confirmed on their third album, *Vagabonds of the Western World*. The record was a quantum leap. Harder and tighter, with better songs, crisper production and a cleaner mix. The growing expansiveness was affirmed by the addition of organ and Fiachra Trench's rich string arrangements.

Refining the harder rock edge of 'Mama Nature Said', 'Gonna Creep Up on You' and the full-length, full-tilt version of 'The Rocker', the title track is pounding Celtic psych-rock, with a menacing bodhrán beat, a cry of *'tura-lura-lura lura-aye'* and a reference to Synge's *Playboy of the Western World*. The song's vagabond anti-hero is a romanticized vision of Lynott's father, ambiguously depicted as an unfettered rake who roams the world seducing women without revealing his name – and is a *'pretty fine dancer, too'*. It's also an idealized mirror image of the singer, the son of a *'gypsy'* who *'gave a girl a baby boy'* and wears an *'earring in his left ear'*.

'A Song for While I'm Away' is an intimate billet-doux from a travelling musician, road-weary but leaving his love a promise of devotion on the pillow where his head never seems to be. It's a classic piece of songwriting and Lynott sings it beautifully, almost crooning, as the strings glide through the air around him. It's so tender, one almost believes him.

> *You are my life, my everything, you're all I have*
> *You are my hopes, my dreams, my world come true*
> *You're all I have*

The most emotive track on the record was 'Little Girl in Bloom', an almost pastoral reflection on a young girl and the child she carries. It's one of Lynott's finest songs, elevated by a tremendous studio performance of understated power. The opening thrum of feedback leads to a slightly off-beam bass figure, overlapping lead vocals and a soon-to-be familiar twining of electric guitars.

'Little Girl in Bloom' is an emblem for Thin Lizzy's newfound maturity and self-confidence. The eight songs on *Vagabonds of the Western World* sounded like a band shaking itself from its slumber. 'It was just a great record,' says Tauber. 'Everything about it was great: the songs, the whole Thin Lizzy ethos, and he worked so hard on the words. Philip was a great rock lyricist. He was the best lyricist that I ever worked with.'

Lynott had become even more focused in the studio since the Slade tour. 'He would push your creativity to the limit,' says Bell. 'Sometimes I would come up with an idea for one of his songs. "No, it's too jazzy." Then I'd say, "Okay, what about this?" "No, it's too bluesy." "What about this?" "No, it's too melodic." "What about this . . . ?" This would go on for about forty minutes and I'd say, "Well, for fuck's sake, that's all I know!" He'd nod and say, "Right." As if to say, "Now you've got to start playing Eric Bell." That was great because it helped me develop a style. Philip was his own talent, but we all chipped in, and he encouraged that. They were his songs, most of them, but it was still a three-piece band. It still hadn't developed into Phil Lynott and Thin Lizzy. He was firm but very, very fair.'

On 'The Hero and the Madman', he demanded that the laidback David 'Kid' Jensen record multiple takes of his spoken-word narrative. 'He could be a tough bugger to work with, but he knew what he wanted,' says Tauber. 'He wasn't vindictive. He wasn't mean, he wasn't spiteful. He just wanted things done the way he wanted them done because he had a vision. You can't really argue with that.'

The vision extended to all aspects of the record. Lynott had originally asked Tim Booth to design the artwork, but when Booth was unable to take it on, he turned to Jim Fitzpatrick, who created a remarkable space-rock sci-fi piece equally influenced by Marvel comics and ancient Celtic art.

An Irish artist working for a local advertising agency in Dublin, Fitzpatrick had made his mark in 1968 designing *Viva-Che*, the iconic red-and-black poster image of a bearded Che Guevara that has adorned T-shirts, placards and the walls of student flats ever since. In 1969 and 1970, before Lynott left for London, he was also creating magazine art and Day-Glo posters for Tara Telephone. When Lynott saw Fitzpatrick's work for Tara Telephone on the wall of a friend's Dublin flat, he was instantly impressed. 'Philip used to come around and stare at them: "Oh man, these are brilliant!"' says Eamon Carr. 'They were the closest thing we had seen to something you'd get in Haight-Ashbury or the Fillmore posters. Two years later he had Jim working on Thin Lizzy's album sleeves. Very savvy! It's a magpie business, and Philip was checking out all sorts of angles and opportunities.'

At the same time as Thin Lizzy were beginning to hit their stride, another angle presented itself. Ritchie Blackmore and Ian Paice had resolved to leave Deep Purple and start a new band with former Free vocalist Paul Rodgers. Blackmore loved 'The Rocker' and Lynott's Jimi Hendrix aura. After coming to see Thin Lizzy live he invited Lynott to be part of the band, tentatively called Baby Face.

Blackmore was unaware of Lynott's previous connection with Deep Purple. In 1972, tempted by an £1,000 offer from a German music executive called Leo Müller, Thin Lizzy had spent a day at De Lane Lea Studios recording an album of five Deep Purple covers, plus an assortment of instrumental jams, including 'Danny Boy' and 'House of the Rising Sun'. Lynott played bass but refused to sing, so they sub-contracted Elmer Fudd vocalist Benny White and the band's keyboard player Dave Lennox to complete the line-up. Released in January 1973, *Funky Junction*

Play a Tribute to Deep Purple felt ever so slightly undignified, but it was easy money. No mention of Thin Lizzy was made on the album, while the cover photograph was of a different band.

A year later, Lynott was jamming with the real thing. 'We had one rehearsal,' he later recalled. 'When it came to the recording, Paul Rodgers didn't turn up, so we put down two tracks as a three-piece.'[9]

The idea quickly fizzled out. Blackmore allowed himself to be talked back into the ranks of Deep Purple, Paul Rodgers formed Bad Company, and the recordings have never been released. Their quality and quantity is widely disputed. According to some sources, there are two or at most three scrappy, unfinished backing tracks in the Deep Purple vaults. Others claim that there are four or five very good completed songs, including a cover of Johnny Winter's 'Dying to Live'. Blackmore's view was that it all sounded like a Jimi Hendrix fan convention.

Quite where this collaboration would have left Thin Lizzy isn't clear. When news of it surfaced, Chris Morrison released a press statement maintaining that Thin Lizzy were not splitting up and that Lynott was committed to the band. Ted Carroll insists it would not have spelled the end of the group. 'It wasn't a secret,' says Carroll. 'He told us about it, but whatever way it went Phil wanted to stick with Thin Lizzy.'

The band dynamic during the making of *Vagabonds* had been good; out on the road, however, they were disintegrating. They toured the UK from late September to late October 1973 following the release of the new album, recorded a quick John Peel session, and then sailed to Germany in November for two weeks of dates. Now heavily involved as Thin Lizzy's agent, Chris O'Donnell was intent on pursuing a more aggressive booking policy. He wanted them to play hipper clubs, and encouraged Lynott to move centre stage rather than loitering out on the margins. His contributions extended to suggesting what they all might wear. 'I thought the band were starting to get more interested in how we looked rather than how we played,' says Bell. Lynott argued, very plausibly, that image was a fundamental element of success. There was a general awareness that in the background the star-making machine was cranking into gear.

'Our management, the record company and everyone got on to us, and said, "You need another hit, otherwise you're going to be a one-hit wonder,"' says Bell. 'That's when Philip really started wanting the fame and fortune. He used to say to management, "When are you going to make me rich and famous?"' He used to say that all the time. We'd had a small taste of it with "Whiskey in the Jar" . . . so Philip started getting hungry for it.'

Bell felt hollow. His professional unhappiness stretched back to the success of 'Whiskey in the Jar'. 'We were flying out to France to mime to records, and Eric just wanted to play guitar,' Lynott said. 'He couldn't understand why we had to do these things. In the end it got to him.'[10]

'I remember how miserable I was on *Top of the Pops*,' says Bell. 'As I was miming to the record I was thinking, is this it? I thought if I ever got to *Top of the Pops*, man, I would be the happiest man alive, and there I was, thinking, what's wrong?'

His girlfriend had left for Canada with their young son, and he had experienced a terrible acid trip, which had made him paranoid and almost suicidal. He was self-medicating. The drug scene around the group had become heavier. 'We were really fucking messed up,' he says. 'Philip was just getting into cocaine for the first time ever at that point, and I was drinking a lot and smoking a lot of very strong dope, all the stuff that everyone was doing anyway. We were completely wasted all the time.'

The mood deteriorated on tour in Germany. The band were presented with three engraved brandy glasses after a show. Bell smashed them all. 'Philip went mad: "What the fuck are you doing?" We drove back to our hotel, we were walking down our corridor to go to bed, and all of a sudden Philip turns around and punches me. We were both rolling on the ground in this German hotel about half three in the morning. They got the police around.' On another night, Bell asked to jam with a German rock band and, when they refused, he jumped on stage and kicked their PA over. 'The guitar player was going to annihilate me,' he says. 'One of our roadies just stopped it as he was about to plant me into the ground.'

When it came to the band's public image, three of Lynott's cardinal rules read: Always be professional. Never lose your cool. Always be in control. 'I never recall seeing him drunk,' says Jim Fitzpatrick. 'He could hold his liquor.' It was a macho point of principle that prevented him showing any empathy for Bell's predicament. 'I can't understand it to this day, because he knew what I was going through,' says Bell. 'He knew my girlfriend had left, and this, that and the other. He didn't give a fucking shite. There was no discussion about it. It was like, "Oh yeah, she's away. Right, just get on with it." Nobody wanted to know. It was, "Let's do the next show. Let's try and get more famous." I started becoming really, really paranoid. In the car, with two of my closest friends.'

Thin Lizzy's end-of-year Irish tour began at City Hall, Cork, on 20 December 1973. The escalating unhappiness, tension and clash of sensibilities reached a head in Bell's hometown, during a show at Queen's University, Belfast, on New Year's Eve. In front of friends and family, the guitarist suffered a breakdown on stage. 'He turned up at the soundcheck fairly drunk – and got drunker,' Brian Downey told me. 'When he got on stage he was *really* quite drunk. I think he realized that, because he was so drunk, he couldn't play too well, and it was his hometown, which made it worse, and so he said, "I'm off, good luck, see you later." He left us, he just walked

off the stage. We were halfway through the show and we had
to play as a two-piece. This was a pretty big old venue, Queen's
University, and he left the two of us to finish the gig.'

'They should have cancelled the gig,' says Bell. 'I couldn't even
stand, never mind play. I was just completely fucking lost. This
voice came into my head and said, "Eric, if you don't get out of
this situation you are fucked." It came to the third song and I just
got my guitar, took it off, and threw it fifteen feet up in the air.
I'll never forget it as long as I live. Turned round, kicked all my
amps off the stage and just staggered off. Collapsed underneath
the stage on some gymnasium mats and just passed out.'

Frank Murray, watching from the wings, went to investigate.
'I was asking him to go back on to finish the set. I said, "Look,
you can leave tomorrow, you can leave in the morning." I was
pleading with him. He kept going on to me about a bottle of
Guinness for some reason.'

Most of those present remember Bell returning for one
song, his guitar out of tune and his mind even more so. 'I can't
remember,' he says. 'I don't remember what happened. It's just
a blank.' He was eventually spirited away in a taxi and dumped
outside his parents' house, before being summoned to the band's
hotel the following morning. 'Philip and Brian were there, all the
roadies, and they all completely ignored me. They just looked
the other way.'

Chris Morrison called from London, and by the end of the
short conversation Bell's spell in Thin Lizzy, the band formed
under his initial impetus, was over. Bell says he left. Others who
were there say he was fired by Lynott. 'I don't think Phil had
much faith in him after that,' says Brian Downey. 'The day after
the show he called a meeting and threw a really big wobbler.
Eric was willing to come back, but Phil said, "That's it, as far as
I'm concerned he's out."'

In the press, Bell's departure was ascribed to 'nervous exhaustion', an industry euphemism which for once wasn't far from the truth. 'I think things were definitely travelling a bit too fast for him,' says Murray.

It could have ended the band. For a short while it did. In the long run, it presented an opportunity, which Lynott took by the scruff of the neck. 'They became a new group, changed their sound,' says Brian Tuite, who was still maintaining an interest from the side-lines. 'I remember saying to Philip when Brian Robertson and Scott Gorham joined, "What's with the two guitars?" Philip said, "The next time one of those cunts walks out there will be another one there. I'm not going to be caught out again." Those were his exact words.'

It was as though he'd already had a premonition that guitarists were going to be both a blessing and a curse.

10

Thin Lizzy was two, arguably three different bands held together by a name, a drummer and a singer. Its first iteration lasted from early 1970 until the first day of 1974. Following Eric Bell's departure Lynott had to build again. He very nearly opted not to bother. In the first few months of 1974 he and Brian Downey seriously contemplated returning to Ireland and setting up something new around the clubs of Dublin.

'I thought that it was time to break up,' he said in the winter of 1975. 'Lizzy was over, finished . . . I wasn't going to use the name. I really didn't give a fuck. It could have been called Joe Soap for all I cared, but everybody wanted us to keep the name so that was it . . . I don't look on Thin Lizzy as a band that's been together for five years. I look on it as a band that's been together a year and three months. Before that, there was another Thin Lizzy.'[1]

New Year's Eve was an ending, but what followed was not quite a new beginning. After cancelling two concerts, Thin Lizzy completed the remainder of the Irish tour in January using Gary Moore, who flew over to Ireland at short notice. Moore was a sufficiently gifted guitarist to cope with the lack of rehearsal. He learned some of the set, jammed the rest, and excelled on covers of things like the J. Geils Band's 'Hard Drivin' Man'.

If Lynott was personally irked by Bell's abdication, it was largely a matter of its manner and its timing. The musical ramifications could be spun into a positive. 'Philip was really philosophical about it,' says Frank Murray. 'He saw it as an opportunity. "Okay, Eric's left. Watch this. I'm going to pull Gary Moore out of my hat." We kind of knew that Gary was always there. We had a super sub.'

Moore stayed on for the band's UK tour in February and March, and for a scattering of dates in April. The new trio worked up a remarkable new song, 'Sitamoia', a derivation of the old Irish tune 'Si Do Mhaimeo' ('Wealthy Widow'). It was a pulsing Afro-Celtic hybrid, unlike anything they had written before. Lynott free-associated Gaelic speaking-in-tongues and West African vocal chants over Downey's extraordinary 6/8 drum figure, while Moore incorporated funk rhythms, power chords and jigs. He played on Thin Lizzy's final single for Decca, 'Little Darling', and on a demo recording of the weeping blues tune, 'Still in Love with You', which in both style and mood owes an enormous amount to his contribution.

There is no question that, in 1974, a settled Thin Lizzy line-up featuring Gary Moore would have been a force to be reckoned with. 'They came on stage and exploded,' says Chris O'Donnell. 'They were amazing. I said to Chris Morrison and Ted Carroll, "We could take on the world with this band." But you never got the sense that Gary was actually *in* Thin Lizzy ever. We always knew that he was fragile and there wasn't 100 per cent commitment. It was always a conduit to something else.'

Moore could be mercurial and unfathomable. 'I was a little frightened of the man that was inside Gary Moore,' says Chalkie Davies. 'I thought, there's something troubled inside you. He was very complex and quite difficult, because everything came out in the music.'

As well as an instinctive musical empathy, there was a fraternal bond and mutual respect between Lynott and Moore, but their interaction involved strategic games of power and status, which stretched back to when they had first met. Moore had made it out of Ireland first with Skid Row and was much the better musician; Lynott was the more charismatic and a superior songwriter. Both were sticklers for detail; both had their demons but where Lynott pushed his down deep, Moore's tended to be written all over his face. The top-dog sparring could turn personal. Following a concert in the north of England, this interim incarnation of Thin Lizzy stayed at the Clifton Grange Hotel. Moore was accompanied by his girlfriend of the time.

'I wouldn't ever trust Phil with my girlfriend, because he tried to get her into bed with him one night,' Moore told me. 'She was sitting on the end of the bed and he said, "Ah, come on now, get in and we'll do this and we'll do that." He was lethal like that. You couldn't leave him alone with a girl. He had two sides to him, a very soft side and a very hard side. He loved his Irish poetry and music and all that stuff, but on the other hand he could be as tough as fuck. If you went around his house and you dropped a £20 note, he would just scoop it up and that would be it.'

Shortly afterwards, Moore informed the management that he was leaving. 'Gary came to see me in April 1974,' says Ted Carroll. 'People from record companies were coming to the gigs and seeing Gary play. He said, "I don't want to sign as part of the band, I want to get my own deal. I think it would be better if I left now." We'd already recorded "Still in Love with You" down at Pebble Beach Studios in Worthing; it was one of the songs we'd been playing to record companies to show what the new band was like. It made sense for Gary, but it immediately left us in deep shit.'

'It was a very high-pressure situation,' said Moore. 'I was taking a lot of Valium, I was having panic attacks, and the band were watching me all the time. "What's wrong with you, Gary, what's wrong with you?" There was a lot of drugs around by that time. It had kicked in. I also wanted to join another band. [Drummer] Jon Hiseman was looking for musicians for his latest venture [Colosseum II], so I called him.'

With a German tour booked in May, Lynott patched together a group with two new guitarists: John Cann from Atomic Rooster, and Andy Gee, a German musician whom Lynott and Downey had met at a party. Shortly afterwards they were all on the overnight ferry to Hamburg, travelling in hope rather than expectation. 'We tried to solve the problem really quick,' said Lynott. 'We went to Germany and it was really bad. Brian Downey said one night, "Let's forget it. Let's go home." So we did.'[2]

Thin Lizzy ground to a halt in the no-man's-land between the old and the new. The makeshift line-up did not gel on stage. Off stage, Downey didn't much care for Cann, whom he regarded as starry and grand; in Thin Lizzy, at least at this point, everyone carried their own cases into the hotel. Any other expectation was liable to put noses out of joint. The shabby venues were the same ones they had played the last time they had visited Germany. The autobahn ground them down. The entire enterprise seemed suddenly aimless and dispiriting. Thin Lizzy, the ultimate road band, ended up cancelling a handful of dates, including a festival in the Netherlands, and coming home. Back in London, Downey told Ted Carroll he was leaving. 'I said, "If you leave now that's the end of it,"' says Carroll. '"Just stay until we get the band back together and then let's see what happens."'

It was an ending of sorts, all the same. With Bell and Moore leaving in quick succession, the folk-tinged, progressive blues-rock band that had its roots in the loose, vaguely bohemian milieu of late-1960s Dublin was over. The group that recorded 'The Boys Are Back in Town', 'Dancing in the Moonlight' and 'Don't Believe a Word' was a very different entity – not only in terms of personnel, but in outlook, aim, image and sensibility. 'Brand new,' says Frank Murray. 'Brand new approach, brand new style of songwriting. Brand new band.'

Certain qualities were lost in the change. There was a tenderness, a starry-eyed innocence and adventurism that did not wholly survive. In time, Lynott realized that something quite different was required. For now, the brief period spent carrying John Cann and Andy Gee clarified his vision for his new group. The idea of having two guitarists began as a belt-and-braces safeguard but, more importantly, it enabled Thin Lizzy to reproduce on stage what they were trying to do in the studio. Songs like 'Little Girl in Bloom' pointed towards a layered style that a trio could not replicate live.

'In the studio we found we were putting down overdubs of rhythm guitars and really we were writing a fourth line,' Lynott said in 1977. 'I was writing the songs as a rhythm guitarist and as [part of] a three-piece. The guitarist was approaching it as a lead guitarist would, so the rhythm line got lost. So I went for two lead guitarists that could sort of divide everything equally and have the taste to know when to lay back because the other guy's taking a solo, when to step forward, and when to do cross harmonies and get into the sort of ideas where there's two lead lines crossing, whether that be a voice and guitar or two guitars crossing. It seemed far wiser than to just have somebody that could play rhythm and one lead guitarist with a huge ego.'[3] The execution of this theory would revolutionize their studio sound, and transform them as a live band.

Having resolved to continue, in late May and into June, Downey and Lynott held auditions for guitarists at the Iroko Country Club on Haverstock Hill, west London. They hired Brian Robertson, an eighteen-year-old from the suburban sprawl of Greater Glasgow. His father was a jazz musician, and from an early age Robertson had displayed remarkable proficiency. He could read music, he studied cello and classical piano to a high level, and by his early teens he was not only an excellent guitar player, but a decent drummer. Before joining Thin Lizzy, Robertson played with Hamish Stuart in Dream Police, which went on to become the Average White Band.

Robertson had an existing connection to the band. He knew Lynott's roadie Charlie McLennan, and had joined the after-show festivities following a concert at the University of Glasgow on 9 February 1974, playing blues with Brian Downey in the hotel room. Peter Fallon, on a visit from Dublin, was sitting in on the auditions at the Iroko when Robertson was given the job. 'He played great, but I remember saying to Philip, "Are you sure you want to be with that guy?" Immediately, I thought, he's not my kind of company to tour the world with.'

'Listen, I was a fucking uppity little git, right?' says Robertson. 'Very sure of myself, except I wasn't really. I was never really that sure of myself, but I'd always come across that way, which points towards a bit of insecurity really. A few drinks and a bit of a jam brought [my aggression] to the fore, but I think Phil quite liked that. Nobody else would argue with him. It was his band, always was and always would be. He was great big black Irishman, and he sang from that position of strength.'

Robertson joined and clicked immediately. Several more days of auditions failed to find him a partner until the arrival of Scott Gorham. Raised in comfort in Glendale, west California, Gorham had spent years playing in garage groups and bar bands. By

1973 he was embroiled in petty crime and hard drugs. Finding himself at a dead end, at the age of twenty-two he left California for Britain on the advice of his brother-in-law, Bob Siebenberg, the drummer in Supertramp. Though he had cleaned up his act, his musical career remained in stasis. Gorham was playing in pubs for £12 a week and was considering returning to the States before his visa expired the following month, when a friend on the circuit, Bees Make Honey saxophonist Ruan O'Lochlainn, informed him that a band called Thin Lizzy were looking for a guitar player.

'I had never even heard of these guys,' says Gorham. 'They weren't being played or written about, so I had no chance to hear them. I walked in that day to a place called the Iroko in Hampstead, which was an African dinner club, of all things. There were all these African waiters laying out the tables, and when I first saw Phil I actually thought he was one of the waiters. I know that sounds horribly racist, but nobody had told me he was black. He turned his head, said, "Are you Scott?" and introduced himself, and all I thought was, "Wow, a black rock and roller!" That just didn't happen back in 1974.

'I was intrigued right off the bat, and after the third song I desperately wanted into this thing. I'm watching how Brian Downey is playing the drums, there's this kid on the other guitar firing out these guitar lines; he'd been there for two weeks, and acting like he'd been there for years. And I was watching this Phil guy in front of me. Even in rehearsal he was already taking command. He dominated right from the moment I met him. When Phil spoke, the two Brians looked up and paid attention.'

Lynott called late that night to offer him a place in the band. Gorham delivered when it came to image. Tall, slender and laid-back, he was quintessentially American, with fine, straight hair falling down to his sternum. Though his playing was not as technically proficient or as forceful as Robertson's, he possessed a fluid and distinctive guitar style.

The first appearance of what most observers would regard as the classic Thin Lizzy line-up took place early in July 1974, in the Lafayette club in Wolverhampton. A handful of people witnessed the show. Within ten days they were touring Ireland, a visit deliberately intended as both a trial and a baptism. With a Scotsman and an American in the band, Thin Lizzy were now an international group, but Ireland would always be the ultimate proving ground.

While back in Dublin, Lynott took receipt of a copy of his first book. *Songs for While I'm Away* was a compendium of lyrics to twenty-one Thin Lizzy compositions, plus an unpublished song-poem. 'A Holy Encounter' recounted a street meeting with two friends in which Lynott, seemingly reflecting on the masks he and we all wear in public, '*gave them my one-man show*'.

There is a lovely, natural photograph taken by Tom Collins on the day the first copies of the book arrived from the printer. Lynott is sitting in Neary's between Peter Fallon and Jim Fitzpatrick, sharing a drink and a joke. 'It was a moment of real excitement,' says Fallon. 'There was another little swagger to his step.'

Songs for While I'm Away was published on Lynott's twenty-fifth birthday, less than five years after he had first summoned up the courage to perform his own work publicly at the Arts Society at Trinity College. The simple, stylish line illustrations were provided by Fitzpatrick and Tim Booth, while the short introduction was written by Fallon, who in 1970 had set up the Gallery Press in Dublin. By 1974 the imprint had already published dozens of elegantly designed volumes of poetry, and would later put out work by such vital and eminent Irish voices as Brian Friel, Seamus Heaney and Paul Muldoon, as well as publishing Fallon's own verse.

Lynott had asked Fallon to publish his lyrics in Gallery Press, but his friend declined. His reasons for doing so lie at the heart of any serious discussion of Lynott's merits and status as a writer.

'These were the times when Bob Dylan wasn't just a songwriter, he was "a poet",' says Fallon. 'Every second person who was good was "a poet". The need for people of that generation of songwriters to place themselves in the realm of poetry was a reaction against Tin Pan Alley and the pop single . . .

'Creative people have a shared currency, and in our early hopes and ambitions and aspirations there was common ground between us [as poets] and Philip. I understood his impulse to be called a poet, but I took the position, which I maintain, that poetry is a different thing. What's wrong with being known as a really good songwriter? So I said to Philip, "I'm not going to publish it, but I can help you with it." I think he understood that. There was no resentment because he knew he couldn't have done it on his own . . . It really was a question of whittling it into shape from a scrappy mess of papers. He gave me everything – things like spelling weren't his forte – and I put into some kind of shape a little book. I came up with the name for it. I wrote a little introduction, which was about some of that era. He was still very excited about it. He decided his record company or management would pay for it.'

Songs for While I'm Away was self-published by Pippen Publishers (a literary twist on the name of Lynott's music publishing company, Pippin) in an initial print run of 1,000 copies: 200 signed hardbacks and 800 paperbacks. It was dedicated to his father.

For Lynott to have his work published in Gallery Press would have classified it unambiguously as literature, a weight the words would struggle to bear. He is still often referred to, perhaps rather casually and usually with good intent, as a 'poet'. Such a description requires context. It is best regarded as an acknowledgement of his status as a popular songwriter who truly cared about words and thought deeply about how he used them.

There was an innate refinement to Lynott's thought process, to his imagination and expressive instincts, which was evident not just in the way he shaped words and phrases, but in his intelligence, his organizational skills, his wit and leadership qualities. These were natural gifts which he exploited, but his songs also draw from an intellectual curiosity not always evident in the non-negotiable trappings of being a rock star.

For a man who left school at fifteen with little to show for it, Lynott was well – and widely – read. 'I don't remember him with his nose in anything flippant,' says Chalkie Davies. In interviews Lynott not only dropped the names of Albert Camus and Jean-Paul Sartre, he pondered the validity of their philosophical tenets in his natural saloon-bar register. 'I am normal, everybody else is different,' he told interviewer Chris Salewicz in 1977. 'I know it's an existentialist point of view: that I am the centre of the world. I was into that for a long time. Figuring I was Number One, and if I die the world ends. I was into Sartre and his pals for a long, long time. I believed what they wrote was correct. Now I'm not so sure.'[4]

'I remember the two of us went to see a production of [John Osborne's] Look Back in Anger at Trinity College, which had a big effect on him,' says Frank Murray. 'He liked Sherlock Holmes, he liked The Great Gatsby.' On moving to Kew in 1978, Lynott filled his shelves with literature: history, poetry, science fiction, biography. Next to the jukebox sat a framed picture of James Joyce, a juxtaposition that conveyed a certain crude but neat symbolism.

On tour, even when life got high and heady, he was rarely without a book. 'Phil did a lot of reading,' says Scott Gorham. 'He never liked to give the impression that he was a bookie kind of guy, but he was. He was a huge history buff, and not just with Ireland, but America and different parts of Europe. On our very first tour of Ireland he dragged me out of the hotel and gave me a history lesson of Dublin . . . He went out of his way to find out things, he was that kind of person.' On downtime in hotels, while the band were watching sports on television, he would invariably be tuned into a documentary.

Just as often, Lynott would absorb information and inspiration second-hand, without paying much heed to the source. 'If I'd read a book and I told him the story and he gleaned some information from it, he'd be really happy with that,' says Frank Murray. 'He wouldn't say, "I must go out and buy that book." He'd say, "That's a great story." He loved the idea of storytelling.'

He liked to learn and he liked – to a point – to be challenged. He could stay up through the night talking politics, cheerfully acknowledging his own contradictions. 'My heart leans to the left,' he'd say, 'But the hand in my pocket leans to the right.'[5] He was a socialist in the broader view: egalitarian in his dealings with people, a natural ally to the underdog, eternally a backer of David over Goliath.

During the ascendancy and prime of Thin Lizzy, Lynott made a concerted effort to do more than the necessary required, even as he moved from wordy introspection to a 'street-opera' vernacular that found beauty in the urban hustle, a carnival of cinematic characters. His later style became steadily tougher and leaner, until eventually Lynott's lyrics betrayed the threadbare amount of time and effort he was applying to them, but throughout the 1970s in the vast majority of his songs a vivid phrase or startling image will leap out. The line in 'Dancing in the Moonlight' about getting *'chocolate stains on my pants'*, both innocent and suggestive, has no need to be there other than to lend a tight, swinging pop song an extra twist of individuality.

Such details mattered to him. He was possessive of his status as the band's lyricist. When the new four-piece Thin Lizzy came into being, says Scott Gorham, 'Phil threw down right at the beginning that he was going to do the lyrics. Nobody but him. So nobody actually even tried . . . He couldn't suffer dumb lyrics. He had to sing things he wrote and believed in.'

It is rich and superior rock lyricism, but it is not poetry as poetry is widely understood, particularly when cut loose from the animating strut of the music and the marvellous textural gradations of Lynott's voice, which possessed a poetry all of its own. His great phrasing guru was Van Morrison, from whom he also learned the value of keeping the listener on their toes. Singing *'gigolo'* with a hard *'g'* sound; the oddly garbled *'if it means to justify the ends'* in 'Dancing in the Moonlight'. You were never quite sure if these eccentricities were deliberate or not, but they worked.

Singing, he was capable of shading in the spaces between the words with an entire spectrum of implied meaning. Naked on the page, stark black on unforgiving white, the same lines appear diminished. 'They are lyrics,' says Tim Booth. 'They have a tempo and a time and a way they are written. They're not really written as poetry.' They are, perhaps, closer to the ballad tradition than the poetic one. They are almost always conceived to be sung.

'His initial works I felt were superb,' says Jim Fitzpatrick. 'As he got busier with Thin Lizzy I felt his writing style deteriorated poetically, [though] as a rock lyric writer he improved hugely. "The Boys Are Back in Town" and "The Rocker" are great, but there were periods [before that] when he was a poetic lyricist, with things like "Little Girl in Bloom" and "Dublin".'

In the long run, *Songs for While I'm Away* caused some discord between Lynott and Peter Fallon, who had agreed to work on it for free. 'Philip did always say that if it made money I would get something. I thought, fine, it doesn't matter. Years later he told me that it had sold 100,000 copies – which I didn't believe and I don't believe – but he kind of waved it at me in a different tone. Like, "It's sold 100,000 copies and you're still not getting anything." I thought, you don't need to do this. It was unpleasant . . . It shifted the chemistry between us.'

He and Fallon were never quite so close again, although they did enjoy an impromptu rapprochement in the year before Lynott died. 'We bumped into each other in the Bailey one night,' says Fallon. 'He said he wasn't using [drugs] anymore. I wasn't convinced, but he was clear enough, and suddenly, whatever distance and awkwardness there might have been just dissolved. We got rid of all that shit. There was a hug, and I felt pleased about that.'

As the singer and lead songwriter in a struggling band with three misfiring albums to their name, clearly the impulse to create a book was not commercial, nor was it to satiate public demand. Published on his birthday, *Songs for While I'm Away* was conceived primarily as a present to himself; it afforded Lynott a shot at a different kind of posterity. He bragged in an interview in 1976 that in two years the book had sold 10,000 (not 100,000) copies. 'I'm incredibly proud of that,' he said. 'I'm more proud of that than, say, I was when ['The Boys Are Back in Town'] got into the charts. I can get the [live] audience, but it's for the moment . . . On record – and with the pen – it's almost for all time. Really a lot more thought has to go into it.'[6]

He published a second volume of lyrics, *Philip*, in 1977, this time with an introduction by John Peel, and collected both titles together in a single volume in 1980, adding a handful of other pieces. More intriguingly, in the late 1970s and again in the early 1980s, he revealed that he was writing prose.

'I started about six months ago to write ten short stories,' he said in 1977. 'Basically they were going to be about the business.

But as opposed to "how I made it in the business" kinds of stories, I was just gonna write about it in an almost – not as good, obviously – but almost like Scott Fitzgerald did. Write about it like, "I happened to be very popular at the time and I mixed with a crowd of other people that was very popular at the time and this is what went on." Like one story would be about the day in the life of a roadie. Or maybe the chick that's followed this guy all the time and goes to the concerts and she gets backstage and meets him, and he makes a pass as her and what does she do? I was gonna write stories like that, about ten of them, and use the language we use today. So as time goes on it will become a period piece. I've done about four chapters of two stories and stopped because there was something else to do. It was a good idea at the time.'[7]

Later, he claimed he had developed ideas for thirteen stories. As late as 1984, he was still talking up the project on television, although the idea did not appear to have developed much beyond its original concept. From 1977 onwards, Lynott increasingly found himself with less time and finally less inclination to devote to lyrics, poetry or prose. He never stopped caring about words, but he was not under any illusions. Poetry? He had read enough of the real thing to recognize that he belonged among the ranks of talented aspirants. 'Poet . . . seems like a whole career,' he said. 'I work in lyrics . . . but poetry in that? Yes, it means a lot to me.'[8] Or, to put it another way: 'If I make it as a poet, I'm a poet. When we die a death, I'm only the bass-player.'[9]

The landscape of Lynott's professional life changed dramatically in 1974. During the first Irish tour with the new line-up, Ted Carroll stood down as Thin Lizzy manager, handing over to Chris O'Donnell and leaving the band in control of 'The Two Chrises' (O'Donnell and Morrison), as they are known by all, for the remainder of their lifespan. Carroll wanted to devote himself to his Rock On store, but he also saw trouble on the horizon.

'As soon as Gary Moore said he was leaving, I had told Chris [Morrison], "Look, I'm out of here. We're always going to have problems with Phil and lead guitarists. I want to get out but I'll stay until everything is sorted." That's what we did. I came to Ireland and saw them play in Ballybunion. I was committed to leaving at this stage, but when I saw them play that night I thought, Hmm, am I making a mistake? They were great, but I had made my mind up. The next day we drove to Galway and Phil came with me in the car, separately from the band, and I told him that I was leaving. He was okay with that. He was surprised, but I told him he still had the same team, and it will be fine.'

Carroll left Thin Lizzy with a parting gift of a new record contract. The path from a disinterested Decca to their new home at Phonogram had not been easy. They had been turned down by Polygram and CBS. RCA offered terms without any advance payment. They came close to signing to Island but a deal had foundered on a general lack of support from within the company. Decca had made a derisory offer to renew their relationship, only to withdraw it when the band dithered. 'We were getting pretty desperate,' says Carroll.

Late in the day, chance intervened. Phonogram's Nigel Grainge was a frequent customer at Rock On. Carroll mentioned in the shop one day that Thin Lizzy were looking for a deal, and within a matter of weeks Phonogram had offered a contract. 'I knew who they were,' says Grainge. 'I wasn't a total fan, but I knew they were a really good live band. They'd had their top-ten record with Decca, but they weren't stars in any way. They sent down a demo tape of two songs, and one was absolutely amazing. That was "Still in Love with You".'

Grainge was particularly moved by the guitar solo. 'We told Nigel Grainge it was the two new guitarists in the band,' Lynott recalled. 'It wasn't, it was Gary Moore.'[10] Grainge didn't discover the truth until years later.

It was do or die. Thin Lizzy were £30,000 in debt. Chris Morrison had to borrow £250 from the bank to cover the expenses for their showcase gig for Phonogram at a broiling Marquee on 9 July 1974. It was so hot that night all the guitars went out of tune, but they played well enough to confirm the deal, even if the advance for a two-album contract only cleared what they owed. 'It was a ridiculously low-budget deal,' says Grainge. 'They ran out of money straight away, so we had to renegotiate immediately.' Thin Lizzy Mk II had barely become accustomed to each other when Phonogram put them in the studio to record a new album.

The arc of Lynott's relationship with Gale Barber can be measured in song. If 'Look What the Wind Blew In' captures the rush, trepidation and wonder of its beginnings, the claustrophobic, bleakly beautiful 'Still in Love with You' encapsulates its sour times and protracted end. 'Philip was a man of two personalities,' says Chris O'Donnell. 'Once inside the flat with Gale, he was incredibly jealous and very guarded about his relationship with her. Then he would walk out the door and put on this swaggering, main-man persona and embrace the lifestyle that goes with that. Chicks in every town, which according to him was fine because that came with the gig. Then he'd go home to Gale and say, "But we're in a relationship!"'

When he was away from London he would sleep with other women. Indeed, he did not always have to be away. Yet the thought that Barber might be unfaithful drove him to distraction. He would assign friends to monitor her movements. While on tour, Lynott would telephone to interrogate her about her whereabouts at specific times. He would say he had called her at nine o'clock last night – why wasn't she there? What had she been doing? And with whom? 'It got to the stage where I thought, I'm going mad, because I was there and the phone didn't ring,' said Barber.[11]

The scenes between them became increasingly ugly. There had been an incident on holiday in Ibiza in 1973, where he and Gale, Philomena and Dennis Keeley had accompanied Frank Murray and his wife Ferga on their honeymoon. Lynott had been best man. One night he discovered that Barber had been dancing – by herself – and lashed out at her.

He claimed that he wanted a child – a boy, always a boy – and marriage, but it was a romantic idyll that bore scant relation to the reality. Nothing in the way he behaved suggested he was ready for that level of commitment. The atmosphere around him was routinely chaotic. One night at Welbeck Mansions a woman turned up on the doorstep holding a new-born baby. She claimed Lynott was the father and was threatening to throw the child onto the marble floor. 'When he was born,' she said, 'I saw a blue light.' Jim Fitzpatrick was staying at the apartment at the time and asked her to leave. The woman jammed her foot between the door and the frame. Lynott came out in his underwear. During the inevitable commotion, the police were called. Prior to their arrival, Lynott threw his stash of dope from the window, no small sacrifice as 'we were living on beans on toast,' says Fitzpatrick. 'We were all taken to the station and then released, and never heard another word about it.'

The woman had claimed that the child was conceived on a ferry – which, as Fitzpatrick notes drily, 'was not beyond the realms of possibility' – but Lynott denied knowing her, never mind being the father of her child. 'That baby was not my baby,' he told Fitzpatrick. 'I don't know that girl from Adam.' Similar scenes were repeated while he was away. Barber also felt that he was surrounded by people who weren't prepared to offer him the unvarnished truth when he needed to hear it. 'Gale knew Philip and understood him better than most people,' says Frank Murray. 'She was a no-bullshitter. Philip at times could be full of bullshit.'

'I talked to her once in the Black Lion in West Hampstead for hours, and she was really upset because she felt Philip was drifting away from her,' says Jim Fitzpatrick. 'There were other women coming in and out. She knew deep down it couldn't work.'

While Thin Lizzy were playing in Germany, Lynott called home to Welbeck Mansions and asked his girlfriend to be gone when he returned. His friends believe that it was a bluff he did not expect Barber to act on. 'She was having none of it, and split up with him,' says O'Donnell. 'She was independent, she wouldn't put up with any of that nonsense. He'd sing "Still in Love with You" about her – like, I'll never get over you – but the reality was he sought fame more than a loving relationship with Gale.'

'He was very insecure,' she recalled later. 'The truth is that he was deep. And he was complicated. There was a big divide between his public and private selves.'[12]

Barber continued to work in West Hampstead, and after the fallout subsided she and Lynott remained in touch. 'That relationship took a long time to end,' says Chris Morrison. 'It seemed to go on past its termination for some considerable time; they would meet up and see each other.' When Lynott married Caroline Crowther in 1980, contact ceased until shortly before he died.

Philomena had always hoped her son would marry Barber, and never quite seemed to accept that he hadn't. Lynott, typically, did not discuss it. After she left Welbeck Mansions, 'Gale's name was mentioned occasionally and quietly,' remembers Chalkie Davies.

'I don't think Phil ever mentioned it, but Frank and I talked about it. Hearts were broken and it was just never discussed. You didn't mention it because you didn't want to upset him.'

His response was to swear off any serious attachment and throw himself into an even more compulsive phase of woman-izing. For the next two years, Welbeck Mansions became the realm of the bachelor. Frank Murray lived there, as did Brian Robertson, Charlie McLennan and many others. There are few among Lynott's group of friends and acquaintances who didn't cohabit with him at one time or another. He did not easily switch into domestic mode.

'Welbeck Mansions was a funny place,' says Murray. 'There were a lot of people there, people who would come over from Dublin and sleep on the sofa for a few nights. There was no real shopping or domestic routine. Philip was really basic in his desires. He liked bacon and egg in the morning. He'd get really pissed off if he went to the fridge and the last piece of bacon was gone. You'd hear him screaming from the kitchen. He liked steak and chips. Beans on toast. I don't recall him cooking meals. He might make you a cup of coffee or a glass of wine. He'd tidy up occasionally.'

'He was never domestic, no,' says Brian Robertson. 'He always had Big Charlie or somebody else there, and he would get them to go to the fish and chip shop. He'd eat half and leave the rest, and get himself a bottle. We had some fine old times, though we argued a lot.' An air of transience hung over it all. Thin Lizzy producer John Alcock remembers 'the place being devoid of any furniture. It was piles of tapes and cassettes and shit all over the floor.' As usual, Lynott was rarely there. As he sang in 'Sweet Marie', in one of his simpler, elegant and truest couplets: *'My home is where my heart is, and my heart is not at home'.*

* * *

Thin Lizzy spent the next year learning how to be the band they wanted to be. Part of the process involved the two new arrivals working out how Lynott ticked.

'Phil was a guy of multiple personalities,' says Scott Gorham. 'He *was* that hard guy from the songs. You didn't say the wrong thing to him at the wrong time. Nobody did. If you were to say anything derogatory to him about Ireland, that was fighting talk. He would not take any shit from anybody about the whole Irish thing. He could be the hard man when it suited him, and wild. He was out every night raising hell. That was the nature of the beast. He was the one who taught me the basic rules of going out at night. I don't think he had any restrictions whatsoever. On the other side of it, he was a real gentle kind of guy too.'

While Thin Lizzy were still in the process of establishing their identity and orientation, they made two records. *Nightlife*, released on 8 November 1974, and *Fighting*, released on 12 September 1975, are half-formed place markers. Produced by Ron Nevison, an American who had worked with Bad Company and the Who, *Nightlife* is a tepid record, the fussy, layered production largely neutering the band's already tentative sense of self. It's a provisional and uncertain work. Phonogram heard the uneven mix of under-powered blues, saccharine ballads, aimless instrumentals and misfiring Sham-rockers and shrugged. Aside from 'Still in Love with You', which became a career-long concert highlight, '*Nightlife* was a pretty mediocre record,' says Nigel Grainge. 'There was no singles material on it, nothing that would take them beyond where they were at the time. We did nothing with it.'

Fighting swung in the other direction. It was an equally self-conscious record in many ways, but stronger and more confident. Much of that assurance stemmed from the six-week US tour Thin Lizzy had undertaken shortly before it was recorded, supporting

Bachman–Turner Overdrive in March 1975. If watching Slade had forced Lynott to reassess his stage craft, then this was a challenge on a far greater scale. Playing arenas and stadiums with capacities rising to 20,000, bottom of a three-act bill which included Bob Seger, Thin Lizzy came of age as a live band. 'The impact on Phil was huge,' says Gorham. 'He couldn't wait to get out there. We hadn't sold any records, but we were on this big tour, playing these arenas, and it hit Phil in a big way.'

The Bachman–Turner Overdrive/Thin Lizzy bill transferred to British venues throughout April and May. By the time prospective producer John Alcock saw the band for the first time later in 1975, he was struck not by the songs – which he felt were average and tended to merge into a homogenized sonic soup – but by the command the lead singer had over the crowd.

'He did that crouch, splitting the legs, and he had a black Fender Precision bass with a mirrored pick-guard on it,' says Alcock. 'He did the thing that every rock band since has done, where you will see the guitar player with the instrument between his legs, pointing it like a machine gun. Because Phil was tall and skinny, it emphasized the look. He was prowling around the front of the stage, pointing this thing like a weapon. I thought, this guy is a rock star. I was very impressed, straight off the bat.'

Lynott was profoundly affected by his first visit to the States. The country that had played such a formative role in shaping his imagination through its popular culture cast an even more seductive spell up close. In Los Angeles, he sought out 77 Sunset Strip, the address which lent its name to the comedy-detective TV series Lynott had loved as a teenager. He went there looking for Kookie Kookson, the show's fictional star, and instead found Dino's Lodge, the Hollywood club named after Dean Martin.

Dino's quickly found its way into a song. Many of America's clubs, bars and restaurants seemed unfathomably exotic: Barney's Beanery, the Rainbow Bar & Grill, the Manhattan Deli, the Troubadour and the Whiskey A Go Go. He immersed himself in the crackling energy of the Chicago blues clubs, relished the blaring Detroit street noise, savoured the cotton-wool heat of the South. The clothes, the buildings, the food, the language, the brazenly upfront women. For six weeks he let it wash over him, recording it all in his notebooks.

There is a distinct whiff of America on *Fighting*. The opening cover of Bob Seger's 'Rosalie' was uncomplicated FM rock, purpose-built for cruising along the freeway. 'He heard it and immediately said, "We could do that,"' says Chris O'Donnell. 'He knew they could take that song and make it their own, and that it contained the seed of something new for them.'

The album has its fair share of dollars and diners, but more significant was Lynott's decision to consciously shape his writing to accentuate his more assertive stage persona. Watching Thin Lizzy's show at London's Roundhouse on 1 June 1975, Chris O'Donnell recognized that Lynott's confident, increasingly theatrical and unashamedly masculine showmanship was a potent weapon. Their manager 'realized that whenever Phil's aggression came through the crowd went wild, yet whenever he trailed off into his more sentimental moments, the audience didn't respond as well. After the show I had a long chat with Philip and I encouraged him to concentrate more on the macho side of his image, because I could see that's what the fans wanted from him.'[13]

Thin Lizzy became a hard-rock band through an act of calculated careerism. 'We knew that we could write soft songs and record them, but we took the decision to unify the whole image, to put the stage and recording image as one identifiable thing,' said Lynott. 'That's the way we planned it. Because the stage act was so live and so raunchy, and we were only doing one slow song, we decided that we'd only put one slow song on an album. We knew we had to make a rock and roll album to make it.'[14]

From the ludicrous cover image – which Lynott loathed – of the band sneering on a building site with their singer baring his puffed-out chest, to the flashes of coiled rock and roll within, *Fighting* reimagined what Thin Lizzy could be. It is a flawed and partial portrait, one which loses momentum towards the end, partly because the songwriting weakens and the music does not punch as hard as the tough boys on the cover would have us believe. Lynott had opted to produce the record himself and he fluffed it, failing to draw out the live power of the band. 'I thought I was experienced enough to handle it,' he said. 'Little did I know.'[15] But the album staked out a path to follow. Thin Lizzy's previous melange of styles confused people. *Fighting* was intended to cohere, if nothing else, and on that level it just about succeeded.

To this end, Lynott proved amenable to compromise. His original idea of a cover featuring close-ups of the four band members bruised and bloodied was shot but rejected by the record company, so he acceded to Mick Rock's 'indescribably bad' alternative. When Thin Lizzy delivered the original album to Phonogram, the band were told it simply wasn't good enough and they would have to record four more songs. Lynott nodded icily. 'He didn't pick me up by the scruff of the neck,' says Nigel Grainge. 'He just said, "What are we going to do?" He wasn't big time in any way. To their credit they went back in, and came back with "King's Vengeance" and a couple of others. The resulting album was much better than the last one. It broke them open and continued on the up. At that stage the band really started to get serious. Live they were going down really well, they had been to the States, and everybody was that much more serious about their career.'

'Really, *Fighting* was the first album where we had a bit of direction,' says Brian Robertson. 'Still hadn't quite clicked, but it was headed [somewhere].'

The songs of vengeance, violence, suicide and fierce independence heralded a burgeoning creative understanding between Lynott, Robertson and Scott Gorham. 'A lot of times he would bring in a chorus and a melody,' says Gorham. 'I would suggest a bridge or a middle eight and we'd go from there. Or I'd bring in a riff and he'd say, rather shyly, "Do you want me to write a lyric to that?" Well, yes, please, Phil! It worked in different ways. A lot of times he had the whole thing done, and your only job was to put on lead guitar or figure out harmony lines to weave in and out of chord patterns or lyrics. He had a rudimentary understanding of the guitar, and he was able to pound down the chords at least enough for me or Brian Robertson to get a sense of where it was going and make some judgements along the way.'

Fighting also marked the first time on record that using two guitar players in tandem started to pay off. The Allman Brothers Band and Wishbone Ash had pioneered a similar close-knitted double harmony style, but Thin Lizzy would mould it into something even more distinctive. 'The two guys were so different,' says Downey. 'Brian was from Scotland and was based on the British blues sound, where Scott was American and into the US West Coast sound. Totally different, but perfect matches in the long run.'

Their growing empathy is particularly evident, if still embryonic, on 'For Those Who Love to Live', 'Freedom Song' and 'Wild One'. 'It was really an accident,' says Scott Gorham.

'Brian was out in the studio doing a take, and the engineer left a delay on his guitar, a millisecond, so he was harmonizing with himself. We thought it was really cool, so we had Brian go out and do his original line, and I went out and put the harmony to it. We kept doing it on other songs, although we weren't thinking about it as a Thin Lizzy sound until we read it in the paper, where the reviewer talked about that "patented twin guitar harmony Thin Lizzy sound". I called Brian and said, "Hey man, we've got a sound!"'

Fighting was not a commercial success. It reached number sixty in the UK album chart and sold something in the region of 20,000 copies in the aftermath of its release, and Scott Gorham still regards the album and *Nightlife* as 'two humongous failures'. Yet it consolidated the breakthrough which everyone sensed was happening on stage, and increased the word-of-mouth acclaim around the band.

When they toured the UK on their Rocktober series of dates in September and October 1975, Thin Lizzy were headlining venues that included the Newcastle City Hall and Manchester Free Trade Hall. At the latter, Lynott walked on stage to be met by a crowd standing virtually in silence. He plugged in his bass, peered into the darkness, and asked, 'Are you out there?'

'It was the first time he had ever said that, and there was this unbelievable roar,' says Chris O'Donnell. 'It kind of threw him a bit. We did the set and went back to his mother's hotel, and he said, "What do you think that was about?" I told him, "The audience want you to take them somewhere. Most of them are boys. You're a gang, and they've decided you are the gang leader. They've given you permission to do that."'

As the headlining act, Thin Lizzy were now playing to audiences who had paid their pound specifically to see the band. They had found their fan base. The thought emboldened Lynott, who grew into the role of Master of Ceremonies. The cry of 'Are you out there?' soon became the ritual call of every Thin Lizzy show, akin to a general summoning his army. He would clench his fist and shake it at the crowd. He asked for their 'helping hands'. He recognized that, framed correctly, the smallest gesture – a raised finger, a twist of his wrist – could make an enormous impact, even right up in the dress circle.

In December they returned to Dublin and sold all 2,500 tickets at the National Stadium, in a concert recorded for television broadcast on RTÉ. The crowd picked up on the aggression of a set that opened with 'Fighting My Way Back' and included 'It's Only Money', 'Suicide', 'The Rocker' and 'Sha La La' by half-tearing the place to pieces. As though engaging in an act of contrition, Lynott then dedicated an epic 'Still in Love with You' to his mother in the crowd.

In a landmark venue situated within walking distance of Leighlin Road, he had irrefutably arrived as a hometown hero. Yet when John Alcock caught up with Thin Lizzy only a few days later on a rainy night in Bracknell, observing the band with a view to producing their next record, his perception was of a group 'that was always around but never really did much. They were a live band, I didn't look upon them as a recording band. Lizzy was always on the road. You opened up the back of *Melody Maker*, where you had page after page of live gigs, and Thin Lizzy was always there, playing all over England, Scotland and Ireland.'

Within the industry, they were still regarded as hardy road-warriors that had fluked a hit with an old Irish pub tune, and were gamely plugging away on the back of it almost three years later.

For that to change, they required a song to match their show.

11

'The Boys Are Back in Town' is the quintessential example of Philip Lynott's ability to transform a blurred Friday night into a showreel of romanticized episodes of enduring clarity. The craft is deceptive. At first hearing, it sounds like verbatim saloon-bar reportage; off-the-cuff, even. Thin Lizzy's most beloved song appears effortless and unforced in the way that all the best conversations do, but its author sweated over every word.

Lynott was rarely without his bag containing notebooks and loose sheaves of paper scrawled with titles, verses, random words and phrases. Often these were recycled. Many early or unreleased versions of Thin Lizzy songs feature lines and ideas that would end up, years later, in a completely different song. In concert, the band would frequently add a third verse to 'Still in Love with You' so that Lynott could road-test new lyrical riffs. Some of these improvisations ended up in 'Sweet Marie' and 'Don't Believe a Word'. Drummer Mark Nauseef, who worked frequently with esoteric jazz artists, electronic experimenters and Indian musicians, rates Lynott as 'an astounding improviser' of words and melodies. 'I don't mean he was just a good jammer, it was like a high-level jazz player improvising on his instrument. He would just take a fragment, maybe even just a word, and run with it. Every time he did it, it would be based on that one motif, but he would build on it.'

'He seemed to have this ability to really pull it out and hone it when it came time to get the job done,' says Scott Gorham. 'I can still see him with his headphones on in the vocal booth – singing a line, playing it back, bending over listening to it – and saying, "All right, let me try it this way", and coming out with a completely different line.'

In common with several other tracks on the *Jailbreak* album, 'The Boys Are Back in Town' went through a series of these semi-extemporized evolutions. Brian Robertson remembers when it was called 'Here in Dallas'. There was another early version called 'G. I. Joe is Back', inspired by the long-running comic-strip hero and action figure G. I. Joe. 'It had the same chord pattern,' says Scott Gorham, 'but it was an anti-war lyric which he quickly dumped for the Friday-night good time thing.' The almost finished version of the song was called 'The Kid Is Back', a longer variant with a different guitar melody towards the end and a slightly different lyric. Lynott knew 'kid' wasn't right. The song simply didn't work until it was switched to 'boys'.

Representations of several aspects of Lynott's own life, and his preferred way of seeing himself, are hard-wired into 'The Boys Are Back in Town'. Written by a man who had by now been a working musician for half his life, it might be the gold-standard portrayal of a touring rock band and its entourage as the modern-day Viking horde.

This was absolutely the atmosphere Thin Lizzy cultivated publicly in the latter half of the 1970s, a volatile mix of fantasy and fact. The legend describes a band and crew sharing the bond of family, and closing ranks as an army. There was no hierarchy. Hotel rooms were open to all, invitations were extended whole-sale and everyone did everything together: drinking, drugging, fucking and especially fighting. It was the domain of the male. Girlfriends and wives were not permitted on tour. They operated as a fiercely close-knit unit, which rolled from town to town defending individual and collective honour in the manner of modern-day musketeers.

'Before I joined that band I'd been in maybe two fights in my whole life,' says Scott Gorham. 'Shit, I got in two fights in the first month in Lizzy. It was a whole attitude that I wasn't quite used to: "This is our game and we're going to stand up and defend it." I had to hold up my end. Most of the time it wasn't down to Phil. It was mostly that the fastest gun in town, out with his girlfriend, wanted to make an impression. Things got stupidly out of hand at times.'

On some primal level, this is how we want every rock and roll band to behave, and at times Thin Lizzy lived up to their billing. At other times, not so much. 'There are a lot of myths,' says Chris O'Donnell. 'There were two fights in the entire fourteen years. After a gig they generally went back to the hotel bar. Drink. Bed. Phil was very private. He'd meet a girl, go back with her to his room, set up his little stereo – and you'd see him next morning at breakfast. We were working.' Often the source of pleasure was disarmingly innocent, such as the warm glow of satisfaction felt by council-estate kids who suddenly realize they're being paid to sit by a hotel pool in California on a Tuesday afternoon while the world toils around them.

The truth runs through both depictions of Thin Lizzy on the road, but 'The Boys Are Back in Town' celebrates the brash, brawling, myth-making part. It captured the gung-ho spirit that enabled the group to get to this point, even as it imagined a new, more muscular identity for them to step inside. As their horizons expanded to encompass territories from Toledo and Tokyo, the song was a potent piece of weaponry to call upon every night.

Both a song of experience and a piece of acute observation, it is, in part, a reflection of the camaraderie the young Lynott felt making his mark in Crumlin, Walkinstown and Clontarf. It also conveys the excitement generated by the returning prodigal on his later visits back to Dublin. 'No matter where he was in the world, he came straight from the airport into the Bailey for his pint of Smithwick's,' says Tom Collins. 'He was interested in finding out what had been happening in Dublin, then he would hold court, then he had to go and see the gran.'

The Quality Street Gang are in the mix, happily exaggerating their exploits in the Biz and Deno's, while the entire song is a celebration of America, Thin Lizzy's new frontier. Dino's Lodge gets a name-check, but the depiction of the United States as one eternal Downtown was inspired by the seedy glamour of the Rainbow Bar & Grill on Sunset Boulevard, a lawless nation state which had seemingly declared every night a long weekend.

What elevates 'The Boys Are Back in Town' to art is Lynott's understanding that the greatest, most enduring legends aren't created in the doing, but in the retelling. In urging his audience to remember *'that time down at Johnny's place'* and *'that chick that used to dance a lot'*, he not only makes it a communal experience, he embellishes and layers, heightening their exploits to the realm of folklore. It is a song about storytelling as much as it is a song telling a story. It's a trick familiar from the great works of Celtic history, but also from long days and nights spent spinning yarns in pubs, cars and dingy dressing rooms.

It is brilliantly conceived and immensely powerful. Has any rock writer better captured the glorious ache of anticipation – of the night to come, of the loves to be loved, of the endless summer stretched out like a benediction – than in the final verse?

The jukebox in the corner blasting out my favourite song
The nights are getting warmer, it won't be long
It won't be long till summer comes
Now that the boys are here again

None of which would matter much if the music failed to play its crucial supporting role. It is a deceptively complex kind of anthem. Brian Downey's snappy shuffle keeps the whole thing swinging, while the crunching power chords have an unorthodox, almost jazzy *joie de vivre*.

'Basically Phil came in with the bones,' says Brian Robertson. 'In "The Boys Are Back . . ." all those fancy minors and diminished chords, I put them in there. The harmonies. The bridge. I did that. He was a great lyricist, nobody can touch him on that, but when it came to the arrangements, [other] people put so much into them, and it should have been acknowledged. I'm not taking anything away from the lyric [but] there was a lot of it to do with other people in the background.'

'Phil came in with the basic chord structure,' says Scott Gorham, 'and there's a couple of turnaround guitar chords I threw in there that he fell in love with. When we first did the demo, there were no guitar harmonies or guitar lines or anything . . . We all realized it needed more, something more interesting musically. That's when me and Robbo started working the whole thing out.'

Jailbreak was, says its producer John Alcock, 'a very collaborative effort'. Four of the nine songs are co-written, and every track relied on the band to bring it fully to fruition. The producer was struck when he visited Lynott at Welbeck Mansions that his musical process was often as fragmented as his lyrical one. 'He played me some stuff live where he would just be singing along, at other times he had cassettes. He had a porta-studio where he put down some very rough ideas. It was all bits. It was a verse here, a chorus there, a bit of instrumental stuff there, a riff here.'

He was also surprised at the distance between the 'ultimate rocker' he had seen on stage in Bracknell and the man he met at home. 'Phil wasn't flamboyant, he wasn't loud,' he says. 'I'd been around a hell of a lot of bands at that time, and the front guy is always the one with the biggest ego. Phil didn't come off like that. He was quiet, reserved and very polite. Kind of introspective. I got the impression that still waters ran deep . . . Even in the whole time that I knew Phil, I always felt that there were several more layers underneath that I didn't know about, but suspected were there.'

After rehearsing for two weeks at Farmyard Studios in Little Chalfont, Buckinghamshire, in January 1976 Thin Lizzy moved into the Who's Ramport Studios in London to start recording. It was the third album in a renegotiated three-album deal with Phonogram, and Lynott sensed this was crunch time. '*Jailbreak* was the sixth album,' says Frank Murray, 'So he owed it to himself, never mind the record company.' According to Brian Robertson, 'we knew that we were on the chopping block'.

Ramport was a converted church. The studio had been purpose-built by John Alcock for use by the Who, and was situated in an unglamorous part of Battersea, where the nearest – indeed only – local distraction was the Butcher's Arms. With no clubs nearby and no hangers-on dropping in, they finished recording in three weeks. Alcock remembers Lynott 'sitting in the control room, rolling joints that he consumed at quite an alarming rate, but it was never out of hand. I had to go down to the local pub every now and then to retrieve them, but they were there to work.'

The songs were packed full of action and adventure, written to play to the strengths of a band which had found its feet. By keeping things relatively loose in rehearsals and allowing the music to spark into life in the studio, Alcock was the first producer to finally harness on record their live power. Robertson and Gorham were now an intuitive unit, combining to give Thin Lizzy a completely distinctive sonic identity. 'On *Nightlife* you can hear strains of that duel guitar sound, and on each subsequent album their trademark became more obvious,' Brian Downey told me. 'When we hit *Jailbreak* it was honed to a "T". We became conscious of it, and because of that Phil decided to write songs in that direction.'

The title song is a powerhouse riff hard-wired to a further refinement of Lynott's recurring leitmotif of bad boys on the lam. The gang are busting out *'dead or alive'*. Best not to get in their way. 'Angel from the Coast' is looser, a funky rock and roll fable starring a femme fatale straight out of a film noir. It ends with a circle of cops and a hail of bullets; inevitably, *'the crook got away'*.

'Romeo and the Lonely Girl' is a more romantic narrative, a study of a handsome ladies' man (Gary Moore believed it was about him, although it is equally convincing as a knowing self-portrait of Lynott) who falls for everyone and ends up with no one. It was the record company's choice for the first single from the album – they wanted to overdub a horn part – and in many ways it is a more immediate song than 'The Boys Are Back in Town'. The same is true of 'Running Back', easily the most concise, insistent pop song Lynott had written to this point. It was adapted from a slow, sad unreleased song called 'Leaving Town', but even its new breezy exterior could not hide the pain at Lynott's break-up with Gale Barber. A vulnerable streak had not entirely been sacrificed on the altar of machismo.

If I said I was sorry
Would you still leave me?
I never thought you'd go till you did
Believe me

When they say it's over
It's not all over completely
'Cause I'd come running
I'd come running back to you again

Where once Lynott drew from the mystic-folk explorations of *Astral Weeks*, now he was explicitly referencing the tight, blue-eyed soul of Van Morrison's *Moondance* and *His Band and the Street Choir*, right down to the song's *'come running'* refrain. It was Thin Lizzy's most nakedly accessible song to date, with a nagging, faux-naif keyboard motif played by session musician Tim Hinkley, laid-back handclaps and background saxophone. Brian Robertson loathed the upbeat arrangement and refused to play on it, a flashpoint that exemplified the growing tensions between Lynott and the Scottish guitar player, still only nineteen.

'Brian Robertson was absolutely phenomenal,' says Alcock. 'I think he's a great guitar player, but a total pain in the arse to work with. Half the time he was drunk, the other half he was depressed. And Phil could be quite high maintenance. To this day I don't know whether he had something wrong with his hearing. We all sat around in the control room swearing up and down that everything was in tune, and Phil was going, "No, no, that's flat, that's flat." We spent hours tuning guitars to the point where tempers got really frayed . . . then Brian Robertson would get even drunker than he was.

'A Scottish guy that was drinking too much and Phil shouting at him all the time because he was constantly out of tune – this did not make for a happy session. But Brian added a tremendous amount. It would never have happened, *Jailbreak*, without Brian Robertson. When he was on, he was great. Unfortunately that came with a price.'

'Fight or Fall' is a soft and rather self-conscious call to arms to Lynott's *'black brothers'*, ending in a vocal refrain that comes perilously close to pastiche. He did not yet know where to align himself with his black heritage, not least because he wasn't entirely sure where those roots lay. On the one hand, Lynott wasn't keen to pursue the topic in public because it forced him to acknowledge a sense of difference in his appearance, which he didn't particularly believe mattered. 'I think questions [about my colour] could make it an issue,' he said. 'I never thought of it as an issue before; it's just accentuating the fact. It's like somebody goes "Do you know you've got a mole on your face", and everybody looks. It's there, but you just don't see it.'[1]

'I don't think he was proud or not proud of being black,' says Scott Gorham. 'When you hung around with Phil, colour was not an issue, it never was. Unless some asshole came up and made a remark, it wasn't talked about. Not that it was swept under the carpet.'

Lynott had been exploring his black identity for songwriting impetus since 'Black Boys on the Corner' in 1972, but readily admitted that 'I haven't got a natural feel for playing reggae or funk.'[2] Lyrically, too, his approach to the subject didn't always ring true. The rhythmic blues of 'Ghetto Woman', written in 1973 and never officially released, felt like a rather dutiful exercise in imitation. In interviews and in private Lynott talked about the 'brothers', in the manner of a man outside the circle of conversation trying to find a suitable entry point. 'I'm very proud of being a Brother, don't get me wrong,' he said. 'But I think that there are a lot of people like Stevie Wonder who're more apt than me to put it across. My cause is more the half-caste cause. You know, a lot of people are really delicate with the questions: "it must be really difficult being a half-caste".'[3]

In 1975 he had written a reggae song called 'Half-Caste', released on the B-side of 'Rosalie'. It's the somewhat tongue-in-cheek lament of a twice-over outsider in multicultural London. He can't click with his black girl in Brixton because he's not black enough, and doesn't quite measure up to the middle-class white girl in Richmond because her father thinks *'the brown boy is born to serve'*. If a proscribed choice of female company was not something Lynott generally had to worry about, the song at least pointed out – however clumsily – the obstacles he felt in wholly aligning himself to any one community, or being accepted in return. Having been raised in a white environment, he would always be most comfortable defining himself as 'an Irishman first, black second'.[4]

The disenfranchised black man was just one of several manifestations of the heroic outsider on *Jailbreak*. 'Cowboy Song' is a variation on the Eagles's 'Desperado' and depicts the touring rock and roller as the modern-day *vaquero*, a high-plains existentialist dedicated to living a life without ties. The thunderous 'Emerald' is perhaps the ultimate Thin Lizzy Celtic epic, all myth and muscle, written collectively in the studio and documenting a terrible triumph of merciless right over vanquished wrong.

> *Down from the glen came the marching men*
> *With their shields and their swords*
> *To fight the fight they believed to be right*
> *Overthrow the overlords*

'Warrior' was similarly heavy, a tribute to a rather dubious heroism that Lynott detected in those musicians who 'gave up everything to make music and live life to the full'.[5] In interviews he namechecked Jimi Hendrix, Robbie McIntosh and Duane Allman as examples, all three of whom conformed to the live-fast-die-young cliché, which Lynott seemed increasingly inclined to find seductive.

'Warrior' was just one strand in a connective thread of rebel songs – 'Cowboy Song', 'Jailbreak', 'Angel from the Coast', 'Emerald', 'Fight or Fall' and 'The Boys Are Back in Town' – in which the protagonists rise up against moral restrictions and accepted social boundaries. Building on the more prosaic aggression of *Fighting*, Lynott had developed a stoned libertarian manifesto that drew from Space Invader arcade games, Marvel comic-book figures, Irish mytho-history, cowboy lore, rock-and-roll rebellion, low-rolling Americana and H. G. Wells's *War of the Worlds*. For the cover image, Jim Fitzpatrick depicted the band breaking loose from a video game gripped by the sinister Overmaster character. The sleeve notes expanded on the theme.

'That warrior aspect fell into the concept of the whole *Jailbreak* album of people constantly trying to escape and being held down by this Overmaster figure,' said Lynott when the album came out. 'The jailbreak thing is about youth and oppression. When you reach the age of 14 or 18, you suddenly find strength that you've never had before. There's aggression, power and rebelliousness . . . It can be put to good use in the right position, where there is an oppressor . . . The whole point was that the Overmaster was bad and we were busting out for the right of freedom of speech, for all that freedom stands for.'[6]

Jailbreak was released on 26 March 1976, midway through Thin Lizzy's headline tour of the UK, which had Graham Parker and the Rumour supporting. Parker's Irish manager, Dave Robinson, was part of the crowd that had run around the Dublin clubs a decade earlier and was in the process of setting up Stiff Records. Lynott liked London's pub-rock scene, enjoyed its rough-and-ready rootsiness, and sensed that what would shortly become 'punk' was fomenting in its kernel. He had turned up to see Graham Parker and the Rumour before one of their early shows in the capital. 'I think he was just really interested in all kinds of music and he was very up on what I was doing from the very beginning,' says Parker. 'We played "White Honey" at the soundcheck, and I sat down on the edge of the stage with the acoustic guitar and Phil started talking. He said, "What's that 'White Honey'? Show me how you play that." So I played him the riff. The swing beat interested him. Then he walked off and the next thing I know we're touring with them.'

Graham Parker and the Rumour was a support act to be reckoned with, a band of musical adepts led by a ball of wiry intensity, but Thin Lizzy were by now one of the finest live bands in Britain. 'After a show, you'd watch them fight over a dropped note,' says Chalkie Davies. '"You dropped a note in the fourth song!" Everyone would be waiting outside the dressing room while they discussed this note. They were a very, very professional unit.'

Their show had become a perfectly paced tour de force. 'You had three albums and when you picked the best, then you had a genius live set,' says Frank Murray. 'Everything kind of fell into place for that tour. There was a great bunch of songs and they all worked really well live. They had a very high standard. Philip never stopped working on the stage. He had learned that if you're playing to a packed house, the crowd are already on your side. You don't have to work too hard to get them to clap their hands or repeat something after you. They want to be part of the show.' They introduced three ramps which reached out from the stage into the crowd, creating a physical and symbolic bridge between band and audience.

'Phil looked forward to going on the road . . .' says John Alcock, 'more than the release of the record . . . He wanted the excitement and that feeling of being in front of people, playing.'

As the tour was gathering pace, the album made an almost immediate impact, reaching the top ten in the UK in April 1976. On 17 April, Thin Lizzy switched continents to begin a string of US dates supporting bands that included Aerosmith, Rush and Styx. Between these commitments, they had a scattering of headline shows in smaller halls. By 2 June, the day of their concert supporting Journey at the Santa Monica Civic Auditorium in California, the ground was shifting beneath their feet. *Jailbreak* was heading for the top twenty in the States, while the previous week 'The Boys Are Back in Town' had broken into the Power Play top fifty in the *Billboard* charts. Having been picked up by regional radio in America, 'it caught on and grew,' says Scott Gorham. 'It was like a bowling ball running down towards the pin. It was pretty cool.'

On the night they played Santa Monica, thoroughly out-performing Journey, the song had risen to number thirty-two. Mercury Records threw a celebratory after-show party at the Old Venice Noodle Company on Main Street. The single continued to climb steadily during the next eight weeks, reaching a peak of twelve on 24 July.

Listening to 'The Boys Are Back in Town', several American critics and DJs drew a comparison between Lynott's writing style and that of Bruce Springsteen. It was something friends had remarked upon much earlier. 'I remember when Springsteen came along, Tim Booth said, "Have you heard this guy? He writes just like Philip,"' says Eamon Carr. Although the first Thin Lizzy album pre-dated the first Springsteen album, *Greetings from Asbury Park, N.J.*, by almost two years, the ebb-and-flow of influence was less clear-cut than that timeline might suggest. Both men were in thrall to Bob Dylan and Van Morrison, and had hit upon a similar style at a similar time. On one level, Lynott took it as a compliment. 'Phil was genuinely excited about that, and touched,' says Chris Salewicz. A music writer covering the West Coast tour for *NME*, he and Lynott became good friends. 'He felt he had moved up a level.'

On the other hand, Lynott tended to be handed the rough end of the comparison. Springsteen had become a huge deal in 1975 with his third album, *Born to Run*, and he was granted seniority to a band only now registering on the American landscape. Lynott was needled, but otherwise the detail surrounding their US success was movie-script perfect. Thin Lizzy were staying in the Continental Hyatt House hotel on Sunset Boulevard, a rock and roll Elysium, and the scene of many of Led Zeppelin's and the Who's most legendary escapades. Lynott did his best to compete. With five minutes to spare before leaving on a chauffeur-driven day out to Disneyland, he selected a random bikini'd blonde from the Hyatt poolside and, with barely a grunt of introduction, took her to his room for a swiftly negotiated sexual diversion before continuing to his audience with Mickey Mouse. It was a grotesque and fabulous distortion of the American Dream. On the radio, in bars, bedrooms and limos, Elton John and Kiki Dee's 'Don't Go Breakin' My Heart' vied with 'The Boys Are Back in Town' for supremacy, providing a constant backdrop to similar scenes from the sex, drugs and rock and roll set text. On stage, the audience response – Thin Lizzy were second on the bill, but had already staged an unofficial *coup d'état* – was rapturous.

When he wasn't immersed in the fallout, Lynott watched it all carefully, with the detachment of a battle-hardened strategist. 'This time, man,' he would say to no one in particular, 'this time, man, we've got to be very careful . . .' He was acutely sensitive to how Thin Lizzy would be perceived, and was desperate to control and shape their own destiny. He checked the contact sheets from photo sessions, selecting the pictures that he felt sent out the right message, vetoing the rest. 'Philip was very careful with the control of the images,' says Chalkie Davies. 'I remember a couple of times pictures weren't used just because he was smiling. He would talk about his propaganda. "Get your propaganda together, control your image, make sure people don't see the wrong thing." He was very, very shrewd. He knew exactly how to be a rock star. Attention to detail.'

He couldn't settle. 'He was very worried,' says Chris Salewicz. 'Very worried. It had all gone pear-shaped after "Whiskey in the Jar" and he was very nervous about it all. He could appear very cool and louche, but he wasn't really like that at all. He was very hard-working and kept an eye on everything. I'd never seen anyone so fastidious, almost to an anal degree.'

'There was a slight panic,' says Chris O'Donnell. 'This was real stuff – not just a fluke single. We were in the album charts every-where. Phil was looking at us, as managers, thinking, "Have I got the back up?" We had to step up. You had to be on your measure with Philip. He said, "Look, Chris, I've got one career. You can go on and manage other bands, but I've got one shot. If you bring something to me, don't drop the ball. Make it happen or don't bring it to me." We would have furious rows about things.'

To capitalize on the momentum, Thin Lizzy planned to extend their American tour from an initial six weeks to twelve. Shortly after the concert at Santa Monica they joined Rainbow, led by Lynott's one-time prospective band-mate Ritchie Blackmore, for a string of dates in the Midwest and eastern seaboard. These would have been critical shows, dove-tailing with their mainstream breakthrough and taking in Ohio, Detroit and a first ever performance in New York City, at the Beacon Theatre. On the eve of the first concert, Lynott was diagnosed with hepatitis.

'He'd been feeling bad for weeks, he was really tired and overly sweating,' says Scott Gorham. 'I remember the day he got diagnosed. We were supporting Rainbow in Columbus, Ohio. He knocked on my door and said, "I'm really sorry, man, I got some bad news and the doctor said I've got to stop." We were in my hotel room and he pulled up his mirrored shades, and oh God, his eyes weren't yellow, they were practically orange. He was in a really bad way. The hepatitis had spread right through him.'

Hepatitis is an infectious liver disease transmitted through contact with contaminated blood or bodily fluids, with intravenous drug use and sexual intercourse both common causes of infection. Symptoms include nausea, sickness, fever, stomach pains and jaundice.

In the summer of 1976, Lynott was nobody's idea of a drug casualty. In common with the entire Thin Lizzy entourage, he was a dedicated drinker, but smoking dope was his only real *habit*. On tour, an ounce of cannabis would be placed on his bedside table by a roadie as soon as he checked into the hotel; it was no more noteworthy than room service leaving a chocolate on the pillow. 'I don't think I ever saw Phil when he wasn't high,' says John Alcock. 'It was perpetual. I would get up in the morning and have a cup of coffee, he would get up in the morning and roll a joint. [But] Phil was totally in control. He could work, he could write, he could do anything.'

In recent months, Lynott had been flying at increased altitude. Success almost instantly altered the environment and atmosphere surrounding the band, and the drugs offered became more varied, particularly in the States. 'Coke came on the scene just after *Jailbreak*, but not in any great measure,' says Frank Murray. 'Nobody went out looking for it [but] you might find a piece at the weekend.'

The high times were essentially extracurricular. The job came first, but Lynott was not a man predisposed to look the other way when new experiences presented themselves. Chris Salewicz says Lynott confided privately that he caught hepatitis from sharing a dirty needle. 'It was from shooting up,' says Salewicz. 'He told me . . . It wasn't something he was regularly doing, it was just what happened on that particular night. He was up for it, basically, [but] mostly he was just a big spliff-head, and cocaine was kind of a professional courtesy.'

Publicly, Lynott put his illness down to an increase in partying in the wake of their success. Having been slightly wary watching 'The Boys Are Back in Town' and *Jailbreak* ascend the charts, 'when I was sure it had happened, I started to go a bit crazy . . . and ended up with hepatitis in a hospital,' he said. 'I was so run down from touring and celebrating, I ended up sick.'[7]

The unfortunate consequence was the cancellation of the second half of the US tour before it had even begun. Lynott was diagnosed in Columbus and was quickly flown back to England, where he was admitted to hospital in Manchester. The rest of the band and crew followed him home shortly afterwards, having effectively been quarantined by Rainbow. Ritchie Blackmore had caught hepatitis a few years earlier and wasn't taking any chances. 'Blackmore wouldn't even let us go down to do a soundcheck because he was convinced he'd get it off the mic,' says Brian Robertson. 'He was really paranoid.'

Because it is not uncommon for chronic hepatitis sufferers to develop cirrhosis or liver cancer in later life, recovering patients are recommended to give up alcohol, ideally permanently. The doctors advised complete abstinence from drink and drugs as Lynott recuperated in hospital under the watchful, worried eye of Philomena. (It was not an entirely conventional convalescence. To lift his spirits, one day his mother arranged for three female triplets to dress up as nurses and visit Lynott in hospital.) In the event, he mustered sufficient resolve to curb almost all of his more destructive habits for twelve months.

'For the rest of us it was a real pain in the ass,' says Scott Gorham. 'He wouldn't be drinking and we'd get in the car in the morning and he would remember every single thing we had done the night before. But he religiously stuck to the year – a year to the day. He still smoked some weed, but as far as coke and all the rest, that was out. I was pretty impressed that he had the willpower to stop everything . . . It made me think he might have been able to do it again near the end.'

According to Frank Murray, Lynott bent the rules when he could. 'Of course, he came out and he was soon saying, "I can't drink, but the doctor said I can drink white wine, maybe, and an odd glass of champagne." He did start asking for champagne in his dressing room because he had the right excuse: doctor's orders.'

'I think he did his best,' says Chalkie Davies, which seems a fair summation.

Lynott was far from oblivious to the ramifications. A year later, he recognized the bout of ill-health as a potentially life-changing episode. 'Standing in bars watching other people getting drunk was a revelationary [sic] experience,' he said. 'Being sober for so long gives you a whole head turnaround. So I went through a few changes, for the better, I hope. It was definitely me body saying, "enough".'[8]

Personally and professionally, the long-term effects of the illness were profound. For Thin Lizzy, the cancellation of the US tour was the first in a series of misadventures that fatally hobbled their attempts to forge a meaningful career in the United States. In the immediate aftermath, it meant that they were not able to capitalize on the momentum built through the success of

'The Boys Are Back in Town' and *Jailbreak*. Not only were the critical taste-makers in New York denied the chance to see the band in their natural live habitat and at the peak of their powers, but the promotional opportunities offered to a rising band were cancelled. It was a hard lesson in the first rule of US success: if you weren't there to grab it, you might as well not exist. 'We were convinced on that tour that all the stars were lined up; we were going to show the US audience en masse what this band could do,' says Scott Gorham. 'We felt we were peaking in terms of our playing abilities and the songs and the arrangements. We had a lot of momentum on our side, we felt in our bones that we were going to crack it in a big way. All of a sudden we were on our way back home. That was one of the lowest lows.'

At least they came home to a hit. Thin Lizzy had already appeared on *Top of the Pops*. The show had broadcast a pre-recorded segment of the band performing 'The Boys Are Back in Town' in a TV studio in the US, intercut with footage of teenagers dancing in the BBC studios in London. Throughout June 1976, Lynott watched from his hospital bed as the single kept climbing, reaching number eight in the first week of July. To celebrate, they arranged a one-off show at the Hammersmith Odeon. 'Thin Lizzy are big time now, and thriving on it,' wrote Harry Doherty, reviewing the 11 July concert in *Melody Maker* and hailing the band's 'arrival as top league rockers'.[9]

'We were looking down and people knew the words,' says Gorham. 'All of a sudden, out of nowhere, we had cracked it. That was a pretty significant high for the band.'

'It was a huge breakthrough for us,' Brian Downey told me. 'Up until then we were still playing smallish venues and we might be second or third on the bill. When *Jailbreak* became a huge international hit we were headlining, which was a big change.' Their guaranteed fee changed almost overnight from three figures to four and sometimes five figures. They could demand as much as 85 per cent of the takings on top.

Lynott couldn't contemplate missing the Hammersmith Odeon party. A sensible recovery period for hepatitis is a year but he appeared on stage a little over a month after being diagnosed. His swift return to frontline action was partly borne from his macho sensibilities but it was indicative, too, of a mindset that would ultimately do few favours for Thin Lizzy, and Lynott in particular: a neurotic anxiety that to take even the shortest break was to risk being forgotten.

The long-term effects on his health are likely to have been significant. Already an asthmatic, Lynott's liver and immune system were now also severely weakened. The constitution he so prided himself on was no longer cast iron and he pushed it harder in the final years of his life. 'What snookered him, I think, was catching hepatitis,' says Ted Carroll. 'He was always in danger after that, but he didn't stop . . . You could advise someone like Phil, but you couldn't tell him what to do.'

Recently, Chalkie Davies was looking through his portfolio of photographs of Lynott. He was particularly struck by one image taken some months after he had left hospital in the summer of 1976. 'I was thinking, there's something weird about him in this picture, and it's because his face was slightly yellow,' says Davies. 'He was still recovering and he didn't quite give it long enough. That affected his health. I honestly think the downward path started there.'

12

'I don't know where my father is . . .'

Success triggered several aftershocks. One was the greater degree of scrutiny that fell on Lynott's private life and family history, especially when he veered away from the music papers and began to be courted by more mainstream publications. In a single-page interview in 1976 with the rather sensationalist weekly human interest magazine *Titbits*, the interviewer's line of questioning focused on his father.

'I haven't seen or heard from him since I was four years old,' Lynott continued. 'He could be anywhere. My mother doesn't talk too much about him. I know he had a lot going for him and a lot of girls after him. He even had a nickname, The Duke. He was South American and a pretty flash dresser. She tells me I've got most of his looks – he was fairly tall and a good dancer – and most of his characteristics. She said he was a good geezer and I should be proud of him.'[1]

At the age of twenty-six, Lynott's perception of his father had advanced little since childhood. He believed that Cecil Parris was living in west London, and may have been working as a barber. Still lacking a name, in 1974 he and Frank Murray had spent a Saturday afternoon visiting barber shops in the

Portobello Road, Ladbroke Grove and Notting Hill Gate, asking staff and customers if they knew a man in his late forties called 'The Duke'. It was a venture doomed to disappointment and a degree of ridicule. 'We failed miserably,' says Murray.

The *Titbits* interview set off a chain reaction that very quickly brought Lynott face to face with some rather prosaic home truths. The myths and mysteries that had been spun around Cecil Parris turned out largely to be a smokescreen. The 'Brazilian seafarer'; the 'Caribbean tap-dancer'; 'The Duke' – the seductive veil of these exotic characterizations fell away upon contact. Lynott's biological father transpired to be a sharp-dressed family man running a hat stall in Shepherd's Bush Market.

After ceasing contact with Philomena and his son, Parris had made a life in London. Members of his family travelled over from British Guiana, including a brother and a sister. In 1955, at a dance at the Lyceum, the vast ballroom situated off the Strand, he had met Irene Lewis, a twenty-three-year-old white woman from London.

Lewis had already been involved in a marriage, which was later dissolved. She and Parris began a relationship, and in time moved in together as common-law man and wife, living at 15 Ashburnham Road in World's End, Chelsea, in west London. In time, Irene changed her surname by deed poll to Parris, and on 21 September 1964 they had a daughter, Sarah Jeanetta Parris, Lynott's half-sister. They finally married in 1984, when Cecil was fifty-nine and Irene was fifty-two.

Before their baby was due, in 1964 the couple moved around the corner to 15 Burnaby Street. World's End was the 'wrong side' of Chelsea. It was at the more ragged end of the King's Road, one of the pre-eminent pendulums of Swinging London in the sixties, and still a vibrant thoroughfare. Malcolm McLaren and Vivienne Westwood's Sex boutique had recently opened nearby. Don

Letts's Acme Attractions clothes store was also close to hand. It was an area with an aura, and one Lynott knew well. Never mind Rio or Demerara. Father and son had been living only five miles apart in London for several years before finally meeting.

According to his wife, Parris was working not as a barber but as a tailor, and for a period had been employed in Savile Row; one truth that did map the outline of the legend was his dramatic sense of style. In 1974 he had set up his own business selling hats.

Irene Parris read the interview with Lynott in *Titbits*. She had always known that her husband had fathered a boy before they had met. When she showed the piece to Cecil, he immediately contacted Thin Lizzy's management at their offices in Dean Street, Soho. 'I was there when he disclosed himself,' says Chris Morrison. 'This guy walked in, wearing a blue denim coat with a sheepskin lining and collar, and a fedora. You could imagine this guy managing a couple of girls. He looked like a pimp, basically.'

Morrison called Philomena, who spoke with Parris and verified his identity. That formality completed, very quickly a meeting between Lynott and his father was set up.

Thin Lizzy were recording a radio session for John Peel at the BBC studios in Maida Vale when Lynott received the news. The band picked up his instant unease. 'He never talked about his dad,' says Gorham. 'And he wasn't happy about meeting him at all, believe me, but he was intrigued. He arranged to meet, but he said to me, "Whatever you do, don't leave me alone with this guy." I said, "Are you sure? You've never even met him. You don't want five minutes alone?" He was sure.'

When Cecil Parris walked back into his son's life he was wearing 'a three-piece all-white suit, white patent leather shoes, a white tie – I think he might even have had a white hat,' says Gorham. 'Real *Superfly* shit. Philip looks at this guy and looks at me, and we both almost start to laugh. The atmosphere is really tense. It was very strange. I don't think they knew what to say to each other.' Gorham eventually stepped outside to get a coffee and to allow the newly reunited father and son a chance to talk. When he returned, Parris was already leaving. 'It couldn't have been more than ten or fifteen minutes. Philip didn't really want to know.'

Despite the natty attire, 'his father's story was radically different to what he thought it was,' according to Midge Ure. 'Philip had a much more glamorous story [in his head] than the reality.' Parris had showed up with his wife and their eleven-year-old daughter. 'I asked him about that meeting with his father, and he was totally nonplussed,' says Jim Fitzpatrick. 'I don't think it was a defensive reaction. It was more like, "Okay, that was interesting. Bye. Now I'm me again."'

His Irish family sensed a similar neutrality in his response. Lynott said little of consequence on the subject to those closest to him, other than intimating that he would not be seeing his father again. In fact, they saw each other on several more occasions, invariably at 15 Burnaby Street, and always with Lynott bringing a chaperone, usually in the form of Charlie McLennan. The family were sent tickets to Thin Lizzy concerts. 'I remember I was at a show once and Philip pointed to a girl in the dressing room and said, "That's my half-sister over there, let me introduce you to her,"' says Frank Murray.

Occasionally, long-submerged resentments bobbed up to the surface. One day Lynott invited Cecil to the studio to watch him work. Parris told him that he would be leaving early to collect Sarah from school. 'He said there was never anybody there to pick him up from school when he was a boy,' Irene Parris recalls.

Relatively quickly, the relationship petered out. 'He was very circumspect with his father,' says Chris Morrison. 'He felt he was after him because [Philip] had made it, after having nothing to do with him before that. Before a show, Philip would phone the office and say, "Get a couple of tickets for me dad, but limit the backstage."' When father and son bumped into one another in the street one day in Chelsea, Irene Parris claims that Lynott 'didn't want to know'.

In 1978 Lynott wrote the words to Gary Moore's 'Parisienne Walkways', providing the song with its bravura encoded opening: '*I remember Parris, back in '49 . . .*' The producer he was working with regularly at the time, Chris Tsangarides, picked up on the resonance but failed to make any headway on the subject. 'He never said anything to me about his father,' he says. 'Never spoke about it. He never did to Gary, either. We used to speak about Phil to each other a hell of a lot after he died, to try and figure out what was going on in his mind. It never came to anything because he just never said.' He followed up the theme with a bleak, unreleased song called 'Blue Parris'.

After their brief intersection with the Lynotts, the Parris family got on with their own lives. In the 1980s they moved to Acton, west London, and Cecil and Irene became grandparents. When Lynott died, early in 1986, they sent flowers to the funeral, but they were not invited to attend. There has been no contact between the families since.

Cecil Parris lived a further twenty-six years. He died, aged eighty-six, on 6 April 2012. At the end of his life he suffered from dementia and was cared for in a nursing home, and his wife and daughter took over the running of the business. The Duke's old stall at Shepherd's Bush Market continues to sell hats, gloves, artificial flowers, swimwear and wedding accessories, and still trades under the Parris name, the middle name of his son.

Johnny the Fox appeared to be ill-conceived from the beginning. In August 1976, after some time spent at the Farmyard working on new material, Thin Lizzy started recording their next album. With two hit singles – 'Jailbreak' was on its way into the UK top forty – a hit album and significantly increased performance fees, the financial rewards were finally beginning to accumulate. The years of Thin Lizzy Ltd working out of one room in Soho with no money were gone. They renegotiated the band's deal with Phonogram for an advance of $750,000 per album, but it would take time for royalties to accrue. 'Philip made all his money on the publishing,' says Chris O'Donnell. 'They barely broke even on the touring because everyone was on a retainer, and it would take eighteen months to recoup on the albums. They were on a salary of £500 a week, but Phil was getting the publishing and the PRS [Performing Right Society royalties], which enabled him to buy a flat while everyone else was living in bedsits. That was the difference.'

In 1976 he left Welbeck Mansions and bought 66 Embassy House, a two-bedroom apartment on the third floor of a modern purpose-built block of flats, once again abutting West End Lane at the junction with Cleve Road. It was a sedate place, full of well-heeled ladies of a certain age, a demographic that Lynott did his best to shake up. Once again, Charlie McLennan lived there with him. He was now Lynott's 'percy', his personal roadie, paid for out of his own pocket and effectively at his beck and call: driver, gofer, drug-dealer, bodyguard, flatmate, wingman, friend and delivery man. The flat was partially furnished with objects that Philomena would send down from Manchester. 'Big brass beds, carpets and wardrobes,' says Chalkie Davies, who later bought the property from Lynott. 'Very nice furniture that was just a little too big.'

The management planned to exploit a tax loophole by recording the next album outside Britain, at Musicland Studios in Munich, situated in the city's high-rise Arabellapark Hotel. The top of the building was a favoured local suicide spot. The bottom was a windowless basement studio complex where the Rolling Stones, Led Zeppelin and Deep Purple had all recently recorded.

The experiment was not a success. The atmosphere was mildly claustrophobic and moderately depressing. Thin Lizzy were accustomed to passing through Germany on tour, but several weeks stuck in an antiseptic environment far from home did not improve their collective mood. There were technical issues with the studio and the tape they were using. After two weeks, John Alcock persuaded the management to abandon Musicland and return to Ramport in London, 'and screw the tax man'.

They came back to Britain with almost nothing usable beyond a handful of drum tracks. In effect the album sessions began again from scratch. 'We did the really good songs first,' says Alcock. '"Don't Believe a Word", "Johnny", "Johnny the Fox Meets Jimmy the Weed". Those were great. Then the problems started, because we had ten or fifteen minutes of blank space. What are we going to do, put out an EP?'

Even without a dispiriting fortnight spent in a high-tech German vault, the odds were stacked against the record. It was only six months since the band had recorded their last album and they had spent most of that time on tour and then, in Lynott's case, in hospital. They were making a record because their newfound success demanded it, not because they were ready.

As the writer, singer and primary focus of a band now expected to fulfil certain goals, Lynott's tension level on *Johnny the Fox* was high, while his energy levels were severely depleted. 'Phil was perhaps a little more quiet than usual, but he didn't strike me as being ill,' says Alcock. 'He was still smoking a lot of dope, and if somebody's smoking a lot of weed, they're kind of introspective anyway. I did suggest modifying the working hours a bit because he was always late . . . "Let's go home at eight or nine o'clock so you get a bit of rest," [but] he said, "No, I don't need it. I'm all right."'

While recuperating from hepatitis, he had used his time in hospital to write several new songs, among them 'Fool's Gold' and 'Massacre', but the quality was inconsistent and the quantity wanting. Relations in the studio began to deteriorate. 'He would come up with ideas and I'd say, "Seriously? Is that the best we can do?"' says Alcock. 'It got really bad when I suggested that we should maybe consider a couple of covers. For Phil that was absolute anathema. That was me mishandling things. You don't say to Phil Lynott of all people, who was more or less a poet, that his writing's not good enough, so how about covering something from Noddy Holder?'

The relationship with Brian Robertson was also breaking down. By his own estimation, Robertson was putting away at least a bottle of Johnnie Walker Black Label a day. Lynott was foresworn from hard liquor but was still smoking dope. Robertson tended towards aggression and provocation when he was drunk, while Lynott had a mean temper but generally maintained an equilibrium. They were running on different fuel and at incompatible speeds.

Lynott still at least nominally strived to make sure everyone felt included in the creative process. 'I feel that in the band, everybody pulls their weight when it comes to the music,' he told Harry Doherty at the time. 'I just happen to write a lot of the songs and lyrics ... I let Thin Lizzy interpret my songs as it wishes. I come down with a song and Brian [Downey] says that he'd like such and such a beat. Then I let the band develop the song and even if I disagree, my power's only a quarter. I'm only a figurehead as far as the press in concerned, but that's the superficial thing. I mean, Brian Downey is the quietest member of the band but if he says he doesn't want to play a number, that's it stumped.'[2]

What was admirable in theory threw up challenges in practice. 'There were a few times when it became a little chicken-shit,' says Gorham. 'If he came up with an idea and no one liked it, he'd say, "Okay, well I'll just quit the band." Oh right! So that was the end of the conversation.'

During rehearsals for the album, Lynott and Robertson had clashed over 'Don't Believe a Word', at the time a slow, bluesy ballad, reminiscent of 'Stand by Me'. Its coordinates were crudely mapped out on acoustic guitar. 'He brought that to us and I said, "I'm not playing that,"' says Robertson. 'I told him it was shit, and he disappeared from the Farmyard for three days. Nobody could find him. I said to Downey, "Listen, we'd better do something about this song because he's pissed off." Downey suggested we do it in a shuffle. There was just two of us in a lit- tle rehearsal room. I wrote the riff. When Philip came back [the song] was a shuffle and a riff, not the slow version, which was really sort of morbid. He was well chuffed with it. Of course, he gets all the publishing.'

With larger sums now being generated, the organization of songwriting credits became an occasional grievance. Because of the increasing discrepancy in earning potential between the principal songwriter and the remaining band members, the man- agement suggested that for one calendar year publishing revenue be split evenly four ways, a civilized compromise which Lynott agreed to, after which the copyrights reverted back to him. 'Phil was very fair about money,' says Ted Carroll. 'He was a man of his word, there was nothing dodgy about him.'

'Don't Believe a Word' was one of the highlights of the record. It was Lynott at his leanest – not street-guy tough, but emotionally ruthless. An unflinching *mea culpa*, it's an anti-love song that sacrifices the songwriter's greatest weapon – sincerity – in favour of a much more unpalatable truth.

Don't believe me if I tell you
That I wrote this song for you
There might be some other silly pretty girl
I'm singing it to

Don't believe a word
For words are only spoken
Your heart is like a promise
Made to be broken

Don't believe a word
Words can tell lies
And lies are no comfort
When there's tears in your eyes

Around this time in interviews he revelled in his image as the lethal lady killer. 'I'm the easiest lay in town,' he'd say, adding that the road crew called him 'Philip Line-'em-up'. 'Sometimes I'm real brutal with chicks, just go after them, get what I want and see you later,' he said. 'Everything I do and say is to get what I want.'[3]

It's an attitude summed up by the bluntly chauvinistic line from 'Jailbreak' – *'Hey you, good looking female, come here!'* – but Chris O'Donnell insists that it offers a simplistic distortion of life on the road. 'These people weren't groupies,' he says. 'There were people we knew in every city we went to. College journalists, women who worked for the promoter or the radio, people who had supported us. They were individuals, they weren't random women picked up for a shag. We met [infamous groupie Connie Hamzy] in Arkansas, she was desperate to meet the band. She said, "You're not a real rock band until you've slept with me." Phil said, "Huh?" He didn't get it at all. Wasn't interested.'

'Don't Believe a Word' is concise and punchy, testament to a rock band in full control of its sonic identity. 'Johnny' and 'Rocky' are similarly hard-edged. The former – originally called 'Weasel's Rhapsody' – explores the dark alter ego of Lynott's perennial protagonist, now a *'juiced up junkie'* on the wrong end of a stand-off with the police. 'Rocky' is an ambiguous portrait of Brian Robertson (*'Cocky Rocky, the rock and roll star / He's got the talent to take him far'*) and comes, aptly, with a trademark twin-guitar break.

'Fool's Gold' ties together Lynott's shared fascination with Ireland and America. His terrifically hammy spoken prologue on the Irish potato famine – where Spinal Tap's 'Stonehenge' collides with Patrick Kavanagh's epic starvation poem *The Great Hunger* – leads to an emigrant's tale of hard times fortune-chasing on the frontier. The fine, pimp-rolling funk-rock of 'Johnny the Fox Meets Jimmy the Weed' is a more contemporary slice of American history, a ghetto hustle full of *'shady deals'* in the parts of town *'where only black men go'*.

In the wake of the tight, controlled aesthetic of the past two albums, there was a conscious effort to be more expansive. Songs arrived fleshed out with strings and backing vocals. The aching 'Borderline' entered country-rock territory familiar to fans of the Eagles, or the Rolling Stones in their more reflective moments. 'Sweet Marie' and 'Old Flame' were limp rather than limpid. 'Boogie Woogie Dance' was unabashed filler.

Johnny the Fox offered the first faint hints that Lynott as a writer was falling back at times on rehashed archetypes. He was over-utilizing the 'Johnny Cool' persona, while the pounding 'Massacre' was essentially a sequel to 'Emerald'. Originally titled 'Little Big Horn', it was another song of slaughter, only this time the battle-lines had moved from ancient Ireland to the nineteenth-century American plains. But even when repeating himself,

Lynott was routinely capable of vividly arresting imagery. 'Massacre' tells of *six hundred unknown heroes killed like sleeping buffalo'*; towards the end of 'Fool's Gold', there is an abrupt and effective switch of scene and tone, as *'the vulture sits on top of the big top circus arena'* watching the *'beautiful dancing tightrope ballerina'*, a Van Morrisonesque tumble of words rendered all the more memorable by Lynott's immaculate phrasing.

Given the circumstances in which it was made, *Johnny the Fox* was good enough. Released on 16 October 1976, it was an act of consolidation, solid rather than spectacular, and in Britain and Europe it maintained the band's upward trajectory. It climbed to number eleven in the album charts and brought the band another hit single in 'Don't Believe a Word', which reached number twelve in the UK in mid-January 1977.

It was a patchy album conceived with an unerring certainty of what would deliver on stage. 'Massacre' worked well enough in the studio, but in the shows that the band undertook in the autumn of 1976 it became a slashing, astonishingly visceral tour de force.

NME sent reviewer David Housham to the concert at Bristol's Colston Hall on 22 October: 'Watching two thousand Bristolians exploding in a spastic frenzy, cheering, stomping, screaming for a third encore, you have to conclude that there is no better bona fide rock band in England, maybe the world, than Thin Lizzy at the moment.' The sold-out UK tour ended with three shows at the Hammersmith Odeon on 14, 15 and 16 November.

These concerts were recorded for future release on *Live and Dangerous*, and represent a high-water mark of unity, power and dynamism. The Thin Lizzy show had become a vivid piece of theatre, tightly choreographed and ritualistic. 'Jailbreak' began amid wailing sirens, police lights and a flurry of flash bombs; a cleverly lit mirror ball showered stars around the theatre on 'Cowboy Song', and Lynott picked out individuals in the crowd with his mirrored bass. The set was a perfectly paced mix of consistent attack and occasional release, the tension only slackening slightly on the semi-improvised audience participation number of 'Baby Drives Me Crazy', and full-tilt encores of 'Me and the Boys Were Wondering How You and the Girls Were Getting Home Tonight' and 'The Rocker', the sole song from the original Thin Lizzy incarnation included in the set.

'They were a real working band,' says Nick Tauber. 'That's why they were so brilliant when they hit the big time, because they were ready for it. Philip honed his stagecraft. He'd got all the patter down. He'd got the way he looked down. He'd done everything he wanted to do.'

The next stop was their first ever headlining tour of America at the end of 1976. On the eve of their departure, Brian Robertson badly cut his hand while socializing at the Speakeasy, defending Scottish singer Frankie Miller from an attack with a broken bottle by a member of funk band Gonzalez. 'Everybody thinks I was pissed as a fart, but in fact I'd only had two whiskies,' says Robertson. 'It was Frankie who was [drunk], I just went to save his face.'

The night of the opening show was three days away. Frank Murray was already in the States, setting up the concerts and organizing the band's biggest round of promotional activity to date. He received the call from Chris Morrison informing him that Robertson would not be able to play guitar for several months, and set about informing press, agents and the record label at a moment's notice that, once again, a crucial Thin Lizzy tour would not be happening. Lynott was 'fucking furious,' says Murray. Injured and isolated, Robertson announced the following March that he was leaving the band permanently. Predictably, it turned out not to be as simple as all that.

A silver lining arrived in the unlikely form of Freddie Mercury. On the night of 26 November, when he should have been subordinating New York to the power of Thin Lizzy, Lynott instead visited Advision Studios in London for the playback of Queen's new album, *A Day at the Races*. The two groups shared a publicist in Tony Brainsby and knew each other socially. By the end of the night, Thin Lizzy had been booked to support Queen on their forthcoming US tour, starting on 18 January 1977 and playing arenas and stadiums with capacities between 5,000 and 20,000. Lynott was pragmatic, viewing the tour as a chance 'to get through to the promoters and remind the kids that we're still alive and well and get some reliability into our reputation.'[4]

Gary Moore was again brought in as a replacement for Brian Robertson, both parties agreeing in advance that it would be a temporary arrangement. Thin Lizzy played a forty-five-minute opening set each night, the distilled essence of a world-class act. 'Freddie Mercury was really, really shocked at how good Lizzy were on that tour,' says Chalkie Davies. 'Their soundcheck time got less and less, because Freddie felt threatened. He knew that Philip had something special as a frontman, in terms of communicating with an audience.'

They were handicapped by the restrictions placed on their light show, soundcheck time, stage boundaries and PA system, but Thin Lizzy still gave Queen a fright in places like Boston and the Nassau Coliseum in Long Island. 'It was their biggest ever tour, and it went great,' Gary Moore said. 'Queen would be sitting at the airport in the morning reading the papers, and we would be getting better reviews than them. It didn't go down too well. Apparently Freddie was stomping around the dressing room going, "Get them off the stage, there's too much applause!"'

The inroads made through 'The Boys Are Back in Town' and *Jailbreak* had not been sustained. 'Don't Believe a Word' did not chart in the States, and *Johnny the Fox* failed to make any meaningful impact. *Creem*'s review of the album was indicative of a general attitude of must-try-harder surrounding the band. 'Ideally, Thin Lizzy should have released an EP, and continued releasing EPs, until they got it right,' wrote the reviewer Susan Whitall. 'They're almost there.'[5]

As Lynott implied with his desire to display 'reliability', with the cancellation of two tours in under six months Thin Lizzy were starting to look like a gamble to their US label, Warner Brothers, who weren't especially inclined to put their promotional muscle behind a band who couldn't seem to get all four members on a stage at the same time. Thin Lizzy didn't help by fluffing their leading lines. When the Queen tour reached its most significant venue on 5 February 1977, New York's 19,000-capacity Madison Square Garden, the band had one of their rare off nights. When it mattered most, they misfired, and did not play an encore.

A greater reality check occurred on their next visit to New York in the autumn, on a US tour with Graham Parker and the Rumour in support, reprising the bill that had travelled around the UK eighteen months earlier. Headlining the Palladium in New York on 22 October, Thin Lizzy were summarily dismissed by the cool metropolitan crowd. 'Unfortunately the audience had come to see us because we were the hip thing in those major cities,' says Parker. 'Half of them walked out for Thin Lizzy. Which sucked. I felt like, oh, you idiots, they're good! They're different from us, but they're still a fucking great rock 'n' roll band. Phil later said our audience were 1960s snobs, and I thought, he's right! I agree, totally. It wasn't good, but it was just New York City. They killed us in Texas, the South and the Midwest.'

All the great shows in Dallas and Phoenix, however, couldn't compensate for two misfiring New York appearances in quick succession, but the music was strong and good, and there was fun to be had each night in the bars, clubs and hotels of each town. Several songs from the autumn dates at the Seneca College Fieldhouse, Toronto, and the Tower Theater, Philadelphia, are preserved on *Live and Dangerous* (in the case of Philadelphia, the entire show was later released as *Still Dangerous*). The Rumour performed with horns, and their Irish saxophonist John Earle would join Thin Lizzy each night to play their new single, 'Dancing in the Moonlight'. 'Thin Lizzy and Graham Parker and the Rumour, plus the horn section, was one of the greatest double bills there ever was,' says Chalkie Davies. 'It was just fantastic. Pure entertainment from both bands.'

'Phil was such a showman and I learned a lot off of him,' says Parker. 'How to grab the audience and stare them in the face. When I started I was nailed behind an acoustic guitar, and gradually I came out of that. Phil was nailed to his bass, but he still looked like he was stalking the stage, *handling* the audience. On top of that, they were an incredibly tight band, and everyone was professional. They all played their hearts out every night.'

Their prospects in Britain continued to thrive. Released on 2 September 1977, *Bad Reputation* was Thin Lizzy's highest charting UK album to date, reaching number four. They had recorded it over the summer in Toronto, slipping through another tax loophole.

They stayed at the Hotel Plaza II on Bloor Street and recorded at Toronto Sound with Tony Visconti, who had worked extensively with David Bowie and Marc Bolan and was one of the most successful and innovative producers around. The choice was a promising one, indicative of Lynott's desire to push the band in new directions. Bowie, readying to make *"Heroes"*, was reportedly baffled by his producer's decision to work with a group he himself did not rate, but Visconti had loved

'The Boys Are Back in Town' and had fallen for Lynott's stoned garrulousness on the sole occasion they had previously met. 'He was Prince Charming,' says Visconti. 'Full of enthusiasm, really outgoing and friendly. He wanted to make it work and oozed with confidence.'

He arrived for preliminary discussions at Visconti's London studio straight from lunch at the Carlton House Hotel, where Thin Lizzy had won the Best Newcomer category at the *Melody Maker* awards – an accolade which amused Lynott, given that they were just about to make their eighth album. The record company had provided a limousine for the day. When Lynott and Gorham climbed out a little the worse for wear, Visconti wondered what he might have got himself into, but he ended up impressed at their organization. 'All the songs were written, and apparently rehearsed,' he says. 'The arrangements were more or less worked out. I might change the length of intros or reorder a few sections of the songs, but they were in great shape. Philip was very methodical.'

They began the sessions in Toronto in May as a three-piece. Lynott had not forgiven Brian Robertson, and was aware that even before the guitar player had cut his hand their combative working relationship had become almost untenable. Gary Moore had been a stop-gap replacement for the Queen tour. In the studio, they decided that Scott Gorham would record all the guitar parts himself, overdubbing whatever was needed. This was how the album started. In the end, on Gorham's insistence, Robertson was drafted in on a session basis, adding guitar and keyboards to several songs. The truce was uneasy.

'Brian Robertson was always on the side-lines,' says Visconti. 'I didn't understand why, I was a bit naive about the group politics, but Brian kept himself separate. He didn't really hang out – he would go to his room and drink. In the studio he would do his solo and go to another room. He wasn't really clicking with the band.' Robertson was deliberately excluded from the punky, bleached-out cover photograph, which showed only Lynott, Gorham and Downey, but the signals were mixed. In June, Thin Lizzy announced publicly that they were officially a three-piece. The following month, they announced publicly that Brian Robertson was back in the band.

Lynott's relatively sober post-hepatitis period was over. During recording, his discipline in the studio, a source of pride for so long, began to waver. 'Philip was a medium drug user on *Bad Reputation*,' says Visconti. 'When we were in Toronto, the drug of choice was cocaine, which was almost impossible to get. So the band smoked and drank. It was mainly an alcohol-fuelled album. There was a period when they were out of control because they were drinking too much. I threatened to leave the album. I called their managers in London, and said, "I can't work with these guys, they're falling down drunk." Chris O'Donnell flew over from London and sorted them out.' 'They just wanted affirmation,' says O'Donnell. 'I just had to say, "It's a great record, it's fantastic, and by the way, that's the single – 'Dancing in the Moonlight'."'

The day after O'Donnell's departure, Lynott came to Visconti to berate the excessive behaviour of the rest of the band. 'I can handle it but they can't,' he said. Visconti told him he was part of the problem, which rather took Lynott aback. He promised to cut down, 'but it's impossible to cut it out completely'.

Bad Reputation does not sound like an undisciplined record. Pleasingly concise at thirty-six minutes and nine songs, the album introduced a tighter, more rhythmic dynamic. It is certainly Thin Lizzy's best-sounding studio record. Visconti, a bass player himself, brought Lynott's lines to the fore throughout, giving his bass a thicker, more contemporary sonic identity on 'Southbound', 'Dear Lord' and 'Dancing in the Moonlight' in particular.

The latter is one of Lynott's greatest achievements. It does not strive to impress, it seeks only to uplift and entertain. It's hard to think of any other rock band of the 1970s in possession of such wit and lightness of touch. Lynott was not entirely sure of the track – he insisted that the hard-driving 'Bad Reputation' was released with it as a double A-side to circumnavigate any accusations of softening up – but it was a timely reminder of his most persuasive and enduring gifts: he was a pop craftsman when it came to mood and melody, and a singer of rare versatility. The way he would bite down on the words, roll them around his mouth, chew on each syllable and stretch it out. It was an art form. It certainly impressed Visconti. 'He was like the Sinatra of the rock world,' he says. 'A highly nuanced voice, and so expressive.' When Supertramp played Toronto, Thin Lizzy asked saxophonist John Helliwell to overdub a horn part, a pitch-perfect textural counterpoint to Lynott's vocal.

'Dancing in the Moonlight' is not just a fond, finger-clicking recollection of teenage misadventure on the streets of south Dublin, but an exuberant love letter to life. Little else on the album contained even a hint at such optimism, veering between razor-edged nihilism and rather oppressive melancholy. *Bad Reputation* shifted Thin Lizzy away from the streets towards a warzone. Aware that he was in danger of self-parody, Lynott had wisely ditched the gum-chewing case studies. 'I wrote so many Johnnies and Rockies that I'll probably drop the character thing for a while till it really interests me again,' he said in December 1977.[6]

In their place, the atmosphere on much of the album is martial, staking out the territory of heavy metal. The wonderfully evocative 'Soldier of Fortune' and less persuasive 'Killer without a Cause' are set in extremity, recounting mercenary lives mired in death and violence. The juddering riff of the title track is a template for the coming New Wave of British Heavy Metal.

'Opium Trail' is equally grim, a romanticized blood-and-thunder account of the heroin trade, written after watching two television documentaries on the Hong Kong Triads and the Golden States of Shan. 'It's an anti-drug song, that's the funny thing . . .' said Lynott. 'It was kind of to make me aware that you can flirt around with these sorts of things but eventually they'll trap you, there's no two ways that it won't trap you.'[7] The words to 'Opium Trail' gave Tony Visconti pause. 'I read the lyrics and I thought, He's trying to tell us something here. I didn't see evidence that he was using an opiate, but I felt he was probably . . . having some kind of internal conflict.'

The sense of a man in turmoil is evident elsewhere. On one level, the tugging Wild West sadness of 'Southbound' works as a sequel to 'Fool's Gold', but cuts closer to the bone. *The gold rush it is over and depression days draw near,'* sings Lynott, *'Drifting like a drover / chasing my career.'* Musically, 'Dear Lord' betrayed the influence of Queen in its mock-pompous opening salvo and stack of layered vocals, provided by Visconti's wife Mary Hopkin, but lyrically it's one long prayer.

> *Give me dignity, restore my sanity*
> *Oh Lord, come rescue me*
> *Dear Lord, my vanity is killing me*

No matter that Lynott's belief in a higher power had been ingrained during his upbringing, and that the sense of a spiritual lack was real, his soul-bearing on *Bad Reputation* was greeted with the kind of critical mockery specially reserved for macho rock stars exploring their sensitive side. Such indulgences were unfashionable by 1977. More acceptable was the sharpened sense of attack displayed elsewhere on the album, and its new-found bleakness. '[Thin Lizzy] make perfect sense in The Age of Punk, just as they did a year or two years or three years ago,' wrote Charles Shaar Murray in *New Musical Express*.[8]

Punk was increasingly on Lynott's mind. He told friends it was just rock and roll wearing different trousers. Immediately before the Queen tour, in January 1977, he had spent an evening jamming at the Hope and Anchor pub in Islington with Rat Scabies from the Damned. 'There was initially going to be a band for Philip and Rat,' says Frank Murray. 'Somewhere along the line that got lost. They didn't rehearse or anything like that, it was probably just talk.' Nick Lowe, whom Lynott revered, was also there that night. A fellow bass player, Lowe's 1976 solo single, 'So it Goes', not only sounded like Thin Lizzy, but began with a description of going to see the band before their gig at the Hammersmith Odeon in 1975.

> *Security's so tight tonight*
> *Oh, they're ready for a tussle*
> *Gotta keep your backstage passes*
> *'Cause your promoter had the muscle*

At the Hope and Anchor, the pair discussed recording a single together for the fledgling Stiff label until 'my managers found out about it and went berserk, and the record company heard about it, so it was shelved,' said Lynott. 'Nick Lowe is just great. I really like him as a person. I like characters. I think it's better to be a character than a drone.'[9]

A few days later, in New York to rehearse for the Queen tour, Lynott had gone to see Talking Heads at CBGBs and Mink DeVille at Max's Kansas City. Back in London, in 1977 and 1978 he fell into friendships with Joe Strummer and Mick Jones of the Clash, Sid Vicious, Paul Cook and Steve Jones of the Sex Pistols, and Malcolm Owen of the Ruts. On 15 April 1978, he guested at the Roundhouse with Elvis Costello and the Attractions, playing bass on 'Mystery Dance'.

Partly this was the kind of canny manoeuvring that harked back to the days when Lynott poked a finger into every pie available in Dublin's arts and music scene. 'Was it calculating?' says Frank Murray. 'Of course it was. Philip could be a very calculating person.'

'I suspect he was interested in both ways,' says Graham Parker. 'I suspect he was interested musically, in terms of, what's going on with this? And I think he might also have thought, what can I take from this? What can I learn? That's a good musician. He didn't discount it. And also, where does this leave me in the grand scheme of things? That means you're smart. You keep your ears and your eyes open.'

Punk operated a scorched earth policy to bands not terribly dissimilar to Thin Lizzy, but while Brian Downey admits that 'we were side-lined a bit by the press', many of the musicians were prepared to overlook the drum solos, long hair and passé 'chick' talk. They gave Lynott a bye because 'he was like a punk anyway,' says Downey. 'He had that kind of image, and the punks realized that.'

Though nobody would ever define Lynott as a politically motivated or particularly socially conscious songwriter, there was an aggression in their recent albums that resonated with the mood of the times. Thin Lizzy played without any pretence. They radiated an aura of independence. They didn't toe the line. The chaos surrounding their line-up, the bar-room brawls and amped-up, confrontational sensibility spoke of a maverick spirit. There was no attempt to crawl to the United States by softening their live sound with female backing vocalists, conceptual stage shows or synthesizers. If they were to make it, they would make it on their own terms.

The attitude chimed with punk, as did the way they interacted with their audience and fellow musicians. Lynott defined Thin Lizzy as the people's band and called fans 'supporters', as though the group were a football team and their concerts were FA Cup finals. The mass chant of 'Lizzy, Lizzy, Lizzy' at the start of *Live and Dangerous* was closer to the terrace than a rock concert.

At his insistence, after each concert they operated an open-house policy. 'It didn't matter how long they stayed in the venue, just as long as everyone who wanted an autograph or photograph got one,' says Chalkie Davies. 'They queued up and they came through the dressing room. That was part of the ritual. He never scribbled: he always signed "Philip" very beautifully. I never saw him rush it. He never acted the star, then he'd hang out in clubs and talk to anybody who would talk to him.' Only occasionally would particularly persistent fans be given short shrift.

Above all, he gained respect from punks through proximity. David Gilmour and Freddie Mercury weren't hanging out at the Camden Palace, Music Machine, Club for Heroes or the Vortex, but as an innately social animal Lynott mixed with them all. He enjoyed their energy and identified with the iconoclastic spirit. 'Everything they're singing about I actually *do*,' he said. 'I do what I want to do. I never wanted to be like anybody else. I don't give a fuck about good, bad or indifferent music, I just like what I like.'[10]

In the short term Lynott emerged personally unscathed by punk, but he was aware that in the long run it left Thin Lizzy more out of step with the times than they had been a year ago. 'The Boys Are Back in Town' had been voted 1976 single of the year in the *NME* readers' poll. Such plaudits would not be repeated again after the great purge of 1977. 'When we came back [from Canada], everything we were aiming for was being shut down by the press and people in the know,' said

Lynott. 'Instead of going for perfect production it was going back to rawness.'[11] It was the beginning of a period where he increasingly tried to orientate himself with fast-changing musical trends.

Shortly before the release of *Bad Reputation*, on 21 August 1977, Thin Lizzy headlined what was billed as 'Dublin's First Official Open-air Rock Festival' (the debacle in 1970 at Richmond Park had clearly been written out of history) before a crowd of 11,000 at Dalymount Park, home of Bohemians FC, in the north of the city. The bill included the Boomtown Rats, Ireland's first break-out punk band, whom Lynott had befriended when they had moved to London. 'I was freaked out when he came down to see us,' says Bob Geldof. 'He always checked out the opposition. Even though we were potential rivals, he befriended us, gave us great advice.' Thin Lizzy had been instrumental in getting the Boomtown Rats a record deal, bringing the band and their demo tape to Nigel Grainge in 1976, who subsequently signed them to his new label, Ensign.

In Dublin for the long weekend, Lynott relished the role of homecoming king. The night before Dalymount was his twenty-eighth birthday. He held court in the Bailey, then jammed with the Boomtown Rats at Moran's Hotel, a stunt organized by his old friend Smiley Bolger. Word spread around Dublin in minutes. Such was the crush – Moran's held no more than 300 people – that Bolger abandoned any attempt at collecting money at the door and let everyone in for free. Later that night Lynott attended a party at Castledown House in County Kildare, owned by the Guinness family. He was entertaining in his accustomed style in the hayloft when the Gardaí entered, looking for drugs. Lynott was searched and, with a certain inevitability, found to be clean.

He enjoyed an aura of invincibility in his hometown, but he wasn't bulletproof. The day after the festival, Lynott was relaxing in the Brazen Head pub with Chalkie Davies and Chris Salewicz, who were covering the events of the weekend for *NME*, when he saw an article in that day's *Irish Independent* concerning the events at Castledown House. The headline read, 'SIX HELD IN DRUGS RAID ON POP PARTY', going on to mention the 'thousands of pounds worth of cannabis and cocaine seized'. Noticing that his own name was prominently dispalyed, Lynott immediately marched across Dublin. 'He went charging up to the newspaper offices,' says Salewicz. 'I remember this very traditional editor in his striped shirt and tie, and Lynott shouting, "My fucking granny saw that, and it's not fucking true, I didn't have any fucking drugs." Obviously it was completely true, he just got someone else to carry them. Blows were struck. It was all very Irish. A local skirmish. But the big thing was, *my fucking granny saw that*.'

The vision of Lynott as the honourable gunslinger pursuing a righteous cause was rather undermined a week later when he attacked a *Melody Maker* journalist at the Reading Festival over disparaging remarks that had been published about him. 'He wasn't the kind of guy who would keep it in,' says Scott Gorham. 'That was not a Phil-ism. If he was bugged you knew about it. It could be acting like an idiot in front of him, or a bad review, or not doing what you said you would. He would rant and rave – "I'll fucking kill this guy, I'll beat the shite out of him" – and let rip. Sometimes he had to be restrained from doing it. He was not the kind of guy you wanted to piss off.' Chris O'Donnell recalls Lynott beating up Charlie McLennan on one occasion because 'he was taking the piss'. Few people ever recall him apologizing. 'Philip never said sorry about anything – ever,' says Scott Gorham. 'His idea of an apology was to say, "Here man, I bought you this." We had some silly-assed business argument once, and he drove over to the house and gave me two bedside tables. That was his way of saying the argument was over.'

The scuffle at the offices of the *Irish Independent* only added to the instantly mythical status of a long weekend that established Thin Lizzy as Ireland's biggest ever band, and crowned Lynott as the country's first genuine rock star. He emerged for the encore at Dalymount with a light, almost ceremonial dusting of white powder on his moustache.

He embraced the role of paterfamilias to the Irish rock scene. For the rest of his life he went out of his way to mentor, encourage and support Irish musicians, be they folk groups, punk bands, electronic acts or rock and rollers. At the time of Dalymount, in a community hall in north Dublin, four teenage boys calling themselves the Hype were trying to master 'Don't Believe a Word' and 'Dancing in the Moonlight'. They would soon change their name to U2, and in little more than a year would be playing with Lynott at McGonagle's and the Stardust Ballroom. Bottom of the bill at Dalymount had been another up-and-coming Irish punk band, the Radiators from Space. Later in 1977 Lynott hired them to open for Thin Lizzy on their UK tour.

He was entirely comfortable being the benevolent sugar daddy, dispensing largesse to those who needed a helping hand up the ladder. He was less secure when it came to dealing with the really big beasts, especially when they came lumbering onto his patch. When the Rolling Stones played Slane Castle in County Meath in the early 1980s, Lynott, his wife, friends, family and colleagues arranged a grand day out to see them. 'All the Lizzy crew turned up, we were all ready to go,' says Helen Ruttle, a close friend and neighbour of the Lynotts when they moved to Dublin. 'But was Philip ready? No. There was somebody much bigger than Philip in town that day and he wasn't interested. We got there just about in time for the Stones. It was always the same if there was an artist bigger than him. He wasn't keen.'

Bob Geldof sensed a shift in mood when the Boomtown Rats started having their own commercial success. In the *Record Mirror* end-of-year poll in 1977, Thin Lizzy and Boomtown Rats were jointly awarded Best Album for *Bad Reputation* and *Boomtown Rats* respectively. Geldof, improbably, was voted best singer; Lynott came in at number two. Even more problematic was the amount of press the motor-mouthed Geldof generated in Ireland. '[Philip] was supposed to be king of the castle on his home territory, but there we were on the telly, in the charts and in all the papers,' Geldof said. 'He was very jealous and suddenly he wasn't so helpful.'[12] Lynott would later admit to friends that he found Geldof tiresome.

Yet no matter who came in their wake, and how much farther they travelled, Thin Lizzy had got there first. Regardless of their chosen form of musical expression, Irish bands looked at Lynott and thought, maybe, just maybe, we can do this too. '*Jailbreak* was the one, and "The Boys Are Back in Town",' says Geldof. 'Then they're off and running. Once they've done that, then you go, "Wow, an Irish band can break through." That was the big thing. It was a breakout.'

By the time Lynott returned from Thin Lizzy's second US tour of 1977 with Graham Parker and the Rumour in early November, those around him noticed a change in his behaviour. It had been a starry year. While rehearsing in New York in January prior to the Queen tour, a limousine, rather than the customary station wagon, had been made available to the band. He rather liked this, and it became his favoured mode of transport in the US henceforth. 'Philip had these philosophies,' says Chalkie Davis. 'Like, even if they didn't have the money, they needed to turn up and leave in a limousine so they looked like stars.'

He observed the mega-watt star power of Freddie Mercury at close quarters. It was a first-hand masterclass in advanced rock diva-dom. By the time Lynott returned to the States in September 1977 on Thin Lizzy's headlining tour, he was starting to flex his muscles, circumnavigating management to demand things he didn't necessarily want or need as a test of loyalty and an affirmation of status. 'Up until then Phil had left it to me and Chris Morrison to deliver what was needed for the band,' says Chris O'Donnell. 'Then Phil started to see if you were incredibly difficult you got treated differently. That became a real sea change.'

'To me, rock is just a game,' he said.[13] He enjoying raising the stakes. Big-hitting industry players like Rod Stewart's manager, Billy Gaff, were turning his head at LA parties. The legendarily combative Don Arden was circling. Lynott stayed loyal to Morrison and O'Donnell, as they did to him, but he made sure they were aware of his pulling power.

'The rock star thing started to raise its ugly head post-Queen,' says Frank Murray. 'They were a band who were far, far bigger than us, and Freddie first of all was a monster star. I just think Philip saw [how] they were being treated and decided, I want a bit of that for myself. Which is natural enough, but I was seeing him as my old friend and I disagreed with an awful lot of his actions. I knew he was only doing them for effect. Stupid things became important, like the size of the hotel bed . . . By the end of 1977, me and him were really niggling each other.'

Having been on the sharp end of Queen's policy of keeping the support band on a tight leash, Lynott meted out similar behaviour to Graham Parker and the Rumour. 'It was obviously the Phil Lynott show,' says Parker. 'He liked to soundcheck quite a long time, and we never got long enough. There's also a trick with being the opening act, you don't get as many lights. You don't get as much of anything. In New York there was a real to-do [over this], but I was the kind of guy who was like, "Hey, I'm having a blast," and Phil was like, "Well, I'm having a blast, too." We didn't get into it personally in any way.'

A disillusioned Frank Murray would shortly leave his role as tour manager. The two men remained friends, but his departure was the start of a gradual exit of some of Lynott's most trusted coterie, a process one member likens to the break-up of a family unit.

The use of cocaine – virtually ubiquitous throughout the music industry by this time – did not help. 'There were drugs every-where,' Brian Downey told me. 'People were coming up with all sorts of dope, and we were just human.' Scott Gorham maintains it was still 'casual stuff', but Lynott was transitioning from dabbler to enthusiast. It was another status symbol: he once paid a vast sum of money for a rock of pure Peruvian flake cocaine. He started taking tranquilizers to take the edge off the highs and to help him sleep, which left him groggy and in a foul mood the next morning.

He could be 'bossy, shouty and arrogant,' says Paul Scully, but on a one-to-one basis, Lynott remained charming, polite, engaged and inquisitive. 'He was a very sensitive person, I thought,' says Parker. 'Certainly he wasn't just a strutting rock star. He brought a lot of intelligence to things. The cocaine phase was a peripheral thing that didn't seem to happen very often.'

'There was still a very tender side to him,' says Chris Morrison. 'My parents came to the Thin Lizzy concert at Lewisham Odeon in 1977, and on stage Phil came forward and said, "There's two people in the audience I'd like to dedicate this to, and that's Mr and Mrs Morrison." And then he played "Still in Love with You". It was a fantastic thing to do. Those kind of things end up meaning more to you than a lot of things that happened.'

Lynott's insistence on practising with an amplifier rather than headphones led to a deterioration in neighbourly relations at Embassy House. Shortly before Christmas 1977, he moved to a rented terraced house on Anson Road in Cricklewood. He shared with Chalkie Davies. In time other people, such as Gary Holton from the band Heavy Metal Kids, moved in. 'He had always been in a gang,' says Davies. 'I don't think he was a loner. He might not come downstairs for a few days, he would just rest and girls would come over or whatever, but he liked to have his mates around him.'

One new resident changed the Anson Road dynamic. Caroline Crowther was the eighteen-year-old daughter of television personality Leslie Crowther, one time *Crackerjack* presenter, and soon to be host of prime-time ITV hits *The Price Is Right* and *Stars in Their Eyes*. Crowther was working at Tony Brainsby's office, and through that connection first met Lynott at a party. She was attracted by the combination of powerful masculinity and the suggestion of something softer, more playful. Lynott almost immediately began showing up more often at the office.

Tall, slender, with an elegant English rose complexion, Crowther lived in Richmond. She was privately educated, intelligent and self-possessed, the antithesis of the stereotypical ditzy PR blonde. Brainsby's office was involved with several punk and New Wave acts. Crowther was working and socializing with a group that included Bob Geldof's future wife, Paula Yates, and Magenta Devine, the girlfriend of Generation X's Tony James, and later the presenter of *Reportage* on BBC2. She ran with a fashionable crowd and had already done her fair share of fast living before she met Lynott.

The relationship quickly became serious. 'It was obvious that he had fallen in love, despite his theoretical, "I'm not going to let that happen again,"' says Chalkie Davies. On 11 February 1978,

Lynott took Crowther to Stamford Bridge to watch Manchester United play Chelsea. 'I went with them and I thought, hmm, there you go,' says Chris O'Donnell. 'He was smitten instantly. She was the one, I just knew.'

13

What had been conceived as a swift stop-gap turned into Thin Lizzy's masterpiece. Lynott wanted to collaborate with Tony Visconti again, but the producer was due to begin work with David Bowie in the spring of 1978, taping a series of concerts for the *Stage* album. Rather than prolong the making of a new studio album by recording either side of Visconti's prior commitment, they decided to make a quick live record.

Bad Reputation was the third album of original material Thin Lizzy had recorded in a little over twelve months. 'I thought he might have been exhausted, but Philip never took time off,' says Frank Murray. 'The only time he'd take time off would be to [make] a record, and that was work.'

'I remember a conversation with Chris Morrison early in 1978, and he was concerned that they weren't giving Phil enough time to sit down with his notebook the way he used to,' says Chalkie Davies. 'He was writing music first and lyrics later, and it shouldn't be like that.'

The next album, at least, relieved that burden. In February, Visconti was given the tapes from several Thin Lizzy shows, dating back to the Hammersmith Odeon in the autumn of 1976, with a view to assembling a live double album. The process was tricky. The concerts had been recorded in Europe and North America using a variety of equipment. 'The tapes were in different formats at different speeds, some had Dolby, some didn't,' says Visconti. 'It was a nightmare. We hit the wall with technical obstacles, but once we'd sorted out what performances we'd be using, Phil started saying, "I'm not too in love with my bass parts. When I sing and play I make mistakes." Which is valid. It's hard to play bass and sing at the same time.'

Which is how what Visconti calls the 'overdubbing miasma' began. *Live and Dangerous* has become notorious for the amount of embellishment grafted on to the raw recordings; somewhat unfairly, given that the majority of live albums are finessed to some degree.

Chalkie Davies watched Lynott leave Anson Road for work each day and wondered why he was taking so long to mix an in-concert record. 'He was spending an inordinate amount of time in the studio, and he always took his instrument with him,' says Davies. 'He didn't just go down and mix. I think it got out of hand. He got obsessive about cleaning it up and making it perfect.' The man who would open a backstage inquest into one stray note was keen to make the album as powerful as it could be.

'We fixed a couple of bass notes, and then Phil said, "That was great, why don't I just replay it?"' says Visconti. 'I'd say he replayed around 50 per cent of the songs, ballpark figure.' Lynott played at full volume and used a radio transmitter, which enabled him to prowl around the top level of the three-tiered control room in Visconti's Good Earth studios in Soho. It was a performance. Then he started replacing some vocals. 'We put up the identical mike that he would sing into live.'

Visconti claims that Brian Robertson and Scott Gorham later asked to flesh out their original guitar parts. 'I can't remember how much. They fixed some mistakes, and also did double-tracking.

So what you hear on the average track on *Live and Dangerous* is a fixed vocal, most likely a replayed bass part, and mostly the original guitars and drums. I know this to be true because I was in the control room at all times. This is no great crime. Everyone does it. The live feel is there, just a few things are fixed, and it still sounds absolutely great.'

The album was finished at Studio Des Dames in Paris. Visconti brought his wife, Mary Hopkin, Lynott brought Caroline Crowther, and they dined on gin and oysters at La Coupole. 'In the end it took longer than five weeks, more like seven weeks,' says Visconti. 'Bowie was extremely pissed off, but at that point *Live and Dangerous* was turning into a work of art and we had to finish it.'

The difference, in the end, was a question of emphasis rather than authenticity. Listening to the original tapes of all three Hammersmith Odeon shows from November 1976, or the full set from Philadelphia's Tower Theater a year later, it is not hard to identify where certain bum notes or glitches have been rectified, but it's equally apparent that no wholesale whitewash or act of dishonesty has occurred. The overall impact of the unrefined recordings remains astonishingly powerful.

Perhaps even more so than *Jailbreak*, *Live and Dangerous* is the record that seals Thin Lizzy's reputation. A double album, it's an alternative greatest hits with an effervescent in-the-room ambience, a document of a band at their peak and in their natural habitat. It routinely features high, and sometimes at the top, of lists of the greatest ever live albums, and is a perennial musicians' favourite. 'Bono and The Edge told me that that album was the primer for their band,' says Visconti. 'It had a massive effect on a lot of people, it changed a few things, and it certainly wouldn't have done that if it had just been a throwaway live album.'

'Nobody wants the warts and all,' says Chris O'Donnell. 'That lasts for a minute. It became a document of a great group that would stand the test of time.' It was a record that made absolute sense in the wake of punk because it captured not just a sound but an attitude that was essentially territorial. The music hits hard, but it also slides on 'Johnny the Fox Meets Jimmy the Weed', swings on 'Dancing in the Moonlight' and sighs on 'Still in Love with You'. Lynott had worked hard to allow room for that kind of space and tenderness. Thin Lizzy had earned the right to be more than just a narrow definition of a rock group, and on *Live and Dangerous* they recouped.

The record felt like the summation of the past four years' hard work. It is the defining statement of the band that had formed in 1974. The only track acknowledging that there had once been *another* kind of band called Thin Lizzy was 'The Rocker', and even that now sounded very different.

Even the title was a masterstroke. Thin Lizzy's management wanted to make a concert film to accompany the live album, featuring the Clash supporting Thin Lizzy at the Roundhouse in London. The idea was to create a 1970s version of the Rolling Stones's 1968 multi-act extravaganza, *Rock and Roll Circus*. The Clash's manager Bernard Rhodes, a dream-spinner and hustler in the finest Svengali tradition, suggested instead that the film showed Thin Lizzy playing live, and then followed the band as they went to watch the Clash performing at the Marquee. It was a joke with a point; the cultural weathervane was spinning. Rhodes went on to declare that the Clash couldn't do a film with Thin Lizzy because 'we are political animals, and everything we do has to have an element of danger about it,' O'Donnell recalls. 'That was it. The light came on.'

Up to that point the album had been called *Thin Lizzy Live*. There is an early proof of the album with that name, with a front cover featuring the group shot that ultimately ended up above the track listing on the back. Inspired by Rhodes, at the last moment the album was given a new title – *Live and Dangerous* – and the cover image was changed to the classic Chalkie Davies close-up shot of Lynott on his knees. Downey and Gorham weren't consulted on the change, and were furious, although they were mollified somewhat by sales of 600,000 copies of the live double album.

Released on 2 June 1978, *Live and Dangerous* reached number two in the UK charts, kept from number one thanks only to the omnipresent cultural phenomenon that was *Grease*. The live version of 'Rosalie/Cowgirl's Song' became a top-twenty single. Its enduring huge success masked more immediate problems. The bulk of the record was recorded in 1976, and only two tracks – 'Southbound' and 'Dancing in the Moonlight' – represented material from the past eighteen months. The rest of the tracks were written pre-1977, although 'Are You Ready?' and 'Baby Drives Me Crazy' had not been released on any previous singles or albums. They were party songs, exclusively reserved for show time.

Lynott was not the only band member who chafed a little at having to reproduce the album's historic track listing night after night on the *Live and Dangerous* tour of the summer of 1978. Notwithstanding the addition of 'Bad Reputation', 'Don't Believe a Word' and a new song, 'S & M', the set adhered closely to the one they had been playing for two years.

It seemed rather odd to be touring a live album in the first place, but then touring was what Thin Lizzy did. That was also becoming a problem. 'We were . . . on the road all the time, there never seemed to be any real downtime,' says Scott Gorham. 'I place that firmly on the shoulders of the management: they always said, if you ever come off the road, people will just forget about you, and that put the fear of God into us. We'd be out there for six, seven months at a pop.'

Gorham and Lynott were their own worst enemies. After a fortnight without any shows they would be jumpy, itching to get back. It had become their reality. In Lynott's case, the band dominated everything. If he had downtime, he would be on the phone to Morrison and O'Donnell to discuss the next move or to air grievances. His mother told him he was working too hard.

'He was the songwriter, the singer, everything,' Philomena Lynott told me. 'When they finished making a record I would ask, "Where's Brian [Downey]?" and he would say, "He's gone fishing, Ma." Brian had two sons and he loved fishing. Philip never had time to do that. He had to think of the next album, the next tour. No time to sleep. When things went awry in the band it was up to him to find replacements.' He would, occasionally, concede that he felt pressurized. 'It's tough to be on top of all this, man,' he confided to Nigel Grainge one night as a party unfolded around him.

The *Live and Dangerous* tour ended on 22 and 23 June with two nights in London at the 12,000-capacity Empire Pool, now Wembley Arena. It was the biggest indoor venue Thin Lizzy had ever headlined, supported by Horslips, the Irish band that included Lynott's old friend and Tara Telephone co-founder, Eamon Carr. 'Philip grabbed me and took me aside, not to chop out lines, but to take a rain-check,' says Carr. 'It happened a few times over the years. It was a case of, "Look where we are!" I used to love that, actually, because it was almost like he was marking his progress, and I was someone he could measure his success by . . . It was strange and touching. I'd never realized there was that kind of sentimentality in him.'

Lynott didn't want to play Wembley. He felt it was too big, too impersonal, and that the 'supporters' would get a raw deal. He was persuaded to change his mind by one of Britain's leading promoters, Harvey Goldsmith, who convinced him that American agents needed to be shown that Thin Lizzy could handle these kinds of venues if the band were to have a shot at re-establishing themselves in the States. To this end, *Creem's* rock critic, Richard Riegel, was flown over. 'They opened with "Jailbreak",' says Chris Morrison. 'Phil walked out through the smoke and the sirens, banged his bass and the roadie had forgotten to turn on his amp. He recovered, but I didn't go near the dressing room that night. I know he saw every roadie one by one.'

Despite the opening-night hiccup, Riegel's feature-length review reported that, yes, hepatitis and recent albums had slowed the band's trajectory in the US, but Thin Lizzy was fighting fit and arena-worthy once again. Almost before his words hit the page, the ground around the band tilted once more. Perhaps the saddest part of *Live and Dangerous* was the fact that within six weeks of its release the line-up that it celebrated – Lynott, Gorham, Robertson and Downey – permanently broke up.

Brian Robertson had been merely tolerated since the incident at the Speakeasy. Chalkie Davies recalls that Lynott had been plotting his departure for some time. 'I remember Philip telling me well in advance that Robbo would be gone, and the next thing I remember Gary [Moore] was at Anson Road with Brush Shiels.' Robertson's behaviour backstage at the Wembley concerts – he was drunk, stoned and abusive to the road crew – was the last straw. His last stand was in Ibiza, on 7 July 1978.

The two remained friends and Lynott harboured a degree of regret over how things had turned out, not just professionally, but personally. Robertson was only eighteen when he joined Thin Lizzy and was given little guidance or advice about how to pace himself. At times, those around the band felt he was goaded into going too far. One legacy of his time in the group was a serious and lasting alcohol problem. When Sean O'Connor of the Lookalikes was touring with Thin Lizzy in 1980, he recalls that 'there was not one day went by when I wasn't offered coke by numerous people. I didn't take drugs and Philip was incredibly protective. I saw him pin a guy against the wall once and say, "If you ever offer Sean coke again I'll fucking have you killed." He would say to me, "I don't want another Robbo on my hands, or on my conscience either."' Darren Wharton and Midge Ure also credit Lynott for keeping them away from drugs when they were part of Thin Lizzy.

Gary Moore joined again, this time as the permanent second guitarist. Privately, Brush Shiels told Lynott that there was no way Moore would last the distance.

To lose one Brian can be counted as misfortune; to lose two suggested a deeper malaise. When Thin Lizzy departed for America for a ten-week tour beginning on 8 August 1978, they did so without Brian Downey, Lynott's ever-reliable rock since the days of the Black Eagles. Downey had decided he wanted out. He was tired, overdoing things and concerned about the escalating drug scene in the band. He had a young family, which he barely saw. He was also disillusioned by the music.

'The direction seemed to be completely lost,' he said in 1979. 'It was very strange with the *Live and Dangerous* set. We'd recorded it two years earlier and we then had to go and promote an album which was two years old.'[1] Downey left and went underground, retreating to a cottage in rural Cork. He spent his time fishing, listening to music, and trying to re-engage with a vague memory of normal life. It was the kind of pause that Lynott never allowed himself. He was furious with the drummer, and regarded his departure as a traitorous act. For a time it wasn't clear whether Downey would want – or would be allowed – to return, but he was back in the ranks by the end of the year.

Rather than cancel another US tour, he was replaced at short notice by American drummer, Mark Nauseef, late of the Ian Gillan Band. Such was Thin Lizzy's momentum, the personnel changes didn't make much discernible difference to the power of the live show. 'Every night we hit,' Nauseef recalls. 'Every single night. Phil was a great manager of the unmanageable. He ran a tight ship. He knew all of our personalities and knew exactly how to steer everyone so that we were all pumped each night and ready.' While in Memphis, Lynott booked the band into Sun Studios and they recorded a handful of early rock-and-roll classics. At soundchecks they worked up a new song, 'Waiting for an Alibi', and quickly threw it into the set. 'He loved to get the fans involved,' says Nauseef. 'They actually became part of the writing process.'

After leaving the United States, the band embarked on their first trip to Australia and Japan. On 28 August they played a free concert to a vast sea of humanity (the myth puts the number at 100,000; more sober accounts suggest it was closer to 30,000) on the steps of the Sydney Opera House. The show was filmed by Seven Network, broadcast on Australian radio, and subsequently released on numerous semi-legal bootleg albums and films. Lynott's songs had made it all the way around the world.

In March 1978, Caroline Crowther became pregnant. With the baby due just before Christmas, they made plans to move out of Anson Road, which was not set up along the lines of a conventional family home. Bob Geldof would visit regularly with Paula Yates. 'It was drug city,' he says. 'Endless coke.' Lynott had recently bought a huge video camera – it was so big he wheeled it around in a supermarket trolley – and one night decided he was going to make a video for the Boomtown Rats's new single, 'She's So Modern'. 'Me and Chalkie stood behind his sofa,' says

Geldof. 'Phil put "She's So Modern" on the record player, me and Chalkie [sang], and you can hear Phil going, "Hur-hur-hur. Roight, now let's do this one," and then you hear, *snnniiiiifff.*'

Later, they attempted to write a song for *That Summer!*, a 1979 film starring Ray Winstone with a New Wave soundtrack. 'We sat on two stools,' says Geldof. 'It's now about two or three in the morning, and we're off our heads. We start writing this Beach Boys' pastiche because the film was called *That Summer!* The words were: *"It came a little late, man / But now it's here, it's great, man / I can hardly wait / Because this summer's here at last."* It was fucking terrible, and we thought it was a work of genius. I fell off the stool, and literally crawled up to the loo and started to tremble and throw up. I didn't know what lines we were doing, and Phil clearly had given me a line of smack. I think he knew he'd given me a line of smack, because he then tried to get into bed with Paula. She told him to fuck off, as I crawled back into bed, trembling. That was *typical* of him. That roguish quality, the glint in the eye. You might think you'd be pissed off, but it was so obvious. "Oh right, man, hur-hur, sorry about that!" It was so blatant, so ludicrous.'

Sid Vicious and his girlfriend Nancy Spungen were also regular guests at Anson Road. 'Sid seemed to always end up at Phil's house for some reason,' says Brian Downey. 'Every time I went around he was there in the corner, out of it.'

'I remember [Gary Moore] saying there was bloodstains up the wall where Sid and Nancy had been jacking up in Phil's toilet,' says producer Chris Tsangarides, who worked with Moore and Lynott in 1978. Chalkie Davies insists punk's *enfants terribles* were not such troublesome house guests. 'Philip had the big old Sony video player, and they would just sit transfixed in the living room and watch old Elvis Presley movies. They were good as gold, they respected Philip. I remember Philip trying to teach Sid some bass lines, and Sid said, "I'm not interested in any of that crap, I'm in the fucking Sex Pistols!"

'People think when I lived with Philip it must have been non-stop partying. No. We slept. People came over, but I don't remember ever having a party. [Paul] Cook and [Steve] Jones might come over, Mick [Jones] and Joe [Strummer], but it was five or six people at most. Admittedly, we didn't unpack very well. Our suitcases were always at the bottom of the stairs, but life at Anson Road was not what people expected. Life off the road was quiet, because you were exhausted.'

In the autumn of 1978, Lynott bought 184 Kew Road, a two-storey, five-bedroom house opposite the Lion's Gate entrance to Royal Botanic Gardens Kew, near Richmond in the far reaches of west London. It cost £250,000. He was in the United States and remained hands-off during the entire process. Crowther found the house and the Thin Lizzy office arranged the mortgage. Lynott didn't actually see the property with his own eyes until he owned it.

The house was protected by high walls and an electric entrance gate. There was room for parking at the front and sizeable gardens at the back, and a garage, which Lynott soon converted into a make-shift recording studio. Chalkie Davies moved in for a short period after leaving Anson Road, but left after their daughter was born. One of Lynott's Dublin friends, Gus Curtis, was installed at Kew Road, more or less full-time. Having bought a blue Mercedes 450 SEL which he couldn't drive, Lynott put Curtis on the payroll as his driver, both on and off tour, a position that encompassed almost every task imaginable.

For all that he was a man of the 'street', Lynott was not necessarily a man of the world. 'The office was there to be all things to all people,' says Chris O'Donnell. 'He had no concept of banks or cashing a cheque. He would get his money by calling us, and we would bike over £500 in cash. Cash was what he understood. We invested £100,000 in Gilts [Government bonds] but he got a bee in his bonnet because his accountant told him they were only worth £80,000 at market value at that time. He freaked out. We told him they were long-term investments – "What the fuck? I need money now!" – and he sold them at a loss. So we didn't get involved in that anymore.'

Kew Road used solid-fuel heating, which confused him when he first moved in. He asked Caroline to call the Thin Lizzy office, where O'Donnell explained they would need to buy fuel. 'He wasn't really a domestic guy,' says Scott Gorham. 'I knew he had money, because I had money, but he had this 1930s kitchen that he never redecorated, and I found that kind of odd. You'd open his refrigerator and there wasn't a hell of a lot in there.'

He installed a jukebox in the corner of his study, which looked out onto the back garden. He would go in to write, carrying his notebooks in his new metal briefcase, and then record in the garage. 'Infamously, it was the only seven-track studio in the world, because one of the tracks didn't work,' says Midge Ure, who had known Lynott since the early 1970s and had become a good friend. 'He never learned how to work it himself, so he kept his sound engineer on a retainer. He never used it that much. I think he just liked the idea that every musician should have their own private studio. It was built by his Irish mates and you could hear the planes flying overhead.'

While enjoying the fruits of his most successful album, Lynott was at the same time forging musical relationships born from his punk ties. Before Thin Lizzy left for the United States in August 1978, Lynott had marked the opening night of Frank Murray's Electric Ballroom club in Camden by presenting a new band, the Greedy Bastards. Making their live debut on 29 July, members included Steve Jones, Paul Cook, Chris Spedding, Bob Geldof, Jimmy Bain, Gary Moore, Scott Gorham and Brian Downey. The idea had been kicking around since late 1977. It was essentially a chance for a group of social friends to play together without having to formalize the arrangement. Their respective managers were side-lined. The band were paid in cash and journalists had to buy their own tickets.

'The thing that bugged us was, none of us ever earned any money doing gigs, even though we were having hits,' says Bob Geldof. 'So Phil said, "Let's form a group called the Greedy Bastards." We'd do a couple of Lizzy [songs], a couple of Rats, a couple of Pistols, and then anything we liked. We'd get cash, and then we divvied it up.'

Chris Spedding – a stalwart session man and sometime solo artist who had played on the Sex Pistols demos – recalls that 'no fee was offered or given, so that message didn't filter through to me! I was happy to do it, though. Phil was master of ceremonies, instigating the whole thing. It was the time of punk, and there were a lot of people of the old guard, dare I say, jumping on the bandwagon. I think Phil was one of those. It was the usual schmooze, all the usual people. It was a social night.'

The set was weighted heavily towards Thin Lizzy material, including 'Jailbreak', 'Cowboy Song' and 'The Boys Are Back in Town', plus the Sex Pistols's 'Pretty Vacant' and 'No One is Innocent' and tracks by, among others, Stevie Wonder, Peter Green and Mink DeVille.

The Greedy Bastards provided the soundtrack to an increasingly hedonistic scene. Of those in Lynott's immediate orbit, Sid Vicious, Willy DeVille of Mink DeVille, Malcolm Owen and Gary Holton were all heroin users. Jimmy Bain, former Rainbow bass player and Brian Robertson's new band-mate in Wild Horses, was living nearby. He and his wife, Lady Sophia Crichton-Stuart, daughter of the sixth Marquis of Bute, would become regular visitors at Kew Road. Bain was also a habitual heroin user, and would come to be regarded by many around Lynott as a wholly negative influence.

And then there was Johnny Thunders, the man given the dubious, if debatable, credit of introducing heroin to Britain's punk scene in the first place. Live-wire publicist and general scene-maker, B. P. Fallon – the brother of Lynott's old friend Peter Fallon – was currently managing Thunders after the break-up of the Heartbreakers, the band Thunders had formed following the demise in 1976 of trashy proto-punks, the New York Dolls. Fallon invited Lynott to play on Thunders's solo album, *So Alone*. Lynott duly arrived at Marble Arch Studios in the summer of 1978 with a lump of hash as big as his fist as an ice-breaker. He played bass on the instrumental 'Pipeline' and sang on 'Daddy Rollin' Stone' with Steve Marriott, once of the Small Faces. Steve Jones was on drums.

'That was pretty crazy,' says the album's producer, Steve Lillywhite. 'Thunders had some heroin on a guitar pick and said, "Do you want to try some?"' During the sessions Lynott was, according to B. P. Fallon, concerned at the state of Thunders – 'He's too out of it, *knowarramean?*' – but he was, as one friend notes, moving almost inexorably towards the centre of the 'circle of smack'.

Shortly afterwards, Lynott was on tour with Thin Lizzy in the United States, where they played three nights supporting Blue Öyster Cult at the Palladium in New York on 29 and 30 September and 1 October. 'When I'd see who was turning up in the dressing room I'd think, oh boy, here we go,' says Mark Nauseef. In hindsight, the journey Lynott took one night in New York assumes a symbolic significance, a trip over some psychological Rubicon.

Taking a midnight ride around Manhattan in the now inevitable limousine, Lynott first checked in on Sid Vicious, who was living in the Chelsea Hotel with Nancy Spungen and playing a series of freak-show gigs at Max's Kansas City to cover bed, board and drug bills. During a break in his set they all took cocaine in the toilets. Later, Lynott cruised to the Greenwich Village apartment of Willy DeVille; shortly after arriving, Lynott's limo was despatched to Harlem to score hundreds of dollars' worth of Dilaudid, pharmaceutical morphine in pill form. The capsules were later melted down and injected.

For Chalkie Davies, who accompanied Lynott and Scott Gorham to DeVille's place, the visit was a 'pivotal moment'. There is a picture of the two men taken that night in the apartment. DeVille, his greased-back coiffure in a state of magnificent dishevelment, wears his shirt open to the waist and stares out with a look of glassy insolence. Lynott is way-high, still chic in his white jacket and skinny tie, but with a dangerous new look in his eye. He brandishes his flick knife towards the camera. 'Those two together, man, was beyond anything you could describe,' says Nauseef. 'They were peas in a pod, although maybe not in a great way.'

Lynott had insisted that Chalkie Davies take the shot, as though it was a moment that deserved its place in posterity. Against everybody's advice, he had also insisted that the sleeve of *Live and Dangerous* feature a photograph from the studio sessions showing a line of cocaine, a five pound note and a straw. 'It was all part of that Keith Richards' thing,' says Chris Salewicz. 'He thought you had to behave like that to be a rock star. He'd go on about being in touch with the "street", this mythical concept. He was very good at self-mythologizing.'

A fortnight after Thin Lizzy's New York shows, Nancy Spungen was dead of a single stab wound to the abdomen, and Sid Vicious had been arrested for her murder. Within six months, Vicious, too, would be dead. DeVille later died of a heroin overdose. But however unsavoury or unstable some of these characters were, Scott Gorham dismisses the notion that Lynott was not master of his own destiny. 'I liked those guys,' says Gorham. 'When you latch on to a group of guys who are doing those kinds of professional drugs, you're going to fall into it, too, and we both did. But trying to keep up with Philip was impossible. He could out-drink you, out-drug you, out-womanize you. It was scary. I think it was [a case of] other people trying to keep up with him, rather than the other way around.'

The Greedy Bastards reconvened on 16 December 1978 at the Electric Ballroom, and then flew to Ireland for an end-of-term blow-out. When they attended the *Hot Press* Christmas party at McGonagle's on 19 December, appearing alongside Thin Lizzy and the two former Sex Pistols were members of the Vipers, the Boomtown Rats, Revolver, as well as Noel Bridgeman and Brush Shiels. U2 were there that night too, ahead of supporting the Greedies at their upcoming shows in the Stardust Ballroom in Artane.

'Phil was a big star, he carried himself with a certain swagger and elegance, the like of which I'd never seen before,' said Bono. 'But there were knowing glances between them which disturbed me, without my understanding what they were . . . One of the Greedy Bastards came off stage, walked straight through the door, threw up into the [dressing] room, and then immediately walked back on stage. There was a mood around them that was so far from our mood.'[2]

U2 were still a baby band, naive and idealistic, yet they were not the only ones who were aware that the atmosphere around Lynott had changed. 'By then it wasn't quite the same,' says Eamon Carr. 'I felt there was the influence of something else going on. At one point Philip took me away from the madding crowd. I said, "Jeez, things are flying for you," and he confided something. He said, "Yeah, but I can't get a buzz. *I can't get a buzz* . . . I'm even trying heroin." I was slightly taken aback. I didn't quite start lecturing him, but I said, "Ah Jesus, Philip, there's no need for that." It was a strange conversation . . . It was almost like he had to boast that he was moving to another level.'

'Was he into smack because he liked smack, or was he into it because he thought there was something cool about it?' says Chris Salewicz. 'I was never certain, and I maybe thought slightly the latter.' Eric Bell shrugs. 'He just enjoyed it. He enjoyed getting smashed, and after a while it was as if he couldn't get out of it enough.'

An incessant, insatiable quality to Lynott's appetites became more apparent to those close to him at this time. 'He couldn't be satisfied,' says Jim Fitzpatrick. In a new song, 'With Love', Lynott sang, *'This roving Casanova's days are over . . . more or less.'* The caveat showed a degree of self-awareness. 'I think [sex] just became another addiction,' says Chris Salewicz.

Lynott had been one of the judges at the Miss World 1978 contest, held on 16 November at the Royal Albert Hall and televised live. Thin Lizzy were working on the *Black Rose: A Rock Legend* album in Good Earth with Tony Visconti. They watched the show in the studio. 'There were shots of him winking at the winner,' Visconti recalls with a laugh. 'It was so funny. He claimed when he came back that he'd had Miss Brazil in either the men's room or the ladies' room. I wouldn't have put it past him. He probably did – but if he didn't, he had to say that he did.'

He would complain about American women on tour because they made it all too easy. 'I miss the old hunt and kill, I really do,' he said. 'I like to feel, okay, I'm getting here, but I got here by my own route.'[3] He could be notoriously predatory around other people's girlfriends, a fact confirmed by Midge Ure, Bob Geldof and Tony Visconti, among others. Graham Parker recalls an occasion on the US tour of 1977 when Parker's companion flew in from Los Angeles to spend time with him. She came along to the soundcheck for that night's show. 'She was pretty hot-looking,' he says. 'She walked in and Phil's eyes were like, *I want that*. I felt a certain pissed-off feeling from him that she was actually with me. I thought, he's really jealous. Why? He's had more women than I've had hot dinners. It was the conquest thing. There was a feeling that if he didn't get a girl, he seemed a bit depressed.'

'I didn't understand,' says Jim Fitzpatrick. 'You can't say Philip wasn't loved. His granny adored him, the women in his family were very strong. He had Carole and Gale, and then Caroline – three amazing, beautiful women, who really cared about him and were no bimbos. But there were plenty of other bimbos. He had a need to go further. It was like he was verifying himself.'

In the space of twenty-four hours on 19 December 1978, the Greedy Bastards played McGonagle's and Lynott became a father. Caroline Crowther gave birth to their daughter, Sarah Philomena Lynott, in the National Maternity Hospital on Holles Street, Dublin. While marriage was not considered necessary, some traditions were to be observed. The child had to be born in Ireland, and would be raised as a Catholic. 'I remember on the night Sarah was born, you could not have been around a more proud father,' says Scott Gorham. 'He carried around a box of cigars. We were going down Grafton Street, and we hit every bar and everybody got a cigar. She really tugged at his heartstrings in a huge way. He loved her so much it was unbelievable, and right away he wrote that captivating little song about her.'

That sweetheart song, 'Sarah', was eventually included on the new Thin Lizzy album, recorded either side of Christmas, at Pathé Marconi in Paris and at Good Earth in Soho. The only Thin Lizzy album to feature Gary Moore, it is also the last Thin Lizzy album to truly be worthy of the name.

Enjoying a rare day off with breakfast at William's Famous Bar-B-Q, Philadelphia. *(Chalkie Davies)*

ith old friend and metimes foe, Gary oore, on stage and f. *(Chalkie Davies)*

Friends and influences: hanging out with Bob Geldof and Van Morrison.

(Chalkie Davies)

'A pivotal moment'. With Willy DeVille in his Greenwich Village apartment, October 1978. Lynott is brandishing his flick knife. Scott Gorham relaxes in the background.

(Chalkie Davies)

The Greedy Bastards behind the Electric Ballroom, Camden, 1978. *Standing, left to right:* unknown, Lynott, Gary Moore, Scott Gorham, Chris Spedding and Brian Downey. *Front, left to right:* Paul Cook, Steve Jones and Jimmy Bain. *(Chalkie Davies)*

e Photograph an. Posing for ott Gorham in e shadow of the dney Harbour idge, October 78. *(Chalkie Davies)*

o sides of Philip Lynott: rock star and Manchester ited fan. *(Chalkie Davies)*

Marrying Caroline Crowther at St Elizabeth of Portugal church, Richmond, 14 February 1980. *(Denis O'Regan / Getty Images)*

With his daughters, Sarah and Cathleen, and (*left*) Thin Lizzy keyboardist Darren Wharton, at Kew Road, 1980. *(Courtesy of Caroline Taraskevics)*

THE LYNOTTS · 82 · JF

Family life at Glen Corr, Dublin, in the early 1980s. *(Courtesy of Jim Fitzpatrick and Caroline Taraskevics)*

Backstage at Slane Castle, 16 August 1981.
(Courtesy of Sean O'Connor)

(*above*) Performing with Laurence Archer as part of Grand Slam, 1984. *(Pete Cronin / Getty Images)*

(*left*) A promotional poster for Lynott's final gig in Marbella, 6 August 1985.

D·I·S·C·O·T·E·C·A
M·A·R·B·E·L·L·A
L · I · V · E
MARTES 6 de AGOSTO 1985 TUESDAY 6th AUGUST 1985
THE BAND FEATURING
PHIL LYNOTT
EX THIN LIZZY

THE BOYS
ARE BACK IN TOWN
ONE SHOW ONLY

cuba

TICKETS en la puerta del Club
TICKETS available at door

Lynott's wife, mother, children and father-in-law, Leslie Crowther, attend his funeral in Howth, Dublin, 11 January 1986.

(Photocall Ireland)

PART THREE

Sun Goes Down

14

'I always think that something was lost,' says Eamon Carr. 'I'm not quite sure what.'

In December 1976, Lynott had participated in the recording of *Jeff Wayne's Musical Version of War of the Worlds*. Taking on the dramatic role of Parson Nathaniel, he contributed hoarse, hammy theatrics to 'The Spirit of Man', a lengthy duet with Julie Covington. Finally released in July 1978, the album has since sold over 2.5 million copies in the UK alone. It was far from Lynott's finest hour, but its commercial success may have solidified the idea of a career outside of Thin Lizzy.

When Lynott signed a solo album deal in 1978, it changed the way he wrote and the way he functioned within the band. Of some 500 unreleased Thin Lizzy tracks recovered by Universal Music Group in recent years, an unusually high proportion were recorded in 1978 and 1979. Where in the past the band had set aside a block of time to record a new album as a discrete entity, now that focus became blurred. Lynott envisioned a rolling series of sessions drawing on a pool of musical talent, then cherry-picking the best of the results for whatever project they most suited.

'It was always, "Let's go to the studio, let's do *something*!"' says Mark Nauseef. 'We cut tons of stuff. Bahamas, London, Dublin,

Memphis. He had so many ideas. It was like a laboratory. He was always experimenting, stocking up tracks.'

Although Lynott's first solo album, *Solo in Soho*, would not be released until April 1980, its influence began to assert itself during the recording of the next Thin Lizzy record, *Black Rose: A Rock Legend*. Two songs – 'Sarah' and 'With Love' – featured Jimmy Bain, Huey Lewis and Nauseef. They were recorded during sessions that did not feature certain members of Thin Lizzy. Written by Gary Moore, with words by Lynott celebrating the arrival of his daughter, the joyful, unashamedly sentimental 'Sarah' was recorded in London at the same time as Moore's first solo album, *Back on the Streets*, to which Lynott contributed heavily. Another song on *Back on the Streets*, the bruised bolero 'Parisienne Walkways', was started at the same sessions and later finished while Thin Lizzy were recording *Black Rose*.

It was a preview of how things would often work from now on. Although Lynott's solo deal was not a source of friction within the band per se, the methodology caused a slow bleed. 'I thought it was a good outlet, because he was getting a little bit frustrated,' Brian Downey told me. 'He had stuff he couldn't play with us and he wanted to do it on his own. I encouraged him, and I played on a lot of tracks on those albums and I was more than willing to do it.'

Despite Gary Moore's claim that 'Philip wanted to be Rod Stewart', Scott Gorham insists that 'Thin Lizzy was always, *always* number one for Phil'. He was, by nature, more pack leader than lone wolf. 'But what was confusing was that some of those tracks ended up on Lizzy albums, and some on the solo stuff,' says Downey. 'It was never cut and dried, and that chipped away at the band a bit.'

Another contributory factor to Thin Lizzy's at first gradual, then increasingly swift descent from the peak of *Live and*

Dangerous was drug-induced. Gary Moore was working with Thin Lizzy in the studio for the first time as they laid down the basic tracks of *Black Rose* in Paris. Moore had cleaned up his act, relatively speaking, and was frustrated almost from the start of the sessions at what he perceived as a general slackness within the group. He noted how Lynott would often struggle to get into the studio, and when he did his bass sometimes seemed out of tune. The singer could take hours to complete a finished vocal, and was eager to knock off early to visit the newly opened Le Palace nightclub in Faubourg Montmartre, Paris's notoriously excessive answer to Studio 54. The patrons opened up one of its VIP rooms to the band and their retinue.

The environment was not a wholly healthy one for Lynott. '*Black Rose* was when [our drug use] became totally professional,' says Scott Gorham. 'In Paris the dealers were beating the door down – and of course, we let them in, which was just madness. I remember Cliff Richard was recording in the same studio, and Phil said, "Come on, let's drag over Cliff and see what he thinks." So we sat Cliff in front of the desk and right behind him there's this fucking drug dealer chopping out a line of smack. I'm looking at Cliff and, God bless him, he didn't look over his shoulder one time, he doesn't even acknowledge that this guy is even in the room. But I thought, this has got to be uncomfortable for him.'

A defining snapshot of the sessions was the image of Lynott singing 'Got to Give It Up' in the studio. It was a song in which he blurred the lines between fact and fiction, casting himself as the beautiful loser '*sinking slow*', a man already lost to alcohol who is '*now messing with the heavy stuff*'. Deliberately close to the bone, it played a flirtatious game of truth or dare with the listener. When Lynott wasn't relating his bad habits with a kind of grim pride, he sounded a little frightened. In the studio, he sang 'Got to Give

It Up' with a joint in one hand and a brandy in the other, snorting lines of cocaine between takes. 'I'm sitting next to Visconti,' says engineer Kit Woolven. 'Tony was no angel at the time, either, but he turns to me and goes, "Got to give it up? I can't work with this fucking hypocrite!" I think that's highly amusing, actually. It's rock 'n' roll, isn't it?'

The song returned to the dubious manifesto of 'Warriors' three years previously. 'I don't condone drugs, really, but I know why artists take drugs,' Lynott said, explaining the 'honest contradictions' of 'Got to Give It Up'. 'Why do people climb mountains? To go to the edge. People always want to go to extremes, and if you go to the edge, you must be prepared to fall off. And lots of guys have. Well, some people don't need it at all – but seemingly all the artists that I rate have, one way or another, gone to the extremes. Some made it back and wrote about that experience, and others didn't.'[1]

'Honestly Philip wasn't really any different to [how he had been] on *Bad Reputation* and *Live and Dangerous*,' says Tony Visconti. 'He *was* ill, though. There were a couple of days when he couldn't get out his hotel room and he'd just stay in bed. Charlie [McLennan] would come in with chicken soup, and Phil refused to see a doctor. I told him I was worried about his health and that he looked like shit, and that he should stop whatever he was doing. He'd be sheepish and promise not to hit it too hard, but it's a hard call to make. The drug of choice was still cocaine, and there were copious amounts of it in Paris. People were doing cocaine openly. If they were doing heroin I'm sure that was covert. I didn't see it, but it would explain his poor health.'

Heroin is an analgesic. Brian Downey was not alone in feeling that Lynott was starting to sink under the pressure of keeping all the balls in the air. He was also missing his girlfriend and daughter. 'He was very, very lonely after he met Caro and he was [away from home],' says Chalkie Davies. In Paris, sometimes he talked to Caroline for so long on the telephone he would fall asleep and wake up the next day still connected to Kew Road.

Black Rose: A Rock Legend was released on 14 April 1979, midway through Thin Lizzy's British tour. It was their second number-two record in a row, and though lacking a certain vital spark of inspiration, it contains some of Lynott's most concise and direct songwriting. The irrepressible 'Waiting for an Alibi' gave the band their biggest hit since 'The Boys Are Back in Town', a song it seemed consciously to mirror. 'Do Anything You Want To' – glam-rock meets New Wave meets Lynott's Elvis Presley impersonation – was another top-twenty single. Attitudinal and aspirational, it aimed a swipe at the critics 'who proceed to blindly criticise you for not doing what they think you ought to be doing,' a theme which was becoming a regular Lynott beef.[2]

The rest was a mixed bag. 'S & M' was throwaway funk, and a further example of Lynott's desire to take a walk on the sleazy side; as well as the potions and powders of 'Got to Give It Up', 'Toughest Street in Town' talked of '*taking smack*'. The vulnerable open-heartedness of 'Sarah', with its light, Stevie Wonder-like jazz lines and major-sevenths, was an anomaly. If fatherhood had relocated the whereabouts of Lynott's sweet spot, it had also made him more intolerant. 'With having the kid now I'm far more protective,' he said. 'It's making me twice as quick to go off the mark with the temper . . . as well as making me very soppy.'[3] Henceforth, these emotional extremes were carried through into his songwriting, which became increasingly polarized: Thin Lizzy was for the rough stuff. His solo albums for the lighter and more reflective material.

The album's title track 'Róisín Dubh (Black Rose): A Rock Legend' was Lynott's final stand as the great Celtic-rock romantic. It was inspired by the poetic symbol of the black rose, the 'dark Rosaleen', the female figure who personified Ireland in its times of need against its oppressors. The opening minutes are the equal of anything from *Jailbreak* or *Johnny the Fox* in terms of sheer scale and power. The musical battery is warlike, as Lynott summons up familiar friends: the ancient kings and queens of Ireland, and Cúchulainn, the man who would *'fight and always won'*. The Troubles had worsened as the 1970s wore on, but still Lynott wanted to hear only *'the legends of long ago'*. Halfway through its seven minutes, 'Róisín Dubh' switches to a turbo-charged ceilidh, stitching together snippets of 'Shenandoah', 'Wild Mountain Thyme', 'Danny Boy' and 'The Mason's Apron'. Later, there are references to 'Whiskey in the Jar' and 'It's a Long Way to Tipperary'. It is another song about songs; a story about stories.

During the long fade, Lynott sums up the track's mix of monumental grandeur and extreme eccentricity by reeling off a list of terrible puns: the Joy of Joyce; William Butler Waits; Oscar, he's going Wilde; Brendan, where have you Behan?; George, he knows Best; Van is the Man.

'Róisín Dubh' was Gary Moore's crowning achievement in Thin Lizzy. His arrangement of the disparate musical elements was technically adroit, and his playing mighty. It was all downhill from there. A handful of dates into Thin Lizzy's summer tour of the US, following a festival show on Independence Day 1979 at Oakland Stadium in San Diego, Moore disappeared.

'He just left, like Eric Bell left,' Brian Downey told me. 'In fact, it was even worse because he left us in the middle of America, and nobody knew where the hell he was. There's no forgiving people leaving halfway through a tour. You don't do that. It really left us in a fix.' The slight was made worse when, upon surfacing, an unrepentant Moore publicly claimed that Thin Lizzy were a band who were no longer fit to perform.

'Gary couldn't settle for anything mediocre, and I think certain things started to bother him,' says Mark Nauseef, who spoke to Moore the day after he left the tour. 'He had high standards in terms of tuning and rhythmic timing. When things would slip a bit, it caused aggro. I sensed real disappointment in him more than anger. It bothered him that his buddy was in self-destruct mode, and I know it bothered him the way he left, but he just couldn't carry on.'

'I was so hurt,' said Lynott. 'I could see from the business side of it how we'd lose by it, but also on the friendship side.'[4] The two men would not speak or play together for a further four years.

The US record company was losing patience. In the States, as well as taking limousines door-to-door, Lynott insisted on the band flying between shows, two good reasons why Thin Lizzy's American tours always ran at a loss. Their management relied on Warner Brothers writing off the costs as a marketing expense. That was a question of goodwill, and goodwill was wearing thin. Earlier in the year, Lynott had demanded that all 150,000 pre-release copies of the *Black Rose* sleeve be withdrawn and replaced because Jim Fitzpatrick's painted rose on the cover was the wrong shade of dark purple. To rectify this minor detail would have cost a fortune and delayed the release.

'It was another Philip thing: *prove it to me*,' says Chris Morrison. 'In the end I told Philip that we did it, but actually we only printed up another 10,000 copies in the different colour. I made sure the band saw them, and we left the rest.' During the same US tour Lynott kicked up a fuss with the American label over access to the VIP area at a concert. 'He swore at one of the girls and did a big star trip,' says Morrison. 'I walked into Warner's the next day and doors were slamming all the way down the corridor. I could see the record company getting alienated.'

Thin Lizzy played four shows as a three-piece, with Scott Gorham stretched to the limits, while they organized a replacement. Midge Ure received a call in London from the management and within forty-eight hours was on stage in New Orleans playing 'The Boys Are Back in Town'. 'I learned two songs on Concorde – it flew too fast,' he says. 'The problem was that every Lizzy song had a harmony guitar part, so it was hairy for the first few nights.'

In 1976, while Ure was a member of glam-rockers Slik, a convalescing Lynott had sent over a signed copy of *Songs for While I'm Away* for him before one of the band's London concerts. By the time Ure joined former Sex Pistol Glen Matlock in the Rich Kids, they had become close, yet he remained a surprising choice for Thin Lizzy. Ure had been working on the first Visage album when he was invited to the States, and had just joined Ultravox, a band in the process of regenerating from post-punk to electronic art-pop. His recruitment turned out to be another of Lynott's magpie moves. By the time Thin Lizzy arrived in Japan on 24 September 1979, Dave Flett, formerly of Manfred Mann's Earth Band, was playing guitar, and Ure had started playing keyboards.

'What the hell were synthesizers doing in Thin Lizzy?' says Ure. 'I kept asking. This was a farce, I shouldn't have been there. You couldn't hear them out front and they didn't add anything, but Phil saw it as a toe-hold in that little world. It was fear driven. Every artist always thinks that their last hit will be the final hit, and you'll get swept away on the next wave, whatever that happens to be. I think that's why he got involved with Sid, Paul Cook and the Greedy Bastards, and then with me and the electronics.'

Lynott may have been thinking more about his solo record than Thin Lizzy when he suggested that Ure join the band. At soundchecks in Japan, he heard the keyboard player toying with a new, surging synthesizer motif, and his ears pricked up. 'Phil said, "What's that then, Midgie-poo?"' says Chris O'Donnell. 'So he nicks it and suddenly it's his new solo single.'

The riff turned into 'Yellow Pearl', completed with Ure in Lynott's home studio in Kew. It was included on *Solo in Soho*, his long-gestating solo album which was finished in the last months of the decade. In June 1979 Lynott had spent two weeks in Nassau, in the Bahamas, with producer Kit Woolven and a handful of musicians, including Scott Gorham and drummer Mark Nauseef. Days generally involved lounging by the pool at the hotel on Paradise Island, before going to Compass Point Studio around eleven o'clock at night.

The bones of 'Ode to a Black Man', 'Jamaican Rum' and 'Talk in '79' were recorded here, but the bulk of the work was completed back in London at Tony Visconti's Good Earth studios in Dean Street, just around the corner from the Thin Lizzy offices above the French House pub. Lynott spent a lot of time in the area. 'He would give girls the office address,' says Chris Salewicz. 'He'd say, "Ah, the old Dean Street address, the old favourite. *Hur hur.*"'

Visconti was busy with other projects and had grown slightly weary of man-managing Lynott and Thin Lizzy, however much he liked them. Lynott, for his part, sought someone more pliable. Visconti was a disciplinarian with an ego. His engineer, Kit Woolven, was less experienced and more amenable. 'For very large periods of time it was just me and Phil in the studio for days,' says Woolven. 'We'd meet up about midday and work through until three, four o'clock in the morning. Just the two of us trying ideas, experimenting with things. It was very enjoyable. He was very charming, very amusing, and we became really good friends.'

Released on 18 April 1980, *Solo in Soho* included Nauseef, Gary Moore, Huey Lewis, Jimmy Bain, Midge Ure, Billy Currie and all of Thin Lizzy among its guests. It was created in a collaborative spirit and for Lynott it marked a return to more playful, multi-dimensional forms of expression. 'I think the *Solo in Solo* record is amazing,' says Paul Scully. 'I wasn't a huge fan of the rock stuff, I always thought Philip was more capable of other things. He was a very poetic man, he could have gone down another road, but he had to be Phil Lynott: rock star. My early memories are of a very creative musical sponge, and a humble person, and I hear some of that on his solo records.'

The styles include reggae, funk, electronic music, folk balladry, pop and rock. 'A Child's Lullaby', a syrupy hymn to God and daughter, is given a lavish orchestral arrangement. There are Minimoog and ARP synths on 'Yellow Pearl', a pulsing, futuristic mood piece with an essentially nonsensical lyric inspired by watching the Yellow Magic Orchestra in Japan and a tepid Manchester United display at Old Trafford ('*Attack, attack, attack . . . is what we lack*').

'Dear Miss Lonely Hearts' is clean, chugging power pop. In later live shows, Lynott would preface the song with snippets of Rod Stewart's 'Some Guys Have All the Luck' and the Police's 1983 hit 'Every Breath You Take', gesturing towards certain similarities in chord structure and melody. 'King's Call' featured Mark Knopfler, a friend who would occasionally drop around to Kew Road. It's a brooding recollection of the night Elvis Presley died, an event Lynott would mark each year. 'On the anniversary of Elvis's death we'd sit up and sing Elvis songs all night,' says Helen Ruttle. 'We'd be singing "Are You Lonesome Tonight?" and Caroline would just go off to bed – "Ah, leave them to it!"'

'Talk in '79', sparse bass-and-drum Beat poetry, is a cloudy distillation of Lynott's plan to write short stories that captured the mood and métier of a particular time, place and scene. *'The Pistols left behind a swindle and a scandal / That nobody wished to handle / Sham 69 were left in a shambles / Generation X was next.'* It's fair to say he had some way to go, although early improvisations recorded in Nassau were more experimental and adventurous. 'He did it in one take,' explains Woolven, perhaps unnecessarily. 'No words, nothing written down in front of him. You could see the cogs turning. That was the calibre of the man.'

Solo in Soho is never quite outstanding, merely sporadically enjoyable. Lynott was working on so much material at the time, he seemed unable or unwilling to ensure that his ideas fulfilled their potential, settling too easily for the casual and approximate.

'Talk in '79' namechecks Steve Strange, the glamorous young Welshman who at the time was working as the doorman at the Blitz club in Covent Garden, immediately prior to joining Visage. After recording in Soho, Lynott would often visit the Blitz, observing the blossoming New Romantic movement and its leading lights, including Strange, Rusty Egan, Spandau Ballet and Boy George. Mick Jagger was once refused entry to the Blitz for 'not being the right kind of person', but Lynott, the eternal hustler, the undeniable night-creature, was always welcome.

An awareness of changing tastes and trends lies at the heart of *Solo in Soho*. He was attempting to freeze-frame a specific time – in his own life and in the wider culture – in the midst of rapid flux. 'I knew his solo stuff was going to be different but I didn't realize it was going to be that different,' Brian Downey told me. 'I said to him, "Why don't you do a reggae album, or a funk album?" "Oh no, can't do that." It had to be a mix of styles. He wouldn't listen. Because it was a solo album, he didn't want to concentrate on one genre. Maybe he should have. He was writing some great funk stuff that I don't think ever saw the light of day. He'd be in two minds over whether even to record it, but he had all the lyrics and the music, and it was ready to go. I think he had lost confidence.'

'Róisín Dubh' had been his last flirtation with explicitly Irish themes. 'I'm getting off that kick now,' he told Irish DJ Dave Fanning in 1980, admitting to being sensitive to criticism that he had overplayed his hand. 'But I'm also tired of doing it. I think I milked it to death.'[5]

'Ode to a Black Man' on *Solo in Soho* was a bellicose blues shout on which Lynott positioned himself as a *'bad black boy'* and bumped fists with Stevie Wonder, Dr Martin Luther King, Muhammad Ali, Bob Marley, Jimi Hendrix, Malcolm X, Robert Mugabe and Haile Selassie. *'I was living on the wrong side,'* he sings, *'But now I'm here.'* It was hardly a weighty manifesto, nor a particularly coherent one, but it was an illustration that he was becoming more roots aware. Chris Salewicz recalls telling Lynott, 'You're not *very* black,' and Lynott replying, 'Well, I can't be grooving around South Africa, Chris!'

Across both his solo albums, Lynott displayed a willingness to engage with black musical forms only rarely evident within Thin Lizzy. Alongside the ever-present blues base there was reggae ('Solo in Soho'), funk ('Talk in '79', 'Together', 'Gino'), calypso ('Jamaican Rum') and lush, upbeat soul on 'Tattoo (Giving It All Up for Love)' and 'The Man's a Fool'. 'I think maybe he felt he missed out on that, growing up in Ireland,' says Brian Downey. 'He got into a lot of black culture, and he loaned me loads of albums. I tried to get as many funk beats as I could off of those records.'

Friends noticed that he started socializing much more frequently with a black crowd. Recording with Thin Lizzy in the early 1980s, Chris Tsangarides recalls times when 'a lot of his black friends would pitch up, and around this bunch of American and English black guys Phil would change a bit'. In 1982, Lynott's first solo touring group was called the Soul Band and featured Jerome Rimson on bass and Gus Isidore on guitar; it was the first and only time he formed a group of predominantly black musicians. 'He started really embracing those roots,' says Midge Ure. 'All of a sudden that side of Phil became very important, whereas previously I think the Irish side had been most dominant.'

Solo in Soho was not a commercial or critical success. It entered the lower reaches of the top thirty in Britain and disappeared after six weeks, while lead single 'Dear Miss Lonely Hearts' barely reached the top forty. 'Simultaneously satisfying and frustrating,' wrote Bill Graham in his review in the generally supportive *Hot Press*, before concluding that the album 'certainly could fall victim to disturbing the band's more conservative fans whilst being over-speedily dismissed by the trendsmiths',[6] a description which almost perfectly describes its fate.

In diversifying, Lynott fell between the cracks. The *NME's* savage review of *Solo in Soho*, which depicted him as a man desperately striving to remain relevant in a post-punk world he didn't understand, drove him to frothing fury. 'The guy reviewing it, he totally fucked up,' he said. 'He didn't know what he was talking about. He had it in for me, you know? . . . I read between the lines and the guy was a total fucking arsehole. If he had have said that to me face I would have stuck him out there and then. Simply because an insult is an insult, not criticism.' In the next breath, he added. 'I honestly feel that I do listen to criticism, other people's points of view, and bear them in mind and make a decision.'[7]

'One or two [reviews] were a bit dodgy,' Brian Downey recalled. 'He was a bit sensitive to that, and I think that might have set him back a bit.' The coolest kid in Dublin, the biggest star in Ireland, was acutely aware of a change in status. One of Chris Morrison's managerial maxims is that paranoia drives the music business. Paranoia that your next record won't be as good as the last one, paranoia that somebody else will have the hit that was destined for you, and paranoia that the world just doesn't understand. It's a spur, but it's also corrosive.

Solo in Soho portrayed the softer side of a man who, amid bouts of unreconstructed hedonism, was lullabying his young child to sleep with silly love songs and was, by the time of the album's release, a married man. 'He fell in love, and we got those records from him,' says Chalkie Davies. 'He tried to pretend that he was still macho, but he wasn't, really. He had changed. Once he met Caro that was it, and then the children. He became a different person, but he struggled to balance the two.'

He married Caroline Crowther on Valentine's Day 1980, at the St Elizabeth of Portugal Church in Richmond, less than half a mile from the house in Kew Road. His bride was almost four months pregnant with their second daughter. 'Knowing the kind of guy that he was, it was always in the back of my mind, is this going to last?' says Scott Gorham. 'He was hard to pin down completely, but I'm pretty sure Caroline knew what she was walking into. I know he loved her dearly.'

His stag night at the Clarendon in Hammersmith was the full rock-and-roll blow-out – strippers, Lemmy and all. Midge Ure, Billy Idol, Brian Robertson and Jimmy Bain were among those also in attendance.

On the day, the bride wore white and the groom a dark pin-striped suit with a white shirt, striped tie and button hole. He carried Sarah in his arms and looked shy and handsome. Scott Gorham was best man, the road crew wore suits with cowboy boots, and the ensemble sang 'Lord of the Dance'. At the reception at the Kensington Hilton, Leslie Crowther and Chris O'Donnell gave speeches. The former's proved the more memorable. 'He was very funny, he endeared himself to the rock-and-roll audience,' says Chris Morrison. 'He said, "Philip came to ask for my daughter's hand in marriage, and I said, 'You might as well, you've had everything else!'"' Bob Geldof's partner, Paula Yates, wrote it all up for *Record Mirror*.

Shortly after returning from honeymooning in Rio de Janeiro, the couple bought a second home in Ireland. Since 1969, the country had offered generous tax breaks to artists domiciled there, while any income on songs or records created in Ireland avoided being taxed at the more punitive British rate. More importantly, Dublin offered Lynott a chance to root his family and consolidate domestic life in a city he had never really wanted to leave. 'He got in his head that he wanted his kids to grow up in Ireland,' says Chris O'Donnell. 'That was his romanticism.'

Before the birth of their second child they bought Glen Corr at auction for £130,000. A long, low, modern dormer bungalow at 10 Claremont Road in Sutton, Glen Corr was on the Burrow Road, which connected the city to the picturesque Howth Head peninsula. Imposing iron gateposts led to a short driveway and substantial but not ostentatious grounds. The front garden was protected by tall trees and hedges, while the rear backed on to the dunes, the Burrow beach and the Irish Sea. 'Glen Corr was a summer house,' says O'Donnell. 'Really, you were buying the land and the access to the beach.'

They moved in before the birth of Cathleen Elizabeth Lynott on 29 July 1980. Not long afterwards, Lynott bought White Horses, a house located nearby in the well-heeled fishing village of Howth, for his mother and Dennis Keeley. Gus Curtis, his wife Maeve and his family also lived very close. Jim Fitzpatrick moved into an apartment on Burrow Road, and started organizing football matches on the beach with old friends like Brush Shiels, Noel Bridgeman and Terry Woods.

'We had some fantastic times,' says Fitzpatrick. 'When they came to live in Ireland I used to spend loads of time with them. It was great for Philip to hang out properly and walk along the beach, which he had a habit of doing. He was trying to get himself fit, and I was under the illusion that he was off drugs.' He became an unmissable addition to the local community, instantly recognizable as he strolled around the village and along the beach with the latest family member, a German Shepherd named Gnasher, or rode his bicycle in rock-star shirt and skinny tie. He told friends that he had cycled to the top of Howth Summit. His wife would laugh and say that he'd barely made it out of the drive.

'He would cycle up to the church and back,' says Fitzpatrick. 'He was promenading again, he liked to be seen around. He had a whole neighbourhood of friends around here, a support system. We had parties down at the house. He did live a rather idyllic life, and he started reaching out to other musicians.'

In the years he spent back in Dublin, Lynott cultivated relationships with numerous local bands and artists, from the renowned to the unknown. He bought the Asgard Hotel in Howth for Philomena to run. It cost £300,000 and was intended as a 'thank you to his mum', says Chris O'Donnell. 'But it wasn't a great investment, and they realized that.' Situated on Balscadden Road, during its brief lifespan the Asgard had a nightclub which hosted dances and live music, and Lynott would turn up from time to time to boost trade and chat to the bands.

In 1980 he produced and played on a single of Jimmy Driftwood's country classic 'Tennessee Stud' with his former Orphanage foil, Terry Woods, recorded at Windmill Lane in Dublin. In the same studio the following year, he cut a version of Ewan MacColl's 'Dirty Old Town' with Brian Downey and the Lookalike's Sean O'Connor. Terry Woods's ex-wife, Gay, had formed a band called

Auto Da Fé, and Lynott later produced three of their singles, 'November, November', 'Bad Experience' and 'Man of Mine'.

He befriended Clann Éadair, an amateur folk group comprised of local fishermen and working men who played traditional tunes in the pubs around Howth. 'He used to come in for a pint,' says the band's piper, Leo Rickard. 'We had a regular residency at the Royal Hotel on a Sunday morning, and he'd walk down with the girls after church and bring them in, get them crisps. It was only a small village, so it was kind of a big deal when he came in, with the big hair and the silver jewellery. People were in awe of him, particularly the women. Everyone wanted to chat with him, get a photograph or an autograph, and he liked it.'

Lynott would sit in with Clann Éadair from time to time, to play something new he had written or a traditional standard. Occasionally they had a high-spirited bash through 'The Boys Are Back in Town'. He offered to produce an album by the band, a project which inched to completion between the early 1980s and his death. One of the musical high points of Lynott's lean final years was 'A Tribute to Sandy Denny', the song he wrote and recorded with Clann Éadair, released as a single in 1984. It's a gentle, stately folk ballad, sung with mournful understatement, a world away from the end days of Thin Lizzy. When the single was released Lynott hustled the band a spot on *The Late Late Show* and appeared with them to sing it, dressed like a bad parody of a rock star but singing from the heart.

'He was very good, because we were nobodies,' says Rickard. 'Philip was very genuine, civilized, down to earth and nice . . . He was an out and out "Dub", and very proud of that. Some big rock stars create an aura about themselves and it's very hard to talk to them, but Phil never had a problem with that. He didn't throw tantrums. He enjoyed the trappings of stardom, but around Howth he was just one of the lads.'

There would be parties for local friends and musicians, and occasionally something a little more full-blooded. 'Oh, he was a good man for a party,' says Rickard. 'There might be forty or fifty people in the house on a Saturday night, but that didn't happen too often. When he came home he'd want to spend time with the family and rest.'

Helen Ruttle lived close to Glen Corr, and introduced herself to Caroline Lynott one day on the beach. 'We started palling around together,' she says. 'My daughter Sarah and her Cathleen were a year apart. They had the same birthday, so we used to celebrate together. Philip was great with all the kids. My son Simon was the only boy in the group, and Philip was very nice to him. He'd take him away off into the study and say, "Come on, the lads . . ." When he was away on tour, he'd come back with presents for everybody. He'd bring *Tintin* books for my son, because he had a little red in his hair. The girls got beautiful clothes, whatever they wanted, they always seemed to fit perfectly. He was a great dad and a nice character.'

At Kew Road, too, visitors would sometimes stumble on scenes of simple domesticity. Lynott's grandmother Sarah would be in the front room watching James Bond movies at ear-splitting volume. Philomena would be running in and out. Phone calls, bustle, family life. 'We made home movies with the kids, watched the football,' says Mark Nauseef. 'We wouldn't even talk about work till much later in the evening. We would eventually go out to the studio in the garage and do some recording, but mostly it was all about the family. He was beautiful at home. I saw another side to him than I saw on the road. He was laid-back and happy.'

Lynott talked fondly, if ruefully, about being the father of two girls. 'I'm going to be jealous,' he said. 'At the moment, I'm hoping I'll be liberal, but I also know there's a streak in me that would scare the life out of the fellas. I'm looking forward to it.'[8]

One of the many notable musicians to appear on *Solo in Soho* was the English guitarist Snowy White, who played on 'Dear Miss Lonely Hearts' and the title track. White was the latest Thin Lizzy recruit, brought in to replace Dave Flett. He was a blues player, reserved by nature, temperate in his habits, laconic and economical in style, who tended to perform with minimal movement. The anti-Brian Robertson. He was a terrific guitarist, but a strange choice for Thin Lizzy. For the ever-competitive Lynott, White's major selling point was that he played with Pink Floyd on tour. Chris O'Donnell pointed out that he had also played with Cliff Richard.

Shortly after White's arrival, Midge Ure left Thin Lizzy to focus on Ultravox, a band which travelled with Egon Ronay guide books rather than a retinue of drug dealers. Ultravox had signed to Thin Lizzy's management company, which caused Lynott some disquiet. While Thin Lizzy were touring Australia in October 1980, he demanded that Chris Morrison come over immediately for a meeting. 'I flew for twenty-four hours and he said, "I'm giving you six months to drop Ultravox and Visage and [just] manage us,"' says Morrison. 'He went on at me for an hour and then never spoke to me for the next three days, then I flew back.' Shortly afterwards, Ultravox's 'Vienna' and Visage's 'Fade to Grey' became huge hits, and the matter was quietly dropped.

Ure's replacement on keyboards was Darren Wharton, brought to Lynott via Joe Leach, one of the Quality Street Gang. Wharton was seventeen and playing at Tiffany's nightclub in Manchester with Bill Tarmey, an actor and club singer famous for portraying Jack Duckworth in the long-running ITV soap *Coronation Street*. 'I didn't get it and I didn't think it would work one iota,' says Chris O'Donnell of Wharton's arrival. 'You find yourself losing patience. A friend of Phyllis's from Manchester?

Give me a break. If we really need a keyboard player let's get a top session guy.' Scott Gorham liked Wharton, but he too was unconvinced that there was any need to have him there. Much of the time the keyboards simply added a third harmony line on top of the two guitars.

The line-up featuring White and Wharton made two albums. *Chinatown*, released in October 1980, and *Renegade*, released in November 1981, are widely regarded as the nadir of Thin Lizzy's career. 'There's some great tracks on both, but Phil's songwriting seemed to be slipping a bit,' Brian Downey told me. 'All that pressure was getting to him and the drugs were starting to take effect . . . For some reason we were becoming a little bit unfashionable as well.'

Thin Lizzy aligned themselves to the New Wave of British Heavy Metal, an evolving strain which filtered the power of 1970s hard rock through the aggression of punk. 'I remember Phil going on about how Lizzy weren't rock enough when the New Metal thing came along and all the rock bands started sounding really thrashy,' says Midge Ure. 'He thought Lizzy sounded weak, but they weren't that kind of band. They were soulful, they wrote great songs. I think he was scared to let it slip through his fingers. The songs started taking a back seat to the production, and that was a big mistake.'

The shift was defined by 'Killer on the Loose', an unlikely top-ten hit in October 1980. In the song Lynott adopted the persona of a sexual predator: *'Don't unzip your zipper,'* he sang. *'You know I'm Jack the Ripper.'* At the time the notorious case of the Yorkshire Ripper dominated the British news. Peter Sutcliffe, a serial killer who targeted prostitutes, murdered the last of his thirteen victims on 17 November 1980, and was finally arrested early in 1981. The video for 'Killer on the Loose' featured Lynott wandering around a back-street stage set in a trench coat while prostitutes writhed provocatively around him. A newspaper spun into view, noir-style, bearing the headline: 'MYSTERY KILLER ON THE LOOSE'.

The conflicted examination of decline detailed in 'Sugar Blues' followed in the tracks of 'Opium Trail' and 'Got to Give It Up'. By now, heroin was a habit. 'Phil had broken the taboo of doing it, and he liked doing it, so it became serious quite quickly,' says Scott Gorham. 'By *Chinatown*, it was a problem.'

At the album launch party, Frank Murray pulled Lynott aside. 'We had this huge row about it,' says Murray. 'I remember I was breaking down crying. I was just pleading with him, "Philip, you've got to stop this." He had the balls to tell me he was okay, he wasn't really doing anything. I was like, "Philip, you're talking to me. I know exactly what's going on."'

The title track, too, was a none-too-veiled reference to heroin, and demonstrated the detrimental effect the drug was having on the quality of his writing:

> *Chinatown, it's a different scene*
> *There are people there, they are so obscene*
> *If you see what I mean*
> *Then they've sold you the dream*

As a lyricist, Lynott was beginning to struggle. He frequently relied on a rhyming dictionary. The final Thin Lizzy records are littered with pile-ups of multiple rhymes, many of which make phonetic rather than literal sense. When he did attempt to engage with a specific concept and put across a coherent point of view, he struggled to rediscover the poetic power and atmosphere of old. Jim Fitzpatrick had read a book, *The Cowboys*, concerning the destruction of the buffalo in America and its catastrophic impact on the culture of the Plains Indians. He passed it on to Lynott, who sought to condense the story and its sentiment into a song. The result, 'Genocide (The Killing of the Buffalo)', from *Chinatown*, was a mess. 'I felt [his lyrics] deteriorated horrendously,' says Fitzpatrick. 'His mind wasn't making the connections it used to make. The lyrics were out of character, but he was out of character with himself. Drugs give you a severe dose of ignorance and bad manners. He stopped being the nice, considered guy he was.'

Lynott's third book, published in 1980 and rather grandly titled *The Collected Works of Philip Lynott*, was a compendium of his first two volumes of lyrics, covering 1970 to 1977. 'You can't just go on getting better and better,' he told journalist Paul Du Noyer shortly after publication. 'Reading the book, I can see that in recent years I have for some reason given up on the heavy love lyrics, the marathon pieces, whether it's because I've been too busy gigging, or too busy getting a new guitarist, or whatever the problems of the last year and a half . . . I have to sit down now and write, and I haven't done that lately . . . Plus a lot has happened to me, I think, like getting married and having the kid, stuff like that. So all I can say is that I may have forgotten about it for a while but I'll be getting back into writing far more. I won't go for the quick rhyme.'[9]

On tour, at least, Thin Lizzy retained a piratical swagger. Darren Wharton observed the dynamic. 'You wouldn't want to cross him, he was obviously the boss and everybody knew it.' Taking their lead from *Monty Python's Life of Brian*, some of the road crew had taken to greeting Lynott with a jaunty 'Morning, Saviour!' 'But he still had a great sense of humour. There was always that childlike element. A twinkle in his eye. He loved a joke and we had some great times.'

On 14 June 1980, after the concert in Southampton, Lynott was hit with a bottle at his hotel. 'There was a wedding reception going on and we all went up to the bar,' says Scott Gorham.

'I guess Phil winked at some girl, and about two minutes later a glass came flying out of the crowd and hit him full in the face. The whole thing kicked off – it escalated out into the parking lot, police and ambulances came, a couple of people got hurt pretty bad. It happened a few times. People wanted to make their name by picking a fight with him.'

Irish power-pop group the Lookalikes supported Thin Lizzy on the *Chinatown* tour. Their singer and guitarist Sean O'Connor was befriended by Lynott, travelling with him in the Mercedes between shows. Lynott sat with a two-pound bag filled with cocaine, which he would attend to more or less constantly, digging his thumb into the contents and applying it to one nostril, then the other. 'He used to live on about two hours' sleep a night,' says O'Connor. 'He was a really sweet, genuine guy if he liked you. He could be very kind, he would give you the shirt off his back and he gave me lots of good advice about the show and our act. But if he didn't like you, you'd better keep away from him, because he could be very nasty. You would reap the wrath and the fury.'

There was a growing sense that, musically, the wheels were beginning to spin. An *NME* review concluded that 'the beat goes on, but nowhere in particular'.[10] 'For the most part the set didn't change,' says O'Connor. 'It was all choreographed, Philip's announcements were all the same. It was a worked-out show.'

The fact that Thin Lizzy's American adventure ended between *Chinatown* and *Renegade* added to an increasing sense of gloom. The tour that concluded in Los Angeles in late December 1980 proved to be their last. The band had a small and enthusiastic fan-base in the States, but their albums and singles had made no inroads since *Live and Dangerous*, and the cost of touring was no longer a viable one. 'You get what you deserve,' said Lynott. 'That's the way it goes. There's no bad luck attached with us in

America, we had a great time, [but] I don't wanna fail. I don't like the word failure associated with Thin Lizzy.'[11]

Once upon a time playing a single show at the Hammersmith Odeon had been a thrill; now three or four nights at the same venue seemed routine. Motivation became a problem. Thin Lizzy had two showcase concerts scheduled for the summer of 1981. They headlined a multi-band bill at Milton Keynes Bowl on 8 August – 'it rained, only 10,000 came, I got there early and got drunk,' was Lynott's blunt assessment[12] – and then travelled to Ireland to play at Slane Castle eight days later, the first of many notable concert events held at the Boyne-side estate of Lord Henry Mountcharles.

If Dalymount Park in 1977 was their formal coronation as Irish rock royalty, Slane Castle was a kind of farewell. They had pushed open the door; now the young pretenders were rushing through. When Thin Lizzy had played at the RDS Arena in Dublin with the Lookalikes in June 1980, the support band sold more merchandise than the headliners. At Slane, a crowd of 18,000 congregated for a bill that also included U2. Lynott descended from the skies in a helicopter, clutching Sarah in his left arm as he strode across from the landing point to the backstage area. His wife, daughters and friends watched the concert from the side of the stage. Thin Lizzy were not quite at their best but the sense of occasion won the day. It would be their last appearance as kings of their own domain. U2 were snapping at their heels and would shortly surpass them.

If the live shows suggested a group happy to settle for efficiency rather than innovation, *Renegade* confirmed it. While making the album, once again the lines of delineation were muddied. 'I'd go into the studio and say to Phil, "Who's in tomorrow?"' says producer Kit Woolven. 'If it was Scott and Snowy, I'm going in with my Thin Lizzy head on. We'd be about halfway through the day and Phil would go, "Let's stick up [a solo track]." Snowy White was actually quite irritated with this, but I found it irritating too because I wanted to try and make sure that the solo album sounded one way, and the Lizzy stuff sounded another way. If you're flipping between things all the time, it's quite confusing. Also, Phil was becoming more irrational, he wasn't the fun person that I used to work with during *Solo in Soho* times. He was changing because of the amount of substance abuse.'

It was eventually agreed that Chris Tsangarides would come in to produce *Renegade*, and Woolven would concentrate on Lynott's solo material. Even then, work in the studio was often far from clear-cut. 'I didn't really know what was what until we finished and I found out what was going to actually make up the record,' says Tsangarides.

Lynott's solo album was held back until 1982 to clear space for *Renegade*, released on 15 November 1981. Writing credits were shared throughout the band; only two tracks were written solely by Lynott. Synthesizers were now an integral part of a sound that was increasingly lacklustre and sterile, while Lynott's voice showed obvious signs of wear and tear.

If the album was artistically weak, if not wholly lacking in merit, commercially *Renegade* was a fully fledged disaster. A misguided cover of Billy Bremner's 'Trouble Boys', championed by Lynott in the face of much resistance from the management, was released ahead of the album and limped to number fifty-three. It was promptly dropped from the record. A second single, 'Hollywood (Down on Your Luck)', reached the same lowly position in March 1982. *Renegade* peaked at number thirty-eight, their worst showing since *Fighting*, and the first album since that time not to certify at least silver.

Thin Lizzy spent a further three months at the end of 1981 on tour, and went out again from February to May 1982. Across the board, band unity was slipping. It had become apparent that Snowy White was not working out, on or off stage. 'He was a great guy and everybody really liked him,' says Darren Wharton. 'I just don't think he felt that the style of Thin Lizzy was conducive to his guitar style. I think after *Renegade* there was a point where he had basically had enough.' In February 1982, in Denmark, Brian Downey was attacked by a bouncer and Mark Nauseef was called in as a replacement until he recovered. Compared to the live-wire band of 1978, 'this was a whole different thing,' says Nauseef. 'It was tough, trying to bring synthesizers into Thin Lizzy, but Phil was still trying. His health at that point was what got me. It was clear that he wasn't as well as I had known him.'

Depression. Boredom. Disappointment. All that downtime, from Inverness to Bremen. Nature abhors a vacuum. Heroin fills it with cotton wool. Lynott wasn't the only one suffering. On 7 March 1982, in Porto, Scott Gorham went on stage unable to play and barely able to stand. He was unceremoniously bundled back to Britain the following morning to address his own addictions. Sean O'Connor filled in during his absence, playing out of sight behind the backline equipment to maintain the illusion that Thin Lizzy remained a functioning band.

During the period where Thin Lizzy began to fracture, Lynott's drug dependency went from a private preoccupation to a more public problem. He had been busted on the morning of 13 November 1980, by drug squad officers posing as Gas Board workers in order to gain access to 184 Kew Road. They found two wraps of cocaine in a jacket in Lynott's bedroom, a quantity of cannabis in his Mercedes, and a cannabis plant growing in the conservatory. According to Chris O'Donnell, 'the police didn't know who they were busting. They weren't out to get Philip Lynott. There had been a public complaint that too many people were slamming car doors at four and five in the morning and it set off alarm bells.' The case came to court on 20 August 1981, Lynott's thirty-second birthday. The fine of £200 set down at Kingston Crown Court was only the start. Lynott had paid Charlie McLennan £2,000 to swear in court that the cocaine, and the jacket it was found in, belonged to him.

It was one of numerous incidents, scrapes and misadventures that signalled a slow dissipation. Lynott was now taking cocaine habitually. In the spring of 1981, he had appeared on *The Late Late Show*. With his mother in the audience, he outlined his new status as a reformed family man, and spoke lovingly about life in Sutton with his wife, children and Philomena close at hand. Wily host Gay Byrne smiled with what looked like benign scepticism.

Eamon Carr accompanied Lynott to the show. Beforehand in the dressing room, he had witnessed an extraordinary scene. 'Philip was fastidious about his appearance,' says Carr. 'He's gone into the toilet, the door's closed, and he's in there for a while. He comes out and he fixes that little bit of hair on his forehead so it hangs down, and he turns to me with his hands out and says, "Well, how do I look?" I say, "Great, but have a look in the mirror." And there's a big trickle of blood coming down from his nostril . . .

'So he's leaning over the sink, tidying himself up, snorting the cold water with practised ease, then suddenly there's a knock on the door. "Three minutes!" The flow couldn't be stemmed, so he went back into the cubicle again and got a big wad of toilet paper. Plugs are made, and inserted right up into each nostril. He stands there for a while and everything seems to be okay. He doesn't seem to be in any panic, because he's sort of buzzing, so it's, "Okay, let's go. Ready to rock!"'

Carr watched the interview from backstage on a monitor, transfixed. 'I thought, any minute now these gigantic plugs of toilet paper are going to erupt like Krakatoa. He managed to get through it, but it was very nasal. At one level it's almost comical, but it's also tragic. From thereon it wasn't nice. It deteriorated, and I got a sense of things going terribly awry.'

When friends met him in London and Dublin, they often left saddened. 'I remember being with him once in World's End [pub] in King's Road,' says Steve Lillywhite. 'We were having a nice conversation, then this greasy little low-life guy came in. He looked at Phil, Phil looked at him, and the urge for that lifestyle overtook his conversation with me. He just said, "Right, I'm going to go."' When Lynott bumped into Tim Booth in the Dockers pub down by the Quays, it took him almost half a minute to recognize his old friend from Dr Strangely Strange. 'That was disconcerting and upsetting,' says Booth. 'We had been reasonably good friends. He was a different kind of a person at that stage. He became a much harder individual.'

Work on Lynott's second solo album was hampered by his appetite for old-fashioned chemical excess slipping towards something more troubling. The control room at Good Earth was frequently full of people uninvolved in the making of the record, many of whom gave the impression of exploiting Lynott's largesse. On one occasion, he counted around the room. Concluding that there were 12 people present, he chopped out twelve lines of cocaine. Looking at each person in turn, Lynott proceeded to snort every line himself. 'Everybody got the message and moved out of the control room,' says Kit Woolven. 'He sat next to me and clenched the edge of the desk. His hands went pure white, he was holding the desk so tightly. It was slightly terrifying. That was unusual, but not unexpected.'

While *Solo in Soho* had been a happy and harmonious experience, this project became a struggle. Lynott's time-keeping was terrible, and his behaviour erratic. It became hard to gauge the emotional metabolism of a man who would buy a crate of whiskey on St Patrick's Day for everyone to share, but would fly off the handle if somebody playfully pinched a chip from his plate.

He would ask Woolven to play a twenty-minute reel of rough mixes of songs and then promptly fall asleep. The sound of the tape clicking off at the end would wake him up, at which point he would ask for it to be played through again. He would then fall asleep. This could go on for hours. Where once he had welcomed ideas from all sources, now he told his co-producer: 'I don't pay you to think.'

'It was so sad,' says Woolven. 'He went from being this very determined, positive, talented person to someone who wasn't any of those things, really. He'd lost the charisma and he wasn't fun to work with. I think he'd lost his spark, but that's what heroin does.'

The summer of 1982 found Lynott in New York, battering on the door of Johnny Thunders's Room 216 at the Chelsea Hotel with a bag of heroin – he called it 'birthday cake' – for them to share. For his solo tour of Scandinavia, Germany and the Netherlands with the Soul Band in October 1982, Lynott invited Jimmy Bain along to play a second keyboard in a group that arguably didn't even require the first one. 'Bain was there for the dope,' says Brian Robertson, who jammed with the group at their show in Varberg on 15 October. 'He was bad news. It said: "Bain: keyboards and vocals." He can't play keyboards. He stood there like Linda McCartney.'

The tour, on which Lynott played a twin-necked guitar that allowed him to alternate between bass and rhythm guitar, was in support of *The Philip Lynott Album*, released on 17 September 1982. Like its predecessor, it was a diverse, disparate and sometimes experimental piece of work. Lynott is listed as playing bass synthesizer, timpani and cymbal, CR 76 computer drum machines, guitar, Irish harp, keyboards, percussion and his eldest daughter's space gun.

After being commissioned as the *Top of the Pops* theme tune in 1981, the remixed 'Yellow Pearl' had become a top-twenty hit in the interim and was included on the new record in its shorter, punchier version. There were two songs inspired by his children. 'Cathleen', a sugar-sweet ode to his second daughter, *'a beautiful Irish girl'*, and 'Growing Up', a fictionalized account of father-daughter growing pains. Lushly melodic, the pair came swaddled in strings and saxophones. 'Ode to Liberty (The Protest Song)' was delivered as a Dire Straits-meets-Bob Dylan pastiche, a point underlined by having Mark Knopfler add his unmistakable guitar lines.

The clear stand-out track was 'Old Town', co-written with Jimmy Bain, and perhaps the best and brightest song Lynott wrote in his later years. With its classic chord changes, baroque piccolo solo – consciously mimicking the Beatles's 'Penny Lane' – and a lovely midnight-blue breakdown in the middle, 'Old Town' returned Lynott to the field of pop craftsmanship, albeit one that graphically illustrated the damage to his voice inflicted by cocaine. When Eamon Carr and Brush Shiels met for a drink, they would sometimes joke about how Lynott appeared to be *'bending'* rather than *'spending'* his money in the old town.

It's a break-up song, but it's also a Dublin song. The seed of the idea dated back to a session in Windmill Lane in 1981, when Lynott was recording his version of 'Dirty Old Town'. 'Brian Downey and I were the rhythm section, Phil was playing twelve-string, and we hit on something,' says Sean O'Connor. 'We played through a few things afterwards, and one of those ideas was what eventually became "Old Town".' David Heffernan's panoramic video transformed the song into something like an elegy for Lynott's home city, trailing him as he strolled around

Grafton Street, over the Ha'penny Bridge, along the Liffey and through Herbert Park. At the end he pulled up his collar and wandered along Howth harbour towards the lighthouse. It felt like a story that had begun with 'Dublin' thirteen years earlier was ending.

Lynott's working title for the album was 'Fatalistic Attitude', but the record company blandly packaged up the ten songs as *The Philip Lynott Album* in the hope of lending it a commercial sheen. In the event, the record was even less successful than *Solo in Soho*, and 'Fatalistic Attitude' came closer to capturing the lingering mood of deflation. The frantic post-punk funk groove applied to 'Together' seemed only to accentuate the song's spirit of gnawing unhappiness. The gloom was even more obvious on the original, unreleased version. '*Oh God forbid if I should never see my children,*' sings Lynott, in the midst of grimly documenting a marriage in decline.

'If you view a solo album as being a portrait of a time in somebody's life, then it does that,' says Kit Woolven. 'Things were going awry.'

Channel 4's new live-music magazine show, *The Tube*, was the antithesis of the BBC's venerable rock programme, *The Old Grey Whistle Test*, and its be-whiskered late-night ruminations. If *The Old Grey Whistle Test* conveyed a mood of mellow virtuosity, *The Tube* was a ninety-minute sugar rush, all youthful clamour and rakish camera angles. Broadcast at Friday teatime and presented by Paula Yates and former Squeeze keyboardist Jools Holland, it was messy but fresh, in love with music but determined not to take musicians too seriously.

On 28 January 1983, Lynott stumbled over this new frontier like a man suddenly unsure of his bearings. Thin Lizzy played 'The Boys Are Back in Town', as well as 'The Sun Goes Down' and their new single 'Cold Sweat', both taken from their forthcoming album, *Thunder and Lightning*. The flashing neon Thin Lizzy sign flared behind them, Lynott threw his shapes in the short-cut black and chequered bolero jacket he favoured these days, and it all passed off well enough, but the tone of his dressing-room interview jarred. Obviously the worse for wear, looking puffy and dissolute, his attempts at roguish humour came across merely as condescending, charmless and faintly ridiculous. The young female interviewer looked at first taken aback, then bored, then swiftly moved on, a reaction which served as a neat summation of the prevailing public attitude towards Lynott and his band.

A few days' later, their pre-recorded performance of 'Cold Sweat' was cut from *Top of the Pops* after a drunken Lynott told the producer, Michael Hurll, to 'fuck off' – twice. Around the same time, during an interview with *Melody Maker*, he demanded that the journalist furnish him with amphetamines, then boasted of gangland contacts in Manchester who could have the man shot. The Asgard Hotel in Dublin had recently burned to the ground, and Lynott put it around town with a wink that it had been torched deliberately as an insurance scam.

In extremis, the knowing swagger had slipped into wounded, churlish bravado. Thin Lizzy's career in the United States was long over. In Britain, it was the age of Duran Duran, Wham! and Spandau Ballet, of New Order and the Smiths. The Jam had just quit at the top of their game. In Ireland, U2 had kept growing after Slane Castle and were about to break big with a new, rather devout form of Celtic rock, which would define the tenor of the decade back home. They started having hits, as Thin Lizzy stopped. Fervour was in; ragged intemperance out.

Lynott seemed unable to wean himself from the symbols that screamed unadulterated rock and roll: the come-here leer, the sleeveless jerkin, the studded wristband and belts from the Pleasure Chest, the 'chick' talk, gypsy chic and Valentino moustache. It was a reductive representation of a man with so much more to offer. Lynott's rocker persona had become a caricature, and he was trapped inside. 'It becomes a gimmick,' says Chalkie Davies. 'That's the sad thing, the Fellini aspect of it all.'

The music was in a similar state of limbo. Snowy White had left in the summer of 1982, unable to adjust to Thin Lizzy's temperamental time zone. Lynott had now brought in John Sykes, a twenty-three-year-old English guitarist who had made two albums as the lead guitarist with Tygers of Pan Tang, another New Wave of British Heavy Metal band.

The new recruit promptly moved into Kew Road, living there alongside Darren Wharton and Gus Curtis. Sykes's first act was to play on *Thunder and Lightning*. Much of the principal recording was done at Pete Townshend's Boathouse Studios in Twickenham, less than a mile from Kew Road. The proximity between work and play was perhaps the worst move on an album full of bad choices.

At times, the ambience of Lynott's London home was closer to a boarding house for oil-rig workers on shore leave than a den of iniquity. They would argue over who had eaten the last of the cheese, take it in turns to make bacon and eggs in the morning, and kick around a football in the garden. At night they would hit the town or entertain indoors.

At other times, it was almost an ordinary family home. The various lodgers tried to keep their distance when Lynott's wife and children were over from Ireland. 'He was always happiest when he was with the kids and Caroline,' says Wharton. 'Obviously something happened along the way, but as far as I could see every time I looked at them, they were great. They made a beautiful couple.'

More often than not, however, the house was now the epicentre of a slow drag on Lynott's health, focus and productivity. The band would arrive in the studio early in the afternoon. He might not turn up until eight or nine o'clock in the evening. 'The condition he was in was just shocking,' says Chris Tsangarides. 'It was really, really bad. I would frequently call up the management and tell them that such-and-such a geezer was hanging around the studio, knowing that he was a drug dealer. [Once Phil] turned around and said, "There are spies amongst us," and started laughing. I turned around and smiled at him. Yup, there sure was. Me, basically. I'm telling on him, and he appreciated that, because he knows I'm trying to do something about it. But he's too far gone down that road to bother.'

They found themselves in a £1,000-a-day studio trying desperately to pull material together. During further recording at Lombard Studios, in Dublin, the mood scarcely improved. Eamon Carr was working night sessions there with Irish group the Golden Horde. One morning, just as Carr was leaving, the payphone in the hallway rang and he picked up the receiver. 'It was a woman's voice asking whether Philip or Gus was there,' he says. 'I said nobody was there yet, and I could feel the voice getting a bit disgruntled. "Leave them a message: Brian Downey won't be coming in." "Will he be in later?" "No, he won't be in at all." "Oh, okay." You could smell straight away that chaos reigned.'

'I think, really, Phil's heart had gone out of it,' Downey told me. 'Some of the members, including myself to be honest, were becoming a little bit impatient with the whole thing. It was becoming harder to do. We were getting on each other's nerves. We'd been together a long time, and relationships started to go a little bit pear-shaped in the band, including between myself and Phil. It was strained. Certainly Phil felt the strain. I know that for a fact because he told me.'

Around this time, Jim Fitzpatrick went for a long walk with Lynott and Gnasher along the Burrow beach. 'Phil said, "Do you have any idea what it's like? There are thirty-five people and their families depending on me to turn up for a gig every single day, and I can't do it." He felt he was being thrown to the wolves.'

Thin Lizzy had always been rather too beholden to the public relations machine for their own good. Tony Brainsby delighted in creating and circulating stories that had only a passing relationship with reality. As far back as 1973, several publications reported that Lynott's career was in immediate jeopardy due to his hearing problems. 'Deaf – never to hear again,' *Music Star* announced solemnly in December 1973. 'Never to hear the funky sounds of rock. Never to listen to the soaring notes of a favourite piece of classical music.'

Somehow he struggled on. When Chalkie Davies accompanied Thin Lizzy to the United States in the mid-1970s, he was asked to filter back any juicy gossip that might keep the band in the British press. 'Tony Brainsby always used to say, "If anything goes on, just let me know." I never did, of course. They thought they needed all that when they were away.'

Lynott could be a willing accomplice. 'He'd say, "I'm going to do this tomorrow, that'll get me in the *Daily Mirror*,"' says Kit Woolven. 'And it worked. He knew how to keep playing it.' In interviews he would outline the latest movie offers he was surveying. One was going to be the next *Raging Bull*. Another was similar to *Guess Who's Coming to Dinner?* He was going to play Jimi Hendrix on at least three separate occasions; in the event, his acting career extended to a stilted fifteen-second cameo opposite Lenny Henry on the BBC sketch show *Three of a Kind*. There was always a hustle, always an angle, always drama. Lynott wasn't just involved in a fight; he was going to lose an eye. 'There were a million stories concocted around Phil and Lizzy,' says Midge Ure. 'Usually around the time when ticket sales aren't going so well.'

The end of 1982 was one such occasion. Thin Lizzy had a UK tour booked to start in early February 1983. Less than half the tickets had been sold. The press were disinterested. Band morale was low. The finances were beyond grim. Resigned, Thin Lizzy announced that their next album and tour would be their last.

There was an overwhelming consensus – largely unspoken, but powerful nonetheless – that they needed to stop, at least temporarily. Scott Gorham was battling his own serious addiction issues and had already endured an unsuccessful stint in a rehabilitation centre. The band didn't sound great. They were getting loaded before shows, making mistakes and not caring. 'It was just a shit attitude to have,' says Gorham. 'After all this work we'd put in and now we don't want to get on stage unless we're fucked up? I told Phil this at a meeting at his house: "This is wrong, we're just dragging the name into the gutter, and I think we need to walk away."'

In one of his occasional bouts of back-me-to-the-hilt brinksmanship, Lynott had also recently threatened to quit in a fit of pique over the record company's refusal to pay for a gatefold sleeve for *Thunder and Lightning*. On this occasion, to Lynott's surprise, Chris Morrison agreed that ending the band might be a good idea. But they would have to do it properly, he counselled. A farewell tour was a financial necessity. According to Chris O'Donnell, Thin Lizzy were half a million pounds in debt to the taxman, trucking companies, equipment-hire firms and other creditors. They had been living beyond their means for years.

'We employed thirty-two people, with seven or eight people on full-time salary, plus the band, and a road crew on retainers,' says O'Donnell. 'Queen had that, but they were touring arenas in America. We were Hammersmith Odeon.' Even at their peak, the money coming in just about covered all their overheads. With sales in decline, cash-flow became more problematic. 'Philip would say, "I don't understand . . ." and I'd say, "But your guitar tech is on call 24/7, he's your drug dealer, for God's sake!" I told him to hire 'em and fire 'em. "Oh, can't do that." It became untenable.'

A story ran in *Sounds*, shortly after the announcement that the *Thunder and Lightning* tour would be the last, claiming the split was a scam designed to gee up the band's flagging fortunes. After a respectable pause Thin Lizzy could announce that – due to popular demand – they were going to continue after all. In effect, their final act was a high-stakes game of truth or dare; one final PR stunt, which badly back-fired. Chris Morrison confirms this was the general plan. 'I said, "You can always reform the band at a later date." I think this was a mistake, but I saw a way out of our financial problems. We announced the break, it was on BBC News, and the tour sold out very quickly.'

By this point, Lynott was having second thoughts, but the idea had already gathered momentum. In effect, Thin Lizzy broke up by mistake. 'It was one of those stupid, stupid management ideas,' says Darren Wharton. 'As far as I was concerned it really wasn't supposed to be the end. I know Scott wanted some time off, Scott had some huge issues, but [breaking up] was the worst thing that could have happened to Phil. It was just really badly handled.'

Whatever the impetus for the announcement, once the idea settled it met with little serious opposition among the nucleus of Thin Lizzy Ltd. Gorham was adamant that he had to leave before he died. Downey was exhausted and disillusioned, while the management had had enough. Morrison was focused on Ultravox. Former tour manager John Salter tried to keep the wheels turning, but they had all run out of energy and patience. Some mornings Lynott would be on the phone to the office for three hours straight, relaying a constant loop of threats, demands and ultimatums, until the only option was to hang up on him.

'Philip became incredibly difficult,' says Chris O'Donnell. 'He tracked me down once on a Bank Holiday Monday, when I was out with my girlfriend. He came in raging, saying he'd been ringing the office all day. I told him it was a Bank Holiday. He said, "There's no Bank Holidays in my life, pal." I was beaten up and tired and bored. I didn't mind Philip ringing me every single day of my life and chipping away at me when we were building something positive, but it became negative. Album-tour-album-tour, without any review. It just didn't work anymore.' Before *Thunder and Lightning* was released, O'Donnell officially severed his ties.

Only Lynott seemed tormented by the decision to disband. 'My attitude was that we could save it, but nobody else in the band thought it was gonna happen,' he told *Sounds* in March 1983. 'Apart from the fans nobody seemed interested in us. The record company and the management were taking us for granted . . . Now we're getting all this attention by saying we're breaking up, it's shown how popular we really are. It'd be funny to say "You want us back? Okay, we'll come back" . . . I'm cheeky enough to get away with it, but at the moment it's definitely the end . . . I don't think I could look at myself in the mirror again if we carried on.'[1]

In an interview with *Hot Press* in April 1983, the same sense of regret is apparent. He talked about being 'driven' to make the announcement, and going through with it only to save face. 'Now if we said we're gonna stay together it would just look like it was some publicity thing, which isn't on, so I think we'll break up [but] I feel I've let the supporters down. I'm the leader of the band and I feel I should have been able to lead them through this.'[2]

'I never got the impression that Philip was on board to end the band,' says Jim Fitzpatrick. 'It broke his heart, and I think he felt an immeasurable sense of failure. It was his soul, music. It's one thing if other people regard you as a failure, but when you regard yourself as a failure – that hurts. I got the sense for the first time that he had actually given up.'

The farewell tour began on 9 February 1983 in Scarborough and covered the UK, Ireland, Germany, Denmark, Sweden and Japan. Tickets sold well, and the crowd response was warm and affectionate. More and more dates were added as the management saw the chance to reduce their debt before winding things up. 'It was an extremely painful tour to do,' says Gorham. 'It seemed to never end.'

Thunder and Lightning was released during the UK leg, on 4 March 1983, and received its strong chart position – number four – more because of the unique circumstances surrounding its creation than for its quality, which was negligible. It had more energy than their previous records, and appealed to a new fan base of young heavy-metal fans as well as Thin Lizzy die-hards, but the contrast to the band in their heyday was stark.

Aside from the atmospheric 'The Sun Goes Down' and powerhouse 'Cold Sweat', the songwriting was rote and the playing blunt. John Sykes was a technically superb guitarist, but he did not offer the light and shade of the twin-guitar interplay. All flash but little feel, his contribution tipped the balance uncomfortably close to outright heavy metal. 'It was hideous,' says Midge Ure. 'Horrible. Sykes sucked everything dry and took all the emotion out of it. It wasn't Lizzy at that point ... The songs became more and more repetitive, they were all interchangeable.'

The inevitable run of shows at the Hammersmith Odeon later in March was recorded for a desultory posthumous live album, *Life*, which Scott Gorham concedes he has never listened to all the way through. Lynott insisted on mixing the album, and spent weeks on it, constantly nodding out at the desk. Says Chris Morrison, 'We were spending £1,000 a day for him to sleep.' *Life* took so long to complete that it came out after the tour had ended rather than during it, ensuring it missed its optimum slot.

The Odeon concerts were an opportunity to round up Thin Lizzy's gang of former guitar players, and featured guest spots from Brian Robertson, Gary Moore and Eric Bell. Snowy White was not invited; his contribution to *Life* dates from 1981. Bell had crossed paths with Lynott on a handful of occasions since their parting of the ways early in 1974. With Downey, they had recorded the throwaway 'Song for Jimmy' [*sic*] together in 1980 to mark the tenth anniversary of the death of their mutual hero, Jimi Hendrix. The same year Bell had jammed on tour with Thin Lizzy on a rare run through of 'Whiskey in the Jar'.

'Fame and drink and drugs absolutely changed the guy,' he says. 'At Hammersmith, he hardly acknowledged my existence, though I suppose I couldn't blame him in a way, because of what I'd done in Belfast. He was like a stranger that I'd never known. I had this photograph in my pocket, a very, very old shot of me and Philip with two girls, taken around the third gig Thin Lizzy ever played. We were all there, tuning up for the soundcheck, and Philip strides in. He walks past me and I say, "Hey, Philip, look at this." He saw the photograph, says, "Listen, don't fucking show that to anybody, right?" and walked off. He didn't want anyone to see the way he used to look. Without the moustache and without the swagger.'

In July and August, billed as the Philip Lynott Band, he broke off from Thin Lizzy's valedictory lap to play thirteen solo dates in Sweden, backed by Downey and Sykes, alongside Mark Stanway of Magnum on keyboards and Irish guitarist Doish Nagle, formerly of the Bogey Boys, who was running in the same circles as Lynott and had similar recreational habits. 'We had a great time,' says Stanway, who, almost inevitably, ended up staying at Kew Road, off and on, for the next eighteen months. 'We did a few Lizzy songs and a lot of Phil's solo stuff, and we did "Sarah", which he never did with Lizzy.'

He came back home for Thin Lizzy's last ever British performance, at the Reading Festival on 28 August. The flashy light show and smoke bombs detonated prematurely, but it still felt like a suitably momentous send-off. The audience was on their side and howled with genuine affection as *'the coyote called'* during 'Cowboy Song', but Lynott's once beautifully warm and supple voice strained in the higher register. The reliance on weary old party tricks like 'Are You Ready?' and 'Baby Drives Me Crazy' told its own story. 'What really persuaded me that we were right to quit was the amount of our set that's old stuff we have to play,' said Lynott. 'That was beginning to drown our creativity. In the end there was no challenge there anymore.'[3] The final song was a poignant, potent, nine-minute 'Still in Love with You', introduced by Lynott as 'definitely the last one, you know?' It was no longer for a woman, but for the fans. By the end, he was in tears.

They travelled on to Germany for three final concerts, finishing at the Monsters of Rock festival on 4 September 1983. Brian Robertson was there with Motörhead, and gathered with all the other musicians at the side of the stage. Roadies cried, fans roared, but Lynott now seemed detached and numbed by it all. It didn't quite feel real. 'We said goodbye at the airport and that was the band – finished,' Brian Downey told me. 'There was no big hullabaloo. It was, "Okay, guys, see you again sometime. Take care. Bye."' It was a Monday morning, autumn was in the air, and after almost thirteen years of constant activity, Thin Lizzy was over.

One day, Caroline Lynott had a T-shirt made for her husband. It read, simply, 'WHERE'S GUS?' 'Because Philip woke up and that was the first thing he said,' says Helen Ruttle. 'Gus was there to do everything.'

Life at Glen Corr, says Ruttle, 'was not a normal family situation'. When Lynott was away, often either Dennis Keeley or

Graham Cohen, who had worked for Philomena since the early days in Manchester, would move uninvited into the house with his wife and children.

During the three years that they had lived in Ireland, Lynott's marriage had deteriorated. While he spent most of his life either on tour or in Kew, his wife spent much of her time in Glen Corr with the two children: Sarah was now aged five and Cathleen three. Increasingly, they lived divided lives. 'Philip once said to me, "My marriage broke up because you work me too hard,"' says Chris Morrison. 'I pointed out that he moved Caroline to Ireland so he could get laid by every woman he'd meet in London. I don't think that helped.'

The move to Sutton was partly intended as a retreat from the rigours of life on the road and the incessant demands of London, but Ireland was not the fairy-land of Lynott's more poetic imaginings. Dublin offered no easy refuge from reality. In the early 1980s heroin flooded the city, from the tower blocks of Ballymun to seaside villages like Howth. Lynott was not protected from his own appetites simply by taking an hour's aeroplane ride west, and neither were those closest to him.

The mood around Glen Corr became less happy and healthy. As with Kew Road, at times the house was filled with strangers and casual acquaintances, sometimes staying for one or two weeks at a time. They were often unsavoury and occasionally intimidating, and would not easily be persuaded to leave. Bono from U2 had recently moved with his new wife, Ali, into a cottage in Howth, just along the road from Glen Corr. He would bump into Lynott and was always charmed but slightly wary. 'He was so kind to me and gentle about our band,' he said. 'He'd say, "Do you want to come down for dinner?" And I didn't. I didn't know what to do, because he had that look.'[4] It may have been for the best. Although he was always polite to Bono in public, Lynott's private comments about him were often far from complimentary.

Caroline Lynott sought some semblance of a social life in her husband's long absences. 'We had to be a little bit circumspect,' says Helen Ruttle. 'He was the jealous type. Nobody was to look at Caroline.'

'My phone would ring at one or two in the morning asking where Caroline was,' says Jim Fitzpatrick. 'I said, "I've just dropped her home, she was out with us." He was really fucking angry: "Who else was there, who was talking to her?"'

'His head went,' says Noel Bridgeman sadly. 'I remember going down to his house to play a football match for the craic . . . There was a cut-out caricature of himself at the hall door, and another one at the top of the stairs. It was very strange. When we were leaving, my car was parked out the front, and Caroline's car was there. He said to me, "Is your car better than Caroline's car?" A very, very strange question. I just remember saying, "Ah, not at all, Philip, don't worry about that." He was acting very strange. Paranoid.'

There were instances of dishonesty and deceit on both sides, complicated by drug dependency, alcohol, distance, mistrust and too many people becoming involved in their lives. 'In the end there were a lot of negatives between the two of them,' says Frank Murray. 'Both of them were bad for the other in certain ways.'

Jim Fitzpatrick remained close to the couple in the period where their marriage faltered. 'I remember having a really long heart-to-heart conversation with Caroline in the Cock Tavern. She was going off the rails herself, she was dealing with break-ups, sorrow and panic. Things had got a bit nasty. It was a quagmire, with a lot of competing interests. It was an extraordinary painful period, two people you care about being torn apart from all sides.'

Shortly afterwards in 1984, while her husband was away, Caroline Lynott wrapped the children in duvets, put them in the car and handed the keys to Glen Corr to a neighbour. They caught the next ferry to England and returned to the Crowther family home at Temple Court in Corston, near Bath.

'Philip simply couldn't deal with it,' says Fitzpatrick. 'We walked on the beach a lot. I remember one time, it was the most personal conversation I ever had with him, and it was essentially him saying that he was going down the tubes – mentally and physically. It was an immensely sad conversation. It wasn't tearful, but it was stark.'

The fact that his wife and the mother of his children was the privately educated daughter of a television celebrity had always aroused a degree of tabloid interest. News of their separation led to reporters and photographers hanging around 184 Kew Road. 'When the press were parked outside Phil would say, "Come on, let's go to your place for the weekend,"' says Mark Stanway. 'We'd drive up to my house in Wolverhampton and he'd play with my kids, kip on my settee. He was a family man behind it all. He was as soft as anything, and he lived for his kids. It could all be quite normal – but just not often enough.'

After the break-up, Chris Morrison organized a legal separation hearing. As part of the settlement, Caroline was given provision to buy a cottage in Bath, and Lynott was granted regular access to his daughters under supervision; his chaperone was usually either one of Caroline's sisters, Philomena or his cousin Monica, who was now living and working as a teacher in London, close to Kew Road. Whenever he saw his children, he made a concerted effort to be lucid, bright and upstanding. When Sarah and Cathleen left, he would retreat to his bedroom at Kew Road and often not emerge for the rest of the day.

The relationship was not irreparably damaged. They cared for each other and remained in contact. His friends and family believe he would never have have pushed for a divorce or contemplated remarrying. 'Phil loved his family, loved his daughters, loved his wife – there's absolutely no doubt about that,' Brian Downey told me. 'He was always talking about them and showing photographs. I just think because of the marriage break-up he was a bit devastated. I've experienced it myself, and it's horrible to go through. I think that took a toll on his health. He just didn't have the wherewithal to deal with it.'

16

'Philip's big problem,' says Frank Murray, 'was, "What do I do next?"'

Lynott had been in a band since he was thirteen. Singing in the Black Eagles, Skid Row and Orphanage had helped him establish his identity as he emerged from the void of his early childhood. Being a member of a group had given shape and significance to his sense of otherness. As Thin Lizzy evolved, the band became his primary means of defining himself, the scaffolding which propped up his perception of who and what he was. Darren Wharton is far from alone in believing that 'Phil wasn't a whole person without Thin Lizzy'.

Which explains why, despite the obvious pitfalls, he resolved to form another group almost immediately. 'He couldn't imagine a life not in leather trousers,' says Bob Geldof, 'with a limousine taking him to work every day.'

There was also pride, or perhaps hubris, forcing him back on the horse. 'I wanted to prove to myself that I could play live,' he said.[1] One might have thought that proving it night after night for fourteen years was enough, but that would have been to underestimate the constant questioning voice beneath the bravado. 'I saw him as being this huge rock star, and yet he said,

"I always feel like I'm trying to make it,"' says Kit Woolven. '"I feel like I'm in this little Irish band that's come over, and we're trying to make it in England. It never leaves you." He had all those insecurities. They don't go, you just gloss over them.'

Within months of the final Monsters of Rock show in Germany, at the end of 1983 Lynott called Brian Downey to discuss the prospect of forming a new band. 'I said, "Well, it's a bit early!"' says Downey. 'I was thinking of taking a couple of months out to be with my family. He got a bit impatient. He said, "Well, do all that, and once you're back we can give it a try."'

In the interim, Lynott recruited for his new venture, which was as yet unnamed but eventually would be called Grand Slam. The original line-up was Lynott, Downey, John Sykes – three-fifths of Thin Lizzy – and Mark Stanway on keyboards. The plan was almost certainly to reform his old band by stealth. Almost immediately, however, Sykes left to take up David Coverdale's offer to join Whitesnake. He was replaced by twenty-one-year-old guitarist Laurence Archer, who had been playing in Wild Horses. 'Phil was very down about John leaving,' says Stanway. 'They were very close.'

In March 1984, the line-up started rehearsing at the local community hall in Howth, with Doish Nagle joining on second guitar. Brian Downey had a sinking feeling from the start. He and Lynott were both living in Dublin, and on several occasions the drummer drove from the other side of the city for two o'clock rehearsals, only to discover that Lynott was still sleeping off the excesses of the previous night. 'We'd just broken up Thin Lizzy for lots of strange reasons, and the next thing you know Phil has formed a band that's not quite as good as what we had. I couldn't understand that. I wasn't really enjoying it. Apparently we had an [Irish] tour coming up, but after about a week of this I said to Phil, "We've only got four or five songs, we're not going to have a set together if you keep not turning up." He said, "Oh, don't worry about it, they're only small gigs, we're only playing to 400 or 500 people." I said, "Well, it's not going to sound great. It doesn't matter how many people are there." He said, "Oh, we can do all sorts of Lizzy stuff, it will be fine."'

Downey proposed cancelling the tour until they got it right. 'He wasn't prepared to do that. He wasn't taking it as seriously as he should have been, so I suggested he get somebody else in. There was no animosity, he understood my position. He said, "We'll always be mates," and we left it at that.' In common with Scott Gorham, still addressing his own addiction to heroin, Downey had no contact at all with Lynott during the next eighteen months.

Lynott recruited Robbie Brennan on drums, whom he knew from his 1982 solo tour and from producing his band, Auto Da Fé. Both Brennan and Doish Nagle were using heroin. Stanway and Archer weren't in quite so deep, but Grand Slam would routinely hit the stage in various states and stages of chemically induced disarray. 'There was a lot of partying going on,' says Stanway. 'I'm no angel, but when it came to the hard stuff I never touched it, but you could certainly tell when Phil had been on it. Glazed eyes, he'd forget words . . .'

The tapes from their tour of Ireland in late March and April 1984 confirm Downey's belief that Grand Slam were nowhere near ready. The set list was an expedient mix of Thin Lizzy songs, Lynott's solo material, a couple of new compositions and a medley of Procol Harum's 'A Whiter Shade of Pale' and Bob Dylan's 'Like a Rolling Stone'. Lynott was playing 'Whiskey in the Jar' again, out of professional necessity. His voice was ravaged. He couldn't get near the high notes on 'Sarah'. Compared even to the final Thin Lizzy shows or his solo tour of Sweden the previous summer, far less *Live and Dangerous*, the sense of a talent in decline was acute.

Booked into clubs and hotels in Lifford and Portrush, in Strandhill and Kilkenny, the mood at the shows was often raw, the room heavy with the febrile ambience of local tribes out for a big night rather than a memorable musical experience. Lynott seemed almost to have come full circle. His former Skid Row band-mates, Brush Shiels and Noel Bridgeman, had settled back into the local scene. They were playing around Dublin, touring Ireland occasionally and making a good living. Like Eric Bell, they had made peace with the more urgent ambitions of their youth. To play well, for the love and the joy of it, was enough. Lynott professed to friends that he would be happy 'doing the pubs' again, but he was accustomed to a more elevated altitude.

Before he had formed Grand Slam, Shiels had offered to help. 'I said, "Why don't we go around the country and do a few numbers? You only have to play for half an hour and I'll give you X amount of money." I was doing very well.' Lynott agreed – 'that'll pay for the windows in the garage, *hur hur hur*' – but then decided he would rather do it under his own steam. 'The unfortunate thing was, he was playing down the road from me, and there was nobody at his gig because it wasn't Thin Lizzy and he was in the wrong venues,' says Shiels. 'You can't just turn up and play some little place and expect everyone to follow. He tried it, and it was a disaster.'

The loss of status was truly humbling. Lynott was still shouting 'Are you out there?' as though commanding the stage at the Hammersmith Odeon, but it was like a man roaring into a deepening void. 'I remember him telling me about playing up in Donegal, and there were thirty-two people,' says Jim Fitzpatrick. 'How do you cope with that?' Paying a social visit to another pub venue, in the spirit of generosity Lynott made an impromptu offer to come back soon to play a show, only to be told by the owner, 'I don't think we'd get a crowd.' 'That hurt,' says Jim

Fitzpatrick. 'Later in the car, I said, "That guy's a prick," and Philip said, "Jaysus, I get that all the time now."'

The lesson he had first learned via the lukewarm reception given to his solo albums was now hammered home even more brutally. 'It's difficult when you leave a very successful scenario thinking you're the main guy, and people will still flock to see you,' says Midge Ure. 'It doesn't work that way. Call it Grand Slam and nobody's interested. It's the same with Mick Jagger. It's the same with Midge Ure. The brand is bigger than any individual. He would have been frustrated and annoyed that he wasn't the centre of attention anymore.'

One of several new songs Lynott had written was called 'Military Man'. It depicts a man in a combat zone, estranged from his loved ones, angry, frightened, confused and resigned to fate. Ostensibly a soldier's song, it also sounds like a despatch from the emotional frontline, a chronicle of Lynott's personal battle. *'If you see my children, tell them I miss them,'* he sings. *'I am writing from war.'*

Lynott had a sound in his head for his new band, a flinty hybrid of rock and rhythm. 'Military Man' edges towards it, but another new song, 'I Still Think of You', perhaps came closest to what he envisioned. It recalled the wiry mix of hard rock, funk and electronics of Prince's recent albums, *1999* and *Purple Rain*. He was listening to the nascent hip-hop of Melle Mel and Grandmaster Flash. He loved what ZZ Top had done with their 1983 album *Eliminator*, streamlining their traditional petroleum blues-rock with the aid of synthesizers, sequencers and drum machines. He noted that Michael Jackson had hired Eddie Van Halen to play guitar on 'Beat It'. He would have loved the collaboration between Aerosmith and Run DMC on their 1986 single 'Walk this Way'.

More often, the tenor of the songs he was writing was reflective, often close to despairing. As he did during 'Military Man', on 'Sisters of Mercy' Lynott called out to his father and mother with a naked need. 'Harlem' possessed something of the sweet, sighing spirit of Marvin Gaye's 'Sexual Healing', but while the musical mood is all silk and red roses, the words are stark. Originally called 'Crumlin', Lynott lifted the first verse from a poem Brush Shiels had written in 1968. Changing it to 'Harlem', the song took on a darker hue, reliving that uptown limo ride in 1978, from Willy DeVille's apartment to oblivion. *'I have often wondered, weary and depressed / Lord help me now, I'm wrecked, reckless / In Harlem / There's a warning.'*

Even when Lynott added words to Clann Éadair's 'A Tribute to Sandy Denny', he somehow managed to turn a eulogy for a late folk singer into a lament for himself: *'I'm heartbroken, torn down/ Oh Sandy, is there more to life than this? / Oh Sandy, I reminisce.'*

Some of the new material displayed flickers of vintage Lynott. Riding a boardwalk bounce reminiscent of Bruce Springsteen's 'Spirit in the Night' and 'Kitty's Back', as well as his own 'Dancing in the Moonlight', 'Gay Boys' was a sympathetic if clumsy character study of a same-sex relationship between Billy and Joey. On stage, he improvised a rather less politically correct rap about picking up a woman who turns out to be a man – *'I was disgusted'* – throwing in a reference to Boy George for good measure. 'I've always got on well with gay people,' he said at the time. 'I hate talking about them as if they were a different species. I find the thought of what they do behind closed doors offensive, but, as people, as mates? Great.'[2]

'Gay Boys' had wit and zip and zest, but 'Nineteen', 'Look in These Eyes', 'She Cries', 'I Don't Need This' and 'Dedication' were more characteristic of Grand Slam's inability to rise above rigid, generic hard rock. Most of their material was middling, often co-written with Mark Stanway, sometimes with Doish Nagle and Laurence Archer. Only a handful were composed solely by Lynott.

On 'Military Man' he sings, '*Papa, take a look at your boy, he's fighting.*' In the autumn of 1984, Laurence Archer claims that Lynott was heroin-free for three months. Lynott also told Frank Murray that he had been off the drug for eight weeks. 'He never went into rehab,' says Chris Morrison. 'He stopped by himself.'

He appeared live on ITV's breakfast show, *Good Morning Britain*, on 13 October 1984, talking about his problems in the manner of a man who had survived a narrow escape. 'I don't particularly think I was an addict, I messed around with it enough and I know enough addicts,' he said. 'Secondly, I don't think the battle is over. It never ends. The frightening thing about heroin is – and without wanting to glamorize the drug at all – it's very enjoyable to take. It cuts off reality if you've got a lot of problems.'[3]

He'd been up all night, arriving at the TV studio straight from a Grand Slam gig in Great Yarmouth. It was eight o'clock in the morning and he was a little 'delicate', as he tended to put it, but he held things together. To the obvious discomfort of his fellow guests, who looked horrified, he continued to explain how good heroin could be until dependency kicked in. His point was sensible and valid: to address the low, it's necessary to acknowledge the high, even if the pastel nursery-world of breakfast television may not have been the most sympathetic environment in which to air these views. 'Mentally, the battle will continue for the rest of my life,' he concluded.[4] Later, Meat Loaf joined him on the sofa, espousing meditation. An amused Lynott explained that he unwound these days by watching Manchester United play on the television.

He talked publicly about the good work of Narcotics Anonymous and pledged support to anti-heroin charities. He also talked to the *Evening Standard* about his brush with the drug, which he again referred to in the past tense. Partly this was an attempt to signal to labels and agents that he was not damaged goods, but he was also trying genuinely to address the problem. 'He was really delighted, proud as punch [that he had stopped],' says Murray. 'He did that by himself. Then [Jimmy Bain] came along to a party one night and shared his stash with Philip. I saw him, and he was gone again.'

Lynott worked hard at Grand Slam. Following the calamitous Irish tour, the band improved. Rehearsing at E'Zee Hire Studios in north London, Lynott drilled them for eight hours a day. 'I heard stories that some of the lads were referring to him as Sergeant Rock,' says Noel Bridgeman. 'He'd be marching up and down, giving out fuck to the band and the crew.'

They toured Britain throughout 1984, invariably billed as 'Phil Lynott's Grand Slam' and, on one particularly optimistic occasion, 'Thin Lizzy (now Grand Slam)'. By the time they played two shows at London's Marquee in mid-June, intended as a showcase for prospective record companies, Lynott had purged almost all Thin Lizzy material from the set, apart from 'Cold Sweat' and 'Sarah'. He opened the show with 'Yellow Pearl' and performed a mixture of new songs and solo material.

They faced insurmountable problems. Grand Slam were a drug band attempting to forge a musical bond in a compressed time period. They were inevitably compared unfavourably to Thin Lizzy. Not the Thin Lizzy of *Thunder and Lightning*, but the vintage model. It was one reason, alongside his own diminished and somewhat *démodé* personal profile, why Lynott felt their future lay in the States. 'If we head over there and work on it for a time then we can come back to England and not have to face the usual crap that gets flung in my direction,' he said. 'I'm not fashionable here anymore so once we complete this tour that should be our next move.'[5]

They never made it to the States, and would not get signed in Britain. The promotional blurb in the music papers' listings sections promised a 'major deal' pending, but none was ever offered. Chris Morrison and Mark Stanway are among those who feel that Lynott's unreliable reputation preceded him. Had he been making truly quality music, however, it would scarcely have mattered.

By the time of Grand Slam's final show at the Marquee on 4 December 1984, *Sounds* reviewer Andy Pell was not alone in hearing mere competence and 'mediocrity'. There was some rancour over songwriting credits. The band drifted away from Lynott, and Chris Morrison stopped bankrolling the project. 'We pushed on and recorded things but it just never happened, and it got to the point where it just wasn't going any further,' says Mark Stanway. 'Phil started to work with one or two other people on studio projects, and I went back to Magnum. It ran its course. He was down-hearted that it didn't happen because he had put a lot of time and effort in.'

Back at Kew Road, he indulged in the traditional distractions. His old Dublin friend Tom Collins was staying with Frank Murray in London, working on Neil Jordan's film *A Company of Wolves*. One day, they dropped in to see Lynott on the way back from Shepperton. 'The house appeared to be full of hangers-on,' says Collins. 'Phil was in bed. We were supplied with some Jack Daniel's and he appeared about an hour later with this goddess. She worked at Stringfellows, so off we trotted later on to drop her off. Of course, Philip got the red-carpet treatment. He was spending quite a lot of time there, I think.'

Lynott had recently appeared in a television advert for Virgin airline's first transatlantic flight. In the commercial, a young woman, sceptical of the opulence promised by Richard Branson's new air route, shrugs, 'I suppose it could be full of rock stars.' On cue, Lynott sits down next to her, smiles at the camera, and says, 'Sometimes.' On 22 June 1984, he was invited to fly on Virgin's inaugural Atlantic crossing to New York, a hedonistic celebrity jaunt which included Holly Johnson, Steve Strange and Boy George. When he arrived, Lynott went straight to the VIP area of the Limelight club, partied on Virgin's tab all night, and returned to the UK the next morning.

Helen Ruttle was in London visiting a family member and was staying at Kew Road. 'There was this beautiful American model type in the house in the morning when I woke up,' she recalls. 'She had met Philip at the party in New York and come back with him. All she had with her was a toothbrush and a credit card. I was so impressed! I remember him saying, "Oh Jeez, are you going to say something to me missus?" I said, "Why would I upset Caroline?" They were split up by then.'

He hoped they might be reconciled, but his mood appeared fatalistic. He had reconfigured 'Harlem' into 'If I Had a Wish' (also sometimes known as 'One Wish'), a smooth soul ballad with a new and almost unbearably resigned lyric.

> *I had a wish, my wish came true*
> *I lost it all when I lost you*
> *Lost in my loneliness*
> *Drowned in my selfishness*
> *Wrecked in my helplessness*

The only artists of any stature with whom Lynott worked in 1985 were two old friends. Lynott had known Huey Lewis since his band, Clover, had supported Thin Lizzy in 1976. Lewis's harmonica can be heard on *Live and Dangerous*, on 'Baby Drives Me Crazy', and he had contributed to Lynott's solo albums.

He was now fronting Huey Lewis and the News, who had broken through in 1984 with their third album *Sports*, which included four US top-ten singles. In January 1985, Lewis set up a week-long session at Record Plant Studios in Sausalito, across the Golden Gate Bridge from San Francisco. Lynott prepared to travel over with Grand Slam guitarist Laurence Archer, but he was in disarray. He had lost his passport so many times that the Irish Embassy refused to issue another one. He was also having visa problems due to his drug history. In the end, Archer flew on ahead and Lynott arrived a few days later after his circumstances had been straightened out. The delay meant he could only contribute to two songs on what was intended to be a three-song session.

Where once Lynott had imposed his will on every piece of music he recorded, here he was a passive presence. With the set and the scenery already built around him he was, in effect, a glorified session singer. The lead track, 'Still Alive', was an old Clover song, taken from their 1977 album *Love on the Wire*. It was chosen for its street-survivor lyrics, part of Lewis's plan to re-introduce Lynott as The Rocker. He and his team had completed the backing track and Lewis had recorded a guide vocal, very much in the vintage Lynott style. The results were well-meaning, a cagey approximation of Thin Lizzy's twin-guitar attack fed through Huey Lewis and the News's slick MOR pop-soul.

Lewis coaxed Lynott through a series of vocal sessions later described by his co-producer, Johnny Colla, as 'painstaking'.[6] In the end, a usable version of the song featuring Lynott's lead vocal eluded them. The second track, 'Can't Get Away', was an unremarkable soft-rock song written by Archer, which had been performed with Grand Slam.

Lynott returned to London with two half-finished tracks. This somewhat meagre return was at least sufficient to interest Polydor Records. John Salter and Chris Morrison now struggle to recall the details, but both believe Polydor offered Lynott a singles deal with an album option. He needed to prove himself. 'They didn't feel he had the material,' says Morrison.

Lynott recorded piecemeal and without focus for much of 1985. It wasn't that he had stopped trying. He may actually have been trying too hard. There was more than enough material for a third solo album, but not quite enough quality. The results included cliché-ridden hard rock ('Freedom Comes', 'Hard Times'), synth-based sketches ('Partner in Crime', 'Catholic Charm') and a handful of tracks he had been playing around with since 1983, written with Junior Giscombe, the young London soul singer who had enjoyed a top-ten UK single in 1982 with 'Mama Used to Say'. They had met in a club and had co-written and demoed new material at Kew Road, including the excellent 'He Fell Like a Soldier'.

In some respects, Lynott still resembled the restless soul who tried on every style for size in late-sixties Dublin. Even in extremis, his curiosity remained sharp. Only days before he fell ill, he recorded two songs co-written with a young Yorkshire guitarist, Steve Johnson, called 'Revolution' and 'No More'. He finally completed production on the Clann Éadair album, though it would never be released, while he honoured a personal commitment to watch a new young Irish group, Hothouse Flowers, play at the Magic Carpet pub in Foxrock, south Dublin, on Easter Sunday. The Celtic-soul band were unsigned but his cousin Monica sang with them sometimes, and Lynott was interested in their story. After the show they all went back to his aunt's house.

Through May and June 1985 he was busy working with Gary Moore. Lynott had been reconciled with Moore in 1983, following a four-year estrangement, after they had bumped into one another at Heathrow Airport. Moore had subsequently participated in Thin Lizzy's farewell shows at the Hammersmith Odeon, and at the end of 1984 Lynott had joined him on stage in Belfast and Dublin. As they started socializing again, Moore got to know Lynott's daughters. 'He'd say to me, "Come on around, Gary, the kids are here,"' Moore recalled. 'They'd do little dances on the window ledge and entertain us. They were really cute little girls.'

Moore asked Lynott to contribute to a song he had written called 'Out in the Fields'. 'I went over to his house and we made a little demo of it on his eight-track,' Moore said. 'He'd come down about two hours late, with a spliff in one hand and a glass of whiskey in the other. That's what Phil was like at that time. I knew him a long, long time, and he changed at the end . . . When Phil started out he was always the first in the studio and the last to leave. He was a bundle of energy. At the end he had gone downhill. I hated to see him like that.'

They recorded the song near Kew, at Eel Pie Island Studios. Lynott bypassed his management and cut a direct deal with 10 Records, taking part for a one-off fee of £5,000, paid in cash. It was a maladroit piece of business that left Chris Morrison exasperated, particularly when the song became a sizeable hit. 'Out in the Fields' reached number five in the UK charts in June 1985, number three in Ireland, and number two in Norway and Sweden.

Lynott's contribution was rather more minimal than advertised. He sang two lines at the start of each verse, and contributed a brief spoken section. It was his idea to wear the crimson military-style jackets on the single sleeve and in the video. 'Out in the Fields' was a gnarly anti-war song that made reference to the ongoing violence in Moore's native Northern Ireland. 'At last you've come out and said something,' interviewer Gaz Top told a whacked-out Lynott during a prickly satellite TV interview. Lynott bristled. 'What do you mean, *at last*? I've been saying things all me bleedin' life.'[7]

Mark Nauseef had dinner with the pair in Hamburg while they were in the city to perform on the *Rock Pop Music Hall* programme. 'It was the same old stuff,' he laughs. 'I could tell there was something going on between them. I didn't even want to ask whose record it was! It was cool, we had fun, but I could see Philip's vitality, his energy, was different.'

The B-side of 'Out of the Fields' was Lynott's own harrowing 'Military Man'. When he played it live with Moore on *Rock Pop Music Hall*, it felt crushing. His confidence and playfulness, his engagement with the audience and the camera – it had all gone.

When he sang '*Mama, take a look at your boy, he's dying*', it seemed horribly apposite. Sweating profusely in his military garb, at times Lynott appeared to be struggling to breathe. Heroin and cocaine clogged up his respiratory system and triggered his asthma, making him cough and wheeze dreadfully. He was not fat by any stretch of the imagination, but his pipe-cleaner frame now had a sizeable kink at the gut. 'I remember seeing him with Gary and his bass was an extra foot away from him, sitting on this paunch,' says Midge Ure. 'That just wasn't Phil. He was the archetypal skinny rock star.'

His face had become waxy and bloated. His eyes were dulled and discoloured. He took to wearing sunglasses, previously a rock-and-roll trapping he would usually avoid, not least because those big, mother-me peepers were his first line of attack when it came to the opposite sex. Now he seemed reluctant to meet anyone's gaze, as though to avoid seeing the expression fixed on the face of the person to whom he was talking. He would get dressed and ask younger friends if they thought he looked all right, a lack of sartorial confidence so at odds with his core character it was almost the most shocking change of all.

Gale Barber was now Gale Claydon following her marriage in 1983, and was about to become a mother. She was producing music programmes at a new satellite station, Sky Channel, and met up again with Lynott after several years of non-communication when he appeared on a show called *Sky Trax* alongside Neil Murray, the bass player in Whitesnake. 'The Philip I'd known was the vainest man on the planet,' she said. 'He would spend hours getting ready to go out, everything had to be exactly right, and the way he looked now was heartbreaking.'[8] She confronted him about his drug use, but he denied it was a problem.

Chris Salewicz bumped into him at an Ultravox party in a modish wine bar in central London. 'I saw him in a terrible state,' he says. 'He looked okay when he arrived, then he went off to the toilet, and he came back just fucking green. He was nodding out, he had snot dripping out of his nose and he just let it curl around his hand . . . He was such a great, warm guy, to see him like that was ghastly. I just stared. I didn't know what to do.'

The last year of Lynott's life was the first full year he had spent without being in a band since 1963. It meant more time at Kew Road. During the final few months Lynott's young cousin Monica was living there, working as a teacher and keeping 'normal' hours. He did his utmost to ensure, not always successfully, that she was shielded from direct evidence of his excesses. Drawings and messages from Sarah and Cathleen were pinned up all over the house. Brian Robertson lived nearby and he would come around with Jesse Wood, the nine-year-old son of Ronnie Wood and Krissy Findlay, whom Robertson was going out with, and they would play with train sets. 'They were close,' says Robertson. 'Jesse loved Philip, and he loved Jesse coming around.'

These were rare elements of stability in an environment increasingly overrun by dealers, addicts and freeloaders. 'I think there was a pathological fear of being alone,' says Midge Ure. 'He always had people around him, which was odd. Unfortunately at the end some of them were very dubious and fed his habits. A lot of hangers-on.'

Gus Curtis had returned to Dublin and Charlie McLennan was no longer on the payroll, although he was still on the scene. Former Thin Lizzy roadie Liam Kelly was another regular presence. He later served a prison sentence for supplying Lynott with Class A drugs. Jimmy Bain was perhaps the most invasive influence. Living close by, Bain did not like to get high alone.

Scores of others came and went. Lynott would pass people on the stairs of his own house and have no idea who they were. Young women from overseas would arrive and not leave; pushers, gofers, roadies and musicians moved in. Between bouts of socializing, Lynott sometimes retreated to his room for days, and spent long spells in bed. He ended up surrounded by people but very alone.

The wretchedness of Kew Road seeped into the carpets and the curtains. It saddened and repelled those who had known him in happier, more innocent days. During the final period of Lynott's life, many of his oldest friends had dispiriting encounters with him, where they struggled to equate the person in front of them with the various versions of the man they loved: the gentle poet; the dedicated, disciplined pro; the heroically vain swordsman; the ball of ideas and energy. Where did he go?

Jim Fitzpatrick made a rare visit to Kew Road one morning while he was in London, and found a young woman lying comatose on the sofa, a crumbling cigarette burning the flesh on one hand. She had apparently been living on Lynott's couch for several months. 'They'd had sex and had been smoking heroin,' he says. 'It was a scene of squalor in a very beautiful house.'

Lynott had not been to bed and seemed unperturbed. He and Fitzpatrick went into the garden to play football, and then came inside to have breakfast. 'I had cereal, he had a bottle of claret. I kept checking on the girl. I thought she was gone, she looked as if she could die at any moment. It was really fucking disturbing. It never sat right with me. When I used to come over to Welbeck Mansions, the house would be spotless, the bins would be full of bottles and cigs and trash. He cleaned up, he was meticulous. That stopped. He changed big time. I thought, what the fuck is going on here?'

Frank Murray was now managing the Pogues and Paul Scully was working as their sound technician. On St Patrick's Day 1985, Lynott turned up with a bottle before the Pogues's concert at the Clarendon, and promised to return for a guest spot on 'Whiskey in the Jar'. He failed to show, and afterwards Murray, Scully and a boisterous Pogues' touring party descended on the house. 'Whenever I'd see him he'd run over and throw his arms around me, always,' says Paul Scully. 'It was great seeing him, but by this time he was a lonely man down at his big house in Kew on his own, surrounded by fellas who would call in just to do what he was doing.'

When Lynott and Frank Murray came into contact, it was almost unbearably painful for them both. Neither man quite knew where to look. 'It would be okay as long as there was just me and him there, or maybe one or two other people,' says Murray. 'Then somebody would inevitably turn up with smack and he'd be pretty useless after that. I would look at him and think, how the fuck did you get into this? Who are these freaks you're hanging around with? It was like the house was infected. You felt like getting a broom and just clearing them out. He can't get out of bed. You'd have to go up to the room and tell him, "You get up," and he would. It was like he was guilty or something. He'd try to be all happy and clappy.'

Lynott was injecting heroin into his toes and legs to avoid marking his arms, but to anyone paying close attention his addiction was blindingly obvious. He was taking cocaine almost constantly. He uttered dire warnings that his mother must never be told what he was doing, but the truth was written all over his face, his lifestyle and his songs. 'The signs were there, we all knew it, but what do you do?' says Chris Morrison. 'I said, "If you ever need any help you just have to ask," but he'd back off and be out the door. He didn't want to know. You can't talk sense to someone on smack. My advice from drug people in those days was to let him hit rock bottom and then ask for help.'

When Scott Gorham had collapsed on stage from the effects of heroin in Portugal in 1982, he had been sent to rehab in a manner which had the scent of shame about it. 'In that era, you weren't manly if you went for help, and I think that was part of Phil's mindset,' Brian Downey told me. 'I think he was bottling a lot of shit up and not letting people know exactly what was going on.'

When confronted, occasionally Lynott would say he was going to kick everything and get healthy. More often, he either got angry or went into denial. Jim Fitzpatrick noticed that after being on the receiving end of a pep talk, Lynott would stop answering the phone to him. Sometimes several months would pass before he allowed contact to resume. True friends became alienated or could not get through. Like many others, Ted Carroll heard about his predicament and sighed. Brush Shiels lost heart. 'He wouldn't talk to me when he was overdoing it, he wouldn't talk to a lot of us,' he says. 'And I have a limited amount of patience, which is not very nice.'

They had their own lives to lead, careers to maintain, their own personal struggles and challenges. Life went on. Paul Scully noticed that, increasingly, Lynott would loop back to the past and talk ramblingly about the old days. 'We were mates from fifteen, sixteen, and I think he was very nostalgic for that kind of innocent time,' he says. 'He was already king of the castle even then, everyone knew him and everyone recognized him walking down the street. He had a different kind of fame then, a lovely fame, more natural, and probably more rewarding than the false adulation that comes with being a rock star.'

The fillip of 'Out in the Fields' was offset by Live Aid. The dual-venue, sixteen-hour charity concert was held on 13 July 1985 at Wembley Stadium in London and JFK Stadium in Philadelphia, in aid of Ethiopian famine relief. A live spin-off from the Band Aid single, 'Do They Know It's Christmas?' released at the end of 1984, Live Aid was organized by Bob Geldof and Midge Ure. No favours were granted. The boy who had collected for the 'Black Babies' wasn't asked to participate in the Global Jukebox.

'I think Geldof made a conscious decision not to involve Philip,' says Chalkie Davies. 'People say, "He might have slurred his speech, he was overweight." You don't understand. When he put that guitar on, no matter how sick he might have been, he would have delivered in spades. I think that was a terrible, terrible shame.'

Chris Morrison was a member of the Band Aid Trust and didn't utter Lynott's name as a prospective participant in the six months leading up to the concert. For Lynott, far worse than being deliberately side-lined was the implication that they had simply forgotten he existed.

'To our dying shame neither Bob nor I even thought about asking Phil to put Lizzy together for Live Aid,' says Midge Ure.

'If he had been in a healthy state, that could have been the Queen moment for them – "The Boys Are Back in Town" at Wembley? Jesus, can you imagine? But it never crossed our minds, and we were both good friends of his. I think he would have felt absolutely betrayed by that. I think if we had done that, Lizzy would have reformed. Why didn't we do it? Was it that psychologically we had given Phil up as gone? It's something that will stay with me for the rest of my life.'

Rock and roll was a winner's game, and Live Aid was about global pulling power. Geldof was nothing if not a pragmatist. He was looking for superstars. If the concert had taken place between 1976 and 1979 then Thin Lizzy would legitimately have been on the bill. By 1985, they were just another decent but deceased rock band who had quit slightly beyond their sell-by date. Lynott spent part of that day visiting RTÉ studios in Dublin, where he donated a bass guitar for auction, which raised £900.

Shortly afterwards, he was on holiday in Marbella with his two children and his mother when he met Irish nightclub-impresario Maurice Boland. They went for a drink, and Boland offered Lynott a booking at Disco Cuba, the local club he managed on the Golden Mile. He claimed that Lynott only agreed on the proviso that the club would contact the other members of Thin Lizzy and book them for the show. The Lookalikes's Sean O'Connor received a call from Boland, and was told that Lynott wanted either O'Connor or Gary Moore to play lead guitar.

In the end, Disco Cuba got Grand Slam redux rather than Thin Lizzy. Doish Nagle and Robbie Brennan were flown out, joining O'Connor (who brought Lynott's bass) and Justin Clayton, a guitarist who played regularly with Julian Lennon. It was a strange set-up. The club was owned by three Glaswegian businessmen; the musicians were paid £1,000 cash and each given free and unlimited use of an apartment.

The backline PA was rudimentary and there was no rehearsal time. Playing to a crowd of 700, Lynott didn't get on stage until after three o'clock in the morning, by which point he and most of the musicians – as well as one well-known professional snooker player – had been rendered virtually insensible by cocaine. 'He was off his trolley,' says O'Connor. 'How he got through the gig I'll never know.' They played an hour of Thin Lizzy's greatest hits in severely deconstructed form. Despite the fact that Nagle and Clayton barely knew the songs, 'it went off okay,' says O'Connor. 'The fact that it was Thin Lizzy material and Phil was singing them, we just about got away with it.'

It would prove to be Lynott's final concert, although he appeared at Gary Moore's shows at Manchester Apollo on 23 September and the Hammersmith Apollo on 27 and 28 September 1985, performing 'Out in the Fields' and 'Parisienne Walkways'. 'That was it,' said Moore. 'I never saw him again after that. It was pretty sad, actually. He said to me, "Gary, I'm going to kick this fucking drug habit, and I'm going to kick all the booze, and we'll go out and we'll play." But it never happened.'

Two days before the Manchester show, on 21 September, Lynott had been described in Kilmainham District Court in Dublin as a 'drugs victim and a tragedy' by his own brief. It was the latest in a line of several well-publicized busts. Lynott was often cavalier about ferrying drugs between England and Ireland, and he was caught in possession of cannabis, methadone and heroin, having been stopped and searched at Dublin Airport the previous May. He was fortunate that the presiding judge, Gillian Hussey, had a progressive view of not sending addicts to jail. 'I am not going to do anything to hamper this man's career,' she said. 'As long as he is only using these drugs himself and not giving them to others he is only destroying himself. I wish he would give them up.'

'I'm notorious for being busted,' Lynott said during a TV interview shortly afterwards. 'But I am anti-drugs for other people. Like [Jimi] says, "Have you ever been experienced?" I wouldn't advise people to do it.'[9]

The very first song on the very first Thin Lizzy album had begun with Lynott reciting a poem. *'The Friendly Ranger paused / And scooping a bowl of beans / Spreading them like stars / Falling like justice on different scenes.'* The last song he ever recorded began rather differently: *'You want it rough? You got it rough / You want it tough? I'm tough / You want it mean? I'm mean / I'm bad / Nineteen.'*

Lynott's first and only solo single for Polydor, 'Nineteen', was released on 6 November 1985. 'Rubbish,' declared *NME* in a review that was not so much scathing as tetchily dismissive. Although the single reached only number seventy-six in the UK charts, Lynott had a handful of promotional commitments to fulfil. He needed a drummer to perform the song on the *Razzmatazz Christmas Special*, a children's television show filmed in Newcastle. He asked John Salter to call Brian Downey, who was surprised that Lynott hadn't called himself, but happy to help.

Downey hadn't seen Lynott since March of the previous year, at the aborted Grand Slam rehearsals. 'I flew over and met him at his house, and I got a shock to say the least,' he says. 'It became obvious that he had changed, physically and personality wise. He had put on lots of weight, I noticed that immediately. He looked a bit unhealthy, and he didn't seem to be his normal self. He was withdrawn, and talking in a fairly negative way. I did say to him, "Are you okay? You've put on a bit of weight there, man." He said, "I've got no time to exercise, I'm pretty busy." I didn't really question it, but I was keeping an eye on him. There was a fair bit of brandy and port being consumed on the plane up to Newcastle. I noticed that. It really stuck in my mind.'

After taping the television show, presented by their old champion, David 'Kid' Jensen, Lynott, Downey and guitarist Robin George flew back to London and returned to Kew Road. Downey took one look at the scene of dissolution that Lynott had allowed to accumulate around him and booked into a hotel rather than stay the night, as had been originally planned. He left for Dublin the next day and never saw Lynott again.

Before they parted, Lynott talked about reforming Thin Lizzy as a four-piece in six months' time, once he had got back into shape. 'The conversation was very positive,' says Downey, 'But I did say, "You'll have to get your health and your fitness back." He realized that.' Lynott rehearsed the same theme with Sean O'Connor, earmarked as a prospective second guitarist, over coffee in London, and again when Scott Gorham came to visit him for the first time since Thin Lizzy had split.

The guitarist had finally succeeded in coming off heroin, using the NeuroElectric Therapy technique pioneered by Meg Patterson, the Scottish doctor who had successfully treated Jimmy Page and Eric Clapton. Gorham knew from the grapevine that Lynott was still using hard drugs, but felt strong enough to see him again.

'He was in his robe and slippers,' he says. 'His face was all puffy, and he was suffering really badly from his asthma. He looked terrible. I was clean now, and glowing with health. I played him some stuff, and he said he had a song he wanted to show me. He picked up his acoustic guitar and played, and I started to play along with it. Then he started to say things like, "We've really got to get back to writing songs and putting the band back together." I'm looking at him and I'm thinking, "Buddy, there's nothing I'd love more, but you're not ready to do this." I think he saw that in my face. He said, "Yeah, I'm going to quit all this drug shit, get healthy. It's all going to be good." I gave him a big hug, and went home.'

At the time, Lynott had another court case pending. He had been arrested for possession of a small amount of heroin. A custodial sentence was a possibility. During the three hours Gorham was with him, Lynott received a call from his solicitor informing him that the charges had been dropped, and celebrated by immediately draining two tall glasses of neat vodka.

Lynott was admitted to Salisbury General Hospital on 25 December 1985. His mother and daughters had arrived at Kew Road two days earlier to spend Christmas with him, but Lynott could not shake off the detritus which surrounded him. He struggled to get out of bed. When he got out of bed, he struggled to get dressed. He was vomiting and listless, frightened and freezing cold.

He deteriorated in the period leading up to Christmas Day. Brian Robertson came over on Christmas Eve with Jesse Wood to deliver a present. 'I walked in the bedroom, and he was totally a mess,' says Robertson. 'I tried to have a chat with him, but it was no good. I went straight downstairs, and said to Phyllis, "You'd better call Phil's doctor. This is not flu or whatever it is he's told you. This is dangerous shit."' He was visited by a doctor, who administered a shot and left.

He declined further. Caroline Lynott was spending the holiday period in Bath, and after calling the house on Christmas Day she drove to Kew to collect her daughters. In the belief that his condition was drug-related, Lynott was taken to Clouds House Treatment Centre in East Knoyle, near Salisbury in Wiltshire. Now comatose, he was swiftly transferred by ambulance to Salisbury General Infirmary.

He remained there for eleven days, drifting in and out of consciousness as his system slowly shut down. Graham Cohen, Charlie McLennan and Philomena Lynott were with him. His wife was in regular attendance, and his daughters visited. Chris Morrison came and waved through the glass; Lynott waved back. Everybody else was kept at arm's-length. 'Charlie had called to say Philip was in the hospital,' says Frank Murray. 'I kind of knew he wasn't coming out. It was terrible because people said, "No, you can't come down." Philip was my friend and I felt really sad that I wasn't there, just to hold his hand.'

'I was keeping in contact with people, and they were saying, "Oh, he's coming out of the coma,"' Brian Downey told me. 'One day he was out, the next day he was in. I said, "I'd love to come over and see what the hell is going on," but I was told, "Not really. Don't come over, it's a family matter. He'll be okay, he'll pull through."'

Lynott died on the morning of 4 January, the first Saturday of 1986, and fifteen years to the day since he had entered Decca Studios in Broadhurst Gardens to make the first Thin Lizzy album. He was connected to a dialysis machine and a respirator. His heart, liver and kidneys had ceased to function. He had pneumonia, abscesses and septicaemia. Shortly before Christmas, Lynott had been at a party where he had fallen over and chipped his elbow. This caused osteomyelitis, a bone infection to which intravenous drug users and those with weak immune systems are particularly vulnerable, and which can lead to blood poisoning if left untreated.

There had been close calls in the past, involving speedballs and cocaine seizures. He was drinking dangerous quantities of spirits, which, given his past history with hepatitis, put his liver under enormous strain. At times his asthma was so bad he could scarcely breathe.

Clinically, it was necessary to put a name to the cause of death, but Lynott had been terribly sick for a long time, and his ailments were many and varied. 'Picasso said he could deal with anything apart from fame,' says Noel Bridgeman. 'I think it destroyed Philo in the end.'

Epilogue
The Ageing Orphan

'Irish funerals are usually a lot jollier,' says Jim Fitzpatrick with a sad smile. 'It was pretty awful. Everyone was devastated.'

Befitting a man with at least two personalities, Philip Lynott had two funerals. On 9 January 1986, the Thursday following his death, there was a Mass at St Elizabeth of Portugal, the Richmond church in which he and Caroline had been married almost six years earlier. Among family and a host of musician friends, Lynott's life was celebrated by Father Raymond Brennan, the same priest who had performed his marriage ceremony. There was a gathering afterwards at the Richmond Hill Hotel.

On the Friday, his body was flown back to Dublin, and as the winter darkness closed in, his coffin was carried through the streets of Howth to a service at the Church of the Assumption.

The following morning, 11 January 1986, a Requiem Mass was held. As he had done countless times before, in the Five Club and the Bailey, Moran's and McGonagle's, Lynott seemed to gather all of Dublin around him. Despite the presence of photographers, journalists, a TV crew and a fair number of gawkers, it did not feel like a showbiz affair. This was raw, local business.

Among the throng of mourners were Lynott's mother, wife and daughters, his extended family, his many friends, and the community of Irish musicians who had so much to thank him for: Bob Geldof and assorted Boomtown Rats; Bono, Adam Clayton and Larry Mullen from U2; Terry Woods and Philip Chevron from the Pogues; Marie Brennan from Clannad; members of Dr Strangely Strange; Paul Brady, Brush Shiels, Eamon Carr and many more.

Taoiseach Charles Haughey and his daughter, Eimear, another old friend from the Clontarf days, paid their respects alongside local fishermen, drinking partners and neighbours. Crowds of fans and local residents gathered outside the church. Inside, the mourners sang 'Praise My Soul the King of Heaven', 'Peace, Perfect Peace' and 'Lord of the Dance'. Clann Éadair played two tunes. The lessons were read by Peter Lynott and Leslie Crowther, whose choice of text from Romans:14 made passing comment on some of the more lurid and unfeeling tabloid stories that ran in the immediate aftermath of his death: 'You should never pass judgement on a brother,' he said, 'Or treat him with contempt as some of you have done.'

From the Church of the Assumption, Lynott's coffin was driven the short distance to St Fintan's Cemetery in Sutton. It was a freezing slate-grey day. The suburban cemetery was bleached of colour and exposed to the wind coming in from the sea. By the graveside, festooned with flowers, Clann Éadair's Leo Rickard sat and piped his friend into the soil with 'The Brendan Voyage', a beautiful air from the *Howth Suite* by Irish composer Sean Davey. 'Jesus, it was terrible,' says Rickard. 'Just terrible.'

The wake was held in the Royal Hotel, Howth. 'It was like we were just waiting for Philip to walk in: *"Jaysus, lads, what're youse up to?"*' says Tim Booth. 'Everyone said that.'

U2 manager Paul McGuinness laid on a limousine for some of

Lynott's oldest friends, and they travelled back into town. 'We got together at a bar and we had a kind of requiem for him,' says Jim Fitzpatrick. 'There were seven or eight of us, his close friends, and we just wanted to be on our own. We still couldn't quite believe it.' That sad smile again. 'Still can't, sometimes.'

Philip Lynott has now been gone for some thirty years, but at times he feels remarkably present. Very few artists, particularly those who never quite made it to the top of the ladder or, conversely, are not endowed with the enduring cool of cult status, have enjoyed such a potent afterlife.

In Dublin, he shares with James Joyce, Patrick Kavanagh and James Connolly the distinction of having a statue erected in his honour. Unveiled in 2005, the life-sized bronze sculpture stands outside Bruxelles in Harry Street, funded by the Róisín Dubh Trust, set up by his mother.

And while Joyce has Bloomsday, the annual celebration of his life and work held on 16 June, Lynott has the Vibe for Philo. The bitter-sweet musical tribute has been held on the anniversary of his death each year since 1987, established and organized by Smiley Bolger and featuring live performances from friends, admiring artists and virtually every musician who ever played in Thin Lizzy or with Lynott.

In 2011, a wonderful and warm exhibition of his life and work, *Still in Love with You*, opened in Dublin and later travelled to London. It has since returned to Dublin again, and has been viewed by over 100,000 people.

On the global stage, a band that split up at a low ebb and which was relatively unfashionable through much of its existence is now regarded as one of the great rock groups. 'The Boys Are Back in Town' belongs to an exclusive canon of songs that instantly raise a smile of pleasure and recognition in bars all over the world. 'Dancing in the Moonlight' and 'Jailbreak' have been passed down through generations. Thin Lizzy's reinterpretation of 'Whiskey in the Jar' is now the standard, a unique blend of the modern and traditional which, somehow, reflects back some of the spirit of Lynott. These songs have entered the bloodstream of popular music.

In Ireland, the *little black boy* who landed in Crumlin aged seven succeeded in his quest to write himself into the history of his country. He has become another Irish folk hero, the Bold Philo, who lived fast and loved hard and died young, as folk heroes must. And like all folk heroes, he left behind a comet-shower of barely credible exploits destined to forever fill the air of Dublin bars, lavishly embellished with each retelling.

There is much myth and sentiment surrounding this version of a very complicated, conflicted man. 'I never saw any fear in the guy,' says Mark Nauseef. 'There's a beauty in that – but you need a little fear, sometimes.'

In the year before he fell ill, Lynott imagined a future away from the hurly-burly of rock stardom and constant touring. 'I'd like to think that at a certain age, I'd have written a book, have a nice little place in Howth,' he said. 'On Sundays I'd go down and play in the jazz band, you know? Have two very exuberant daughters, one an athlete with a gold medal . . .'[1]

He would have found his place, with or without Thin Lizzy. He was a young man when he died and he would not be old even now. Rock music is not the youthful preserve it once was. It grew up, and so did its practitioners. The best of Lynott's contemporaries – Elvis Costello, Bruce Springsteen, Van Morrison, Graham Parker – stayed true to their course. 'If only he had known,' says Chalkie Davies. 'I don't think he ever really understood how loved he was.'

Afterword

I met Philip when I was eighteen and he was twenty-seven. I am now fifty-seven, I have remarried, have two more children, and the children I had with Philip have children of their own. Time has moved on, and my life now could not be more different than the life I shared with Philip.

I do not dwell in the past and reading this book has re-immersed me in a period of my life which was turbulent, confused and ended very very sadly. I recognize the man in this book – which I think is accurate and very well-researched – and I mourn his loss all over again.

Who knows what it is that draws people to one another? For me Philip was a challenge, a powerful man with an air of mystery. He was shy and sensitive and the soft voice and those big eyes drew me in. But he was such a mass of contradictions – a man who loved to seduce women but seemed afraid of intimacy. We spent so little time alone together. Invariably one of his male friends/employees/coterie would be there too.

He laughed like Muttley and had a wicked and sometimes very silly sense of humour, but his mood could change without warning and he could be dark and frightening when he was unhappy. He was a Catholic who loved to go to church with his family while maintaining his own moral compass that perhaps didn't quite conform to the tenets of the religion!

I think we both cherished a dream of a traditional family life together. It seems bizarre to me now, remembering the reality of our existence. But there were sometimes hints of the normal life we yearned for in his beloved Dublin – bicycle rides and walks along the beach with the dog. There were Sunday roasts and friends with children who came over to play. There were big family Christmases – he loved to buy presents and was very generous.

But drugs have a way of spoiling everything, even while they're telling you they're going to make it all better. As life became crazier and crazier, I managed to pull myself out of there and start over. For Philip that was not possible. Which remains an enduring sadness for me.

When I think of Philip I think of the man rather than the musician. For me his legacy is not just the great catalogue of music he created, but the two beautiful, strong, funny, creative and loving girls we made together, of whom he would be so very, very proud.

Caroline Taraskevics, November 2015

Bibliography

There is an enormous amount of audio, visual and written material available on Philip Lynott and the career of Thin Lizzy. Among several film and television programmes dedicated to his life, David Heffernan's *Renegade: The Phil Lynott Story*, made in 1982 for RTÉ, remains easily the best and most incisive, not least because it was made during Lynott's lifetime and with his participation. Shay Healy's documentary from 1996, *The Rocker: A Portrait of Phil Lynott*, is also of value.

On the web, Peter Nielsen's online fan-site, www.thinlizzy-guide.com, is a vast and an admirable resource. Among the acres of magazine and newspaper reportage on this subject, special mention goes to the archives of *Hot Press*, and the feature writing of Harry Doherty and Chris Salewicz, whose pieces written during Thin Lizzy's heyday, for *Melody Maker* and *New Musical Express* and *Creem* respectively, provide particularly vivid accounts of Lynott, the band and the wider culture at that time.

The following short list mentions just some of the many biographies, reference works, novels, anthologies and history books that proved useful during my research.

Baillie, Stuart, *Ballad of a Thin Man* (London, 1996).

Behan, Brendan, *The Complete Plays* (London, 1978).

Byrne, Alan, *Philip Lynott, Renegade of Thin Lizzy* (Dublin, 2012).

——, *Thin Lizzy* (London, 2004).

Curtis, Maurice, *The Liberties: A History* (Dublin, 2013).

Donnelly, James, *Jimmy the Weed: Inside the Quality Street Gang* (Preston, 2011).

Doyle, Roddy, *The Commitments* (London, 1988).

Dunphy, Eamon, *Unforgettable Fire: The Story of U2* (London, 1987).

Gantz, Jeffrey, *Early Irish Myths and Sagas* (Harmondsworth, 2000).

Geldof, Bob, *Is That It?* (London, 1986).

Gorham, Scott and Harry Doherty, *Thin Lizzy: The Boys are Back in Town* (London, 2012).

Heaney, Seamus, *Opened Ground: Poems 1966–1996* (London, 1998).

Lynott, Philomena with Jackie Hayden, *My Boy: The Philip Lynott Story* (Dublin, 2011).

O'Connor, Ulrick, *Brendan Behan* (London, 2014).

Puttenford, Mark, *Phil Lynott: The Rocker* (London, 1994).

Stokes, Niall, *Still in Love with You* (Dublin, 2014).

U2 with Neil McCormick, *U2 by U2* (London, 2005).

Visconti, Tony, *Bowie, Bolan and the Brooklyn Boy* (London, 2007).

Wall, Mick, Getcha Rocks Off: *Sex & Excess, Bust-Ups & Binges, Life & Death on the Rock 'n' Roll Road* (London, 2015).

Acknowledgements

I would like to thank everyone who spoke to me about Philip Lynott between 2010 and 2015. Their memories and insights are the heart of this book.

They include: John Alcock, Robert Ballagh, Peter Bardon, Eric Bell, 'Smiley' Bolger, Tim Booth, Noel Bridgeman, Eamon Carr, Ted Carroll, Tom Collins, John D'Ardis, Chalkie Davies, Brian Downey, Martin Duffy, Roy Esmonde, Peter Fallon, Hugh Feighery, Jim Fitzpatrick, Bob Geldof, Jeffa Gill, Scott Gorham, Nigel Grainge, Kevin Horan, Macdaragh Lambe, Johnny Lappin, Steve Lillywhite, Søren Lindberg, Philomena Lynott, Gary Moore, Chris Morrison, Frank Murray, Mark Nauseef, Liam O'Connor, Sean O'Connor, Chris O'Donnell, Michael O'Flanagan, Graham Parker, Ivan Pawle, Suzi Quatro, Fran Quigley, Pat Quigley, Leo Rickard, Brian Robertson, Helen Ruttle, Chris Salewicz, Paul Scully, Brush Shiels, Chris Spedding, Mark Stanway, Carole Stephen, Caroline Taraskevics, Nick Tauber, Chris Tsangarides, Brian Tuite, Midge Ure, Tony Visconti, Darren Wharton and Kit Woolven. Thanks also to those who preferred to speak off the record.

Many people took the time to assist me in other ways: setting up interviews, passing on contact information or forwarding material of interest. Their goodwill is much appreciated. Thank you to Mark Addis, Duff Battye, Nick Clark, Ted Cummings, John Foyle, Martin Foyle, Barry Keevins, Aisling McKone, Andrea O'Hara, Ken Sweeney, Ace Trump and Phillippa Watson.

To everyone who provided personal effects and memorabilia, in particular Ted Carroll and Brian Tuite, sincere thanks. I am indebted to Chalkie Davies and Roy Esmonde for being so generous with their wonderful photographic archives.

I am grateful to Simona Vezzoli for her expert assistance on the subject of migration from British Guiana; to Emory University, Atlanta, GA, and to Morningside Library, Edinburgh; to Lola Smith-Welsh for transcribing a number of interviews so diligently; to Howard Watson for his assiduous copy-editing and making many improving suggestions; and to Nick Hasted for access to his Geldof tapes.

Many thanks to my editor at Constable, Andreas Campomar, to Claire Chesser and Linda Silverman – and to my agent, Matthew Hamilton, at Aitken Alexander. I'm particularly grateful for the input of Caroline Taraskevics and her family, who offered the support of the Lynott Estate without imposing any caveats or conditions.

Finally, heartfelt thanks to my family, particularly to my mother, who went to see Thin Lizzy at Inverness Ice Rink in 1981 and reported back to her curious young son with infectious enthusiasm; and above all to my wife Jen and our three children for their love, patience, advice and support.

Notes

All quotations are from interviews conducted by the author unless credited otherwise in the text or noted here. A handful of interviews – including those with Philomena Lynott and Brian Downey – were conducted originally for a feature which appeared in the February 2011 issue of *Uncut*. The vast majority were conducted in 2014 and 2015.

Introduction
1. Roddy Doyle, *The Commitments* (London, 1987).

Chapter 1
1. Philomena Lynott with Jackie Hayden, *My Boy: The Philip Lynott Story* (Dublin 2011).
2. Lynott with Hayden, *My Boy*.

Chapter 2
1. Peter Silverton, 'Thin Lizzy: Joints', *Sounds* (16 December 1978).
2. *The Rocker: A Portrait of Phil Lynott*, directed by Shay Healy (1996).

3. Niall Stokes, *Philip Lynott: Still in Love with You* (Dublin, 2014).
4. Chris Salewicz, 'Thin Lizzy: A Peep into the Soul of Phil Lynott', *New Musical Express* (10 September 1977).
5. Ibid.
6. Salewicz, 'Thin Lizzy: A Peep into the Soul'.
7. *Hot Press* (1 April 1983).

Chapter 3
1. Ibid.
2. Harry Doherty, 'Thin Lizzy: Lizzy Break 'Em Up', *Melody Maker* (3 April 1976).

3 Interview, *Dave Fanning Show*, RTÉ Radio 2 (April 1980).
4 *The Rocker*.
5 Salewicz, 'Thin Lizzy: A Peep into the Soul'.
6 Stokes, *Philip Lynott*.
7 Ibid.
8 Mark Puttenford, *Phil Lynott: The Rocker* (London, 1994).
9 Harry Doherty, 'Thin Lizzy: The Thin Man', *Melody Maker* (24 April 1976).

Chapter 4
1 Jon Young, *Trouser Press* (July 1978).
2 Keith Altham, 'Thin Lizzy: And Now a Drop of the Real Hard Stuff', *New Musical Express* (10 March 1973).
3 Interview, *Dave Fanning Show*.
4 Salewicz, 'Thin Lizzy: A Peep into the Soul'.
5 *Woman's Way* (December 1969).

Chapter 5
1 Jan Etherington, *Titbits* (22–8 January 1976).
2 Chris Salewicz, 'Thin Lizzy: Who Needs Springsteen When You've Got Johnny Cool?', *Creem* (November 1976).
3 Pete Makowski, 'Thin Lizzy: Buzy Lizzy', *Sounds* (27 March 1976).
4 Tony Visconti, *Bowie, Bolan and the Brooklyn Boy* (London, 2007).

5 Harry Doherty, 'Thin Lizzy: The Irish Question', *Melody Maker* (20 December 1975).
6 Makowski, 'Thin Lizzy: Buzy Lizzy'.
7 Ibid.
8 Interview, *Dave Fanning Show*.

Chapter 6
1 Harry Doherty, 'Deutschland Liebt Lizzy', *Melody Maker* (16 June 1979).
2 Stokes, *Philip Lynott*.
3 Harry Doherty and Scott Gorham, *Thin Lizzy: The Boys Are Back in Town* (London, 2012).
4 Ibid.
5 *The Rocker*.

Chapter 7
1 Ibid.
2 Doherty, 'Thin Lizzy: The Thin Man'.
3 Ibid.
4 Stokes, *Philip Lynott*.
5 Salewicz, 'Thin Lizzy: A Peep into the Soul'.
6 Interview, *Dave Fanning Show*, RTÉ Radio 2, April 1980.
7 Makowski, 'Thin Lizzy: Buzy Lizzy'.

Chapter 8
1 *Hot Press* (1 April 1983).
2 Stokes, *Philip Lynott*.
3 Makowski, 'Thin Lizzy: Buzy Lizzy'.
4 Etherington, *Titbits*.

Chapter 9

1 Makowski, 'Thin Lizzy: Buzy Lizzy'.
2 Interview, *Dave Fanning Show*.
3 Altham, 'Thin Lizzy'.
4 *Hot Press* (1 April 1983).
5 Interview, *Dave Fanning Show*.
6 Makowski, 'Thin Lizzy: Buzy Lizzy'.
7 Stokes, *Philip Lynott*.
8 *Irish Times* (26 April 1973).
9 Young, *Trouser Press*.
10 Interview, *Dave Fanning Show*.

Chapter 10

1 Doherty, 'Thin Lizzy: The Irish Question'.
2 Interview, *Dave Fanning Show*.
3 Don Snowden, *Los Angeles Times* (February 1977).
4 Salewicz, 'Thin Lizzy: A Peep into the Soul'.
5 *Hot Press* (4 May 1984).
6 Salewicz, 'Thin Lizzy: Who Needs Springsteen'.
7 Pete Makowski, 'Thin Lizzy Rule at Reading OK?', *Sounds* (27 August 1977).
8 Salewicz, 'Thin Lizzy: A Peep into the Soul'.
9 Doherty, 'Thin Lizzy: The Irish Question'.
10 Interview, *Dave Fanning Show*.
11 Stokes, *Philip Lynott*.
12 Ibid.
13 Puttenford, *Phil Lynott*.
14 Doherty, 'Thin Lizzy: The Thin Man'.

15 Interview, *Dave Fanning Show*.

Chapter 11

1 *Hot Press* (4 May 1984).
2 Garry Bushell, 'Thin Lizzy: The Liz', *Sounds* (14 April 1979).
3 Salewicz, 'Thin Lizzy: A Peep into the Soul'.
4 *Hot Press* (1 April 1983).
5 Doherty, 'Deutschland Liebt Lizzy', *Melody Maker* (16 June 1979).
6 Doherty, 'Thin Lizzy: The Thin Man'.
7 Interview, *Dave Fanning Show*.
8 Salewicz, 'Thin Lizzy: A Peep into the Soul'.
9 Harry Doherty, *Melody Maker* (17 July 1976).

Chapter 12

1 Etherington, *Titbits*.
2 Doherty, 'Thin Lizzy: Lizzy Break 'Em Up'.
3 Makowski, 'Thin Lizzy Rule'.
4 Snowden, *Los Angeles Times*.
5 Susan Whitall, *Creem* (January 1977).
6 Charles Shaar Murray, 'Thin Lizzy: Gobi Gobi Hey!', *New Musical Express* (17 December 1977).
7 Makowski, 'Thin Lizzy Rule'.
8 Murray, 'Thin Lizzy'.
9 Makowski, 'Thin Lizzy Rule'.
10 Salewicz, 'Thin Lizzy: A Peep into the Soul'.

11. Interview, *Dave Fanning Show*, RTÉ Radio 2, April 1980.
12. Puttenford, *Phil Lynott*.
13. Doherty, 'Thin Lizzy: Lizzy Break 'Em Up'.

Chapter 13

1. *Hot Press* (4 October 1979).
2. U2 with Neil McCormick, *U2 by U2* (London, 2005).
3. Salewicz, 'Thin Lizzy: Who Needs Springsteen'.

Chapter 14

1. Doherty, 'Deutschland Liebt Lizzy'.
2. Bushell, 'Thin Lizzy: The Liz'.
3. Paul Du Noyer, *New Musical Express* (5 July 1980).
4. *Hot Press* (1 April 1983).
5. Interview, *Dave Fanning Show*.
6. *Hot Press* (25 April 1980).
7. Du Noyer, *New Musical Express*.
8. *Hot Press* (4 May 1984).
9. Du Noyer, *New Musical Express*.
10. *New Musical Express* (7 April 1979).

11. Interview, *Dave Fanning Show*.
12. *Hot Press* (4 May 1984).

Chapter 15

1. Garry Bushell, 'Thin Lizzy: Lizzy's Last Stand?' *Sounds* (12 March 1983).
2. *Hot Press* (1 April 1983).
3. Bushell, 'Thin Lizzy: Lizzy's Last Stand?'.
4. U2 with McCormick, *U2 by U2*.

Chapter 16

1. *Monsters of Rock Show*, Sky (May 1985).
2. *Hot Press* (4 May 1984).
3. *Good Morning Britain* (13 October 1984).
4. Ibid.
5. *Kerrang!* (June 1984).
6. http://www.trcjt.ca/ap960/ lizzy2/HLNalive.html.
7. *Music Box TV* (11 June 1985).
8. Stokes, *Philip Lynott*.
9. *Music Box TV* (11 June 1985).

Epilogue

1. *Hot Press* (4 May 1984).

Index

All references relate to Philip Lynott (PL).